D1563226

ESQUISSE DE L'HISTOIRE DE L'HARMONIE

An English-Language Translation of the François-Joseph Fétis History of Harmony

Portrait of François-Joseph Fétis. 1831 Lithograph by J. B. Madou.
Used with permission, Royal Library, Brussels.

ESQUISSE DE L'HISTOIRE DE L'HARMONIE

An English-Language Translation of the François-Joseph Fétis History of Harmony

Translated, Annotated, Edited

and with an Introduction by

Mary I. Arlin

HARMONOLOGIA SERIES No. 7

PENDRAGON PRESS

STUYVESANT NY

Other Titles in the Series *HARMONOLOGIA: Studies in Music Theory*

No. 1 *Heinrich Schenker: Index to Analyses* by Larry Laskowski (1978) ISBN 0-918728-06-1

No. 2 *F. W. Marpurg's* Thoroughbass and Composition Handbook: *A Narrative Translation and Critical Study* by David A. Sheldon (1989) ISBN 0-918728-55-X

No. 3 *Between Modes and Keys: German Theory 1592-1802* by Joel Lester (1990) ISBN 0-918728-77-0

No. 4 *Music Theory from Zarlino to Schenker: A Bibliography and Guide* by David Damschroder and David Russell Williams (1991) ISBN 0-918728-99-1

No. 5 *Musical Time: The Sense of Order* by Barbara Barry (1990) ISBN 0-945193-01-7

No. 6 *Formalized Music: Thought and Mathematics in Composition* (revised edition) by Iannis Xenakis (1992) ISBN 0-945193-24-6

Library of Congress Cataloging-in-Publication Data

Fétis, François-Joseph, 1784-1871.

    [Esquisse de l'histoire de l'harmonie. English]

    Esquisse de l'histoire de l'harmonie : an English-language translation of the Franéois-Joseph Fétls history of harmony / translated, annotated, edited and with an introduction by Mary I. Arlin.

        p.   cm. -- (Harmonologia series no. 7)

    Translation of a work originally published in installments in the Revue et gazette musicale de Paris, 1840.

    Includes bibliographical references and index.

    ISBN 0-945193-51-3

    1. Harmony--History. I. Arlin, Mary I., 1939- . II. Title. III. Series.
ML444.F4813 1994
781 .2'5'09--dc20   94-10964
                                 CIP
                                 MN

Copyright Pendragon Press 1994

TABLE OF CONTENTS

ILLUSTRATIONS

ACKNOWLEDGEMENT

The author wishes to express her sincere appreciation to all who have helped complete this work, to those who have encouraged as well as those have assisted in a tangible way. This translation is essentially that in my doctoral dissertation, which was completed at Indiana University under the guidance of Dr. Vernon L. Kliewer. I am especially grateful to him for his invaluable assistance with the study, patient advice, kind criticism, and personal interest through the years. I am also grateful to Professor Françoise Gebhart (Ithaca College) for assuring that French idioms found appropriate English expression and to Professor Marianne Kalinke (University of Illinois) for reading the German translations and offering helpful suggestions. In revising the translation and introduction, I benefitted from the careful reading and kind suggestions of Joel Lester, editor of the Harmonologia Series, and the insightful comments of my colleague Professor Mark A. Radice.

I am also deeply indebted to the Interlibrary Loan Department of Ithaca College; the staffs of the Libraries of the Royale Albert Ier and Royal Conservatory of Music in Brussels for their kind cooperation and assistance. Special thanks are due to the librarians of the Royal Conservatory of Music, the late Dr. Albert Vander Linden, and Mr. Paul Raspé, for their gracious help. I am singularly indebted to Mr. Raspé for furnishing me with prints of the *Esquisse*. Last, but certainly not least, to my mother, to whose memory this volume is dedicated, and without whose patience assistance, assurances, and encouragement this work would not have been possible.

M.I.A.

ABBREVIATIONS

BUM	*Biographie universelle des musiciens*, 2d ed.
JAMS	*Journal of the American Musicological Society*
JMT	*Journal of Music Theory*
MGG	*Die Musik in Geschichte und Gegenwart*
MQ	*The Musical Quarterly*
MTS	*Music Theory Spectrum*
NHarvard	*The New Harvard Dictionary of Music*
NGrove	*The New Grove Dictionary of Music and Musicians*
RGM	*Revue et Gazette musicale de Paris*
RM	*Revue musicale*

INTRODUCTION

On 19 April 1841, François-Joseph Fétis wrote to Charles-Edmond-Henri de Coussemaker (1805-1876): "I have the pleasure of sending you a copy of the *Esquisse de l'histoire de l'harmonie*, which I have published in articles in Schlesinger's *Gazette musical*, and of which I have had 50 copies in octavo printed for my friends and a few scholars. It is a new work by its content, and the subject matter is one of the most important in the history of music."[1] This "new work," a chronicle of the theoretical tenets of harmony from Franco of Cologne to 1840, is the first history of harmonic theory.[2] Fétis' *Esquisse*, which Matthew Shirlaw called "... a real history of harmonic theory, and of harmonic systems,"[3] predates Hugo Riemann's impressive *Geschichte der Musiktheorie im IX.-XIX. Jahrhundert* by more than fifty years.[4] Yet, aside from some isolated quotations in Shirlaw, little is known about Fétis' *Esquisse de l'histoire de l'harmonie*, and few copies are extant.[5]

Fétis was eminently qualified to undertake writing a history of harmony. As "one of the most lucid musicologists of this time" and "one of the first to consider the past with an artistic interest,"

---

[1]This letter is bound into Coussemaker's copy of the *Esquisse* in the library of the Conservatoire Royal de Musique, Brussels, KK 9620.

[2]In the *Vorbericht* of his *Deutliche Anweisung zum Generalbaß* (1772), C. G. Schröter gives an abbreviated abstract (20 pages in octavo) of the history of harmony. Since Schröter's work is a very cursory overview rather than a dedicated study, it cannot be considered the first history of harmonic theory.

[3]Matthew Shirlaw, *The Theory of Harmony*, 2d ed. (DeKalb, Illinois: B. Coar, 1955), vii.

[4]1898. 2d ed. Leipzig, 1921; Facs. Hildesheim: Olms, 1961.

[5]The book was printed in installments in the *Revue et Gazette musicale de Paris*, 1840, nos. 9, 20, 24, 35, 40, 52, 63, 67, 68, 72, 73, 75, 76, and 77. Book 4 of Fétis' *Traité complet de la théorie et de la pratique de l'harmonie*, 7th ed. (Paris: G. Brandus and S. Dufour, 1861), "Examen critique des principaux systèmes de génération et de classification des accords" (201-54), is based on the *Esquisse*, but the opening 73 pages of the *Esquisse* were deleted from Book 4. Although the reader frequently is referred to specific pages in the *Esquisse* for additional information about a theorist or his theories, Fétis does include some theorists and treatises in Book 4 of the *Traité d'harmonie* that were omitted from the *Esquisse*.

Fétis knew and understood the historical aspects of the art.[6] As a composer and teacher of composition, he understood the need for a systematic presentation of musical materials. As a theorist, he had examined and studied the writings of theorists throughout the ages. In the Preface to his *Traité complet de la théorie et de la pratique de l'harmonie* (ix), Fétis stated that " . . . in the space of twenty years" he had read and studied more than 800 works dealing with harmony before attempting to write his own. Moreover, to ascertain that ". . . the history of the art was in accord with my system," Fétis analyzed "compositions of every genre . . . and arranged them by epochs and by categories of transformations of the art."[7] As a result of his research, he expressed the fundamental idea that he stated in various forms in numerous works: "Art does not progress, it is transformed."[8]

As the first history of the theory of harmony, this volume needs no excuse for being. The *Esquisse* demonstrates Fétis' mastery of the literature of music theory and his skill in distilling the salient information contained in that literature. In light of Fétis' influence as a theorist, this translation is based upon the need to provide access to Fétis' ideas on the most important concepts in the history of harmony by making the *Esquisse de l'histoire de l'harmonie* available for general reference.

BIOGRAPHICAL SKETCH

François-Joseph Fétis, the second child of Antoine-Joseph and Élizabeth Desprets, was born into a family of musicians in Mons, Belgium on 25 March 1784. François-Joseph's grandfather, Simon-Joseph, was an organist and organ builder; and his father, Antoine-Joseph, who was born in Mons in 1756, was the organist at Saint-Wandru, concertmaster of the theater orchestra, and conduc-

---

[6]Robert Wangermée, "François-Joseph Fétis," *Encyclopédie de la musique* (Paris: Fasquelle, 1959), 2:52.

[7]This preface, which was added to the third edition, is dated 13 January 1849.

[8]*BUM*, 1st ed., 1:xxxiii.

tor of the village concerts. "Destined to follow his father's profession"[9] because one "was a musician more by tradition than vocation" at this time,[10] François-Joseph began his musical studies at an early age, receiving instruction in piano, violin, and organ from his father. "The first instrument that was put into his hands was the violin; at age seven he wrote some duos for this instrument and began to study the piano." Early in 1793 the nine-year-old Fétis played a Davaux concerto with the orchestra, and a few months later he and his father performed Viotti's Symphonie Concertante in F at the Concert des Abonnés. Yet even Fétis was forced to admit that he was not a child prodigy; he did not demonstrate talent for any particular instrument. "What engrossed me then was the desire, to be more exact, the *need* to compose."[11]

During the second invasion of Belgium by the French (1794), the subscription concerts were canceled, but Antoine-Joseph formed an orchestra of about twenty artists and amateurs to perform compositions written for chamber orchestra. The musicians, who met in the Fétis home, paid the elder Fétis to lead them in the study of the works. François-Joseph, who was asked to double the bass parts on the keyboard and to realize the harmony, studied and memorized about thirty symphonies of Haydn, about twenty of Pleyel, as well as overtures and piano concertos of C. P. E. Bach, Kozeluch, Mozart, and Viotti's violin concertos. "Even today, I can perform the majority of these works on the piano without having the music in front of me, in spite of the sixty years that have elapsed since the time of which I am speaking."[12] The younger Fétis was particularly struck with the works of Haydn and Mozart, because in them he found ". . . the secrets of a new and lively harmony of which he had no idea at all previously."

---

[9]Unless noted otherwise, the material in this section, including quotations, has been extracted from Fétis' autobiographical article in the *Biographie universelle des musiciens et Bibliographie générale de la musique*, 2d ed. (Paris: Didot Frères, Fils et Cᶦᵉ, 1862), s.v. "Fétis, (François-Joseph)."

[10]Robert Wangermée, *François-Joseph Fétis, Musicologue et Compositeur* (Brussels: Palais des Académies, 1951), 8.

[11]François-Joseph Fétis quoted in Wangermée, *François-Joseph Fétis*, 11.

[12]François-Joseph Fétis quoted in Wangermée, *François-Joseph Fétis*, 12.

Fétis, who had had no formal training in harmony or composition, imitated the style of these men in his own compositions: two piano concertos, a Symphonie Concertante for two violins, viola, bass, and orchestra; piano sonatas, a Mass in D, a *Stabat Mater* in g for two choirs and orchestras, and three violin quartets. One of his piano concertos was performed at the Concert des Abonnés in 1797, and, in 1799, Fétis heard a performance of his Symphonie Concertante.[13]

In October 1800, yielding to the entreaties of friends, the family sent sixteen-year-old Fétis to Paris to matriculate in the recently opened Paris Conservatory. There Fétis studied piano with Adrien Boïeldieu and, after Boïeldieu became director of French opera for the Russian imperial court, with Louis Pradher. Jean-Baptiste Rey, a devotee of Rameau and orchestra conductor at the Paris Opera, taught Fétis harmony, and in the following year (1801), Fétis received the first prize in that discipline. About this same time, he developed a keen interest in the history and theory of music; he read Catel's newly published *Traité de l'harmonie* and compared it to Rameau's *Traité de l'harmonie*.

> The initial result of my efforts was discouragement; because if, on one hand, I found a more philosophical method in Rameau's writings, I saw the art's natural facts twisted to adjust them to the principle of a system; and, on the other hand, if Catel gave me an order of facts more consistent with the feeling of harmony and the practical processes of the art, this advantage was balanced by the shortcomings of a purely empirical method whose illusory foundation lay in the arbitrary divisions of a sounding string.[14]

Fétis continued his research and studied German and Italian so that he could compare the harmonic systems of Catel and Rameau to those of Kirnberger and Sabbatini.

At the beginning of 1803, Fétis left Paris to travel and ". . . to study counterpoint and fugue according to the German school in the

---

[13]Paul Hooreman, *François-Joseph Fétis et la vie musicale de son temps 1784–1871* (Brussels, Bibliothque royale Albert Ier, 1972), xxi.

[14]Preface of the *Traité d'harmonie*, i.

writings of Marpurg, Kirnberger, and Albrechtsberger," because his study of Bach's, Handel's, Haydn's, and Mozart's compositions had generated an ". . . impassioned inclination for this school's style."[15] Encouraged by Cherubini, Fétis then concentrated on the music of Palestrina and composed some sacred works modeled after his manner. Simultaneously, he read ". . . attentively all of the works of the Italian pedagogues, particularly those of Zarlino, Zacconi, Cerrato, and . . . of P[adre] Martini and Paolucci."[16] During this time Fétis continued to compose secular music; he wrote a symphony, an overture, some piano sonatas and caprices, and some pieces for eight wind instruments.

In 1806, at a publisher's request, Fétis began a revision of the plainsong of the Roman Catholic Church and the preparation of a *Graduale* and *Antiphonale* that was more in keeping with the traditions of medieval manuscripts. The fruition of his labors and patient research had to wait, because of interruptions, nearly thirty years.

Fétis married Adélaïde-Louise-Catherine Robert, a young woman of considerable fortune in 1806, and in 1807 he won the second prize (later called the *Prix de Rome*) in composition. Fétis believed that easy circumstances would permit him to devote his time to composition, but in 1811, pecuniary difficulties precipitated by the loss of his wife's fortune forced Fétis to leave Paris. They settled in Ardennes, where he studied philosophy which ". . . seemed indispensable for the exposition of the principles of the theory of

---

[15]Wangermée writes that Fétis left Paris in 1802 (*François-Joseph Fétis*, 15). Fétis gives 1803 in *BUM*.

[16]Gioseffo Zarlino, *The Art of Counterpoint, Part III of Le Institutioni harmoniche*, 1558, trans. Guy A. Marco and Claude V. Palisca (New Haven: Yale University Press, 1968). Lodovico Zacconi, *Prattica di musica seconda parte* (Venice, 1622). Scipione Cerrato, *Dialoghi armonici pel contrapunto e per la compositione* (1626), Ms.; *Dialogo armonico ove si tratta . . . di tutte le regole del contrappunto et anco della compositione de più voci, de' canoni, della proportioni, et d'altri* (1631), Ms. Padre Giovanni Battista Martini, *Esemplare ossia saggio fondamentale pratico di contrappunto sopra il canto fermo*, 2 vols. (Bologna, 1774–75). Giuseppe Paolucci, *Arte pratica di contrappunto dimonstrata con esempi di vari autori e con osservazioni*, 3 vols. (Venice 1765–72).

music, and for the analysis of the facts of the history of this art."[17] His research in harmonic theory led him to the conclusion that ". . . tonality is the sole foundation for this combination of sounds, and that the laws of this tonality . . . are absolutely identical to those that control melody."

In December 1813, Fétis accepted the position of organist at Saint-Pierre in Douai and professor of singing and harmony at the municipal school. Having to give harmony and singing lessons made Fétis focus on pedagogical techniques and materials, and he began the work that culminated in his *Solfèges progressifs avec accompagnement de piano, précédés de l'exposé des principes de musique* (Paris: Schlesinger, 1827) and *Méthode élémentaire et abrégée complet de l'harmonie et d'accompagnement, suivie d'exercices gradués dans tous les tons, par l'étude desquels l'on peut arriver promptement à accompagner la basse chiffrée et la partition* (Paris: Petit, 1824). "In order to carry out so many works [teaching and writing], Fétis, from the time of his arrival in Douai, regularly devoted sixteen or eighteen hours to them each day. Since then his life has followed the same routine without interruption, except his travel." Still hoping to earn his way as a composer, Fétis returned to Paris in 1818 where his stage-works, mostly comic operas, met with more or less success although they ". . . have not satisfied their composer."[18] On 22 August 1821, following the death of André Eler (1764-21 April 1821), Fétis accepted an appointment as professor of composition at the Paris

[17]In a letter to Eugène-Théodore Troupenas, Fétis wrote (17 October 1838) that he had read Wronsky, Fichte, Schelling, Zeunemann, Aristotle, Ziedemann, Ritter, Rischen, Kant (*Critique de la raison purè, Critique du jugement, Philosophie du droit, sa morale; Métaphysique des moeurs*), Plato, Leibnitz, Descartes, Herder, Hegel and that he was reading the aesthetics of Bouterweck, Krause, and Krug. Fétis felt so confident about his competence in philosophy that he wrote, "I can say, my dear Troupenas, that I have now arrived at the point whereby I could teach philosophy at a university, and could perhaps excite some interest." (Archives, Paris Bibliothèque nationale, DUR-F1; copy in Bibliothèque royale Albert Ier, Brussels.)

[18]Fétis' most successful opera was *La Vieille*. This one-act opera was premiered on 14 March 1826 at the Opéra-Comique in Paris and presented until 1840; it was revived again on 11 October 1851. *La Vieille* was given in New York in 1827, in Calcutta in 1837, and in Rio de Janeiro in 1846. The work was translated into German and English for performances in Germany (Berlin, 1827) and England (London, 1828). (Alfred Loewenberg, *Annals of Opera 1597–1940*, 3d ed., rev. and corrected [Totowa, N.J.: Rowan and Littlefield, 1978], col. 701.)

Conservatory, and in 1824, at Cherubini's request, Fétis wrote and published his first important work, *Traité de contrepoint et de la fugue*, which was selected as the official text for the Conservatory.[19]

To augment his salary as a composition professor, Fétis asked to be appointed as François-Louis Perne's successor as the Conservatory librarian. He applied first on 5 January 1824, and in November 1826 he finally obtained the honorary appointment; commencing 1 January 1829 Fétis was compensated 1,000 French francs annually for his work. Fétis, who frequently was absent doing research,[20] was removed as librarian in 1831 and replaced by Bottée de Toulmon on 15 August 1831.[21] An inventory of the library's holdings by de Toulmon revealed numerous missing volumes as well as the mutilation of a number of books, presumably by Fétis. By mid-1833, "L'Affaire Fétis" had begun—an attempt that continued unsuccessfully until 28 October 1871 to recover the numerous books and manuscripts that Fétis had permanently "borrowed" from the Conservatory Library (as well as the Royal and Mazarine libraries in Paris).[22]

Fétis' concern for the lack of a French journal dedicated exclusively to music motivated him to fill the void, and from Tuesday, 13 February 1827 to 1 November 1835 Fétis wrote and published virtually single-handedly the weekly journal the *Revue musicale*.[23] "Between 1827 and 1835[24] more than 200 articles appeared in the

[19]Facs. Osnabrück: Otto Zellner, 1972.

[20]Fétis took an extended trip to London in the spring of 1829, and his eight letters to his son "Sur l'état actuel de la musique à Londres" were published in the *Revue musicale* 5 (1829): 313–19, 361–9, 385–92, 409–17, 457–64, 481–88, 529–36, 560–67.

[21]J.-D Prod'homme, "Fétis, bibliothécaire du Conservatoire," *Revue musicale*, 116 (June 1931): 18–34.

[22]See François Lesure, "L'Affaire Fétis," *Revue belge de musicologie*, 28–30 (1974–76): 214–21.

[23]This was not the first musical periodical in France; *Revue musicale* was preceded by *Journal de Framery* (1770), *Correspondance des amateurs* (1802), and *Tablettes de Polymnie* (1810), all of which were very short-lived.

[24]In 1835 the *Revue musicale* and the eleven-month-old *Gazette musicale de Paris* merged and were renamed *Revue et Gazette musicale de Paris*. Fétis was a featured writer for the latter until his death in March 1871. The *Revue et Gazette musicale de Paris* ceased publication on 31 December 1880.

Revue musicale over Fétis' signature; many others appeared anonymously—but in 1833 Fétis clearly asserted that '. . . I always take
responsibility for anything that does not carry a signature other than
mine.'"[25] Fétis continued to contribute articles to two Parisian newspapers, the *Temps* and the *National*; on several occasions he wrote
three different articles on the same day (approximately twenty-five
printed pages in octavo), each dealing with a different aspect of a
new opera, and each article appeared in either the *Revue musicale*,
the *Temps* or the *National* the morning after the performance. The
publication of the *Revue musicale* and his newspaper articles helped
to make Fétis renowned, and in the succeeding years he had considerable influence on the Parisian musical life, not as a composer
or teacher but as a critic.[26]

Fétis was a polemicist: he had an opinion about the direction
that music should take. His acid critic's pen was feared and detested;
he was frequently the target of considerable criticism by composers.
Berlioz, a man with whom Fétis was often at odds, thought Fétis
squelched creativity and innovation because he was ". . . a pedagogue
who, hopelessly involved in his [own] theories, could not come to
grips with the new art."[27] In his *Mémoires*, Berlioz reported that
during a debate between Fétis and the critic Zani de Ferranti, when
the latter cited the Pilgrims' March in *Harold* as one of the most
interesting things of Berlioz that he had ever heard, Fétis answered,
"'How can I be expected to approve of a piece in which one is
constantly hearing two notes that are not part of the harmony?" (He

---

[25]Peter Bloom, "A Review of Fétis's *Revue musicale*" in *Music in Paris in the
Eighteen-Thirties*, ed. Peter Bloom (Stuyvesant, NY: Pendragon Press, 1987), 73.

[26]Fétis' articles frequently appeared in translation in Germany and England. As
Peter Bloom has noted (Ibid., 74), "Such formal and informal borrowing and
exchange among newspapers and other publications from various countries . . .
was an extremely common practice among moguls of the 19th-century press." For
a discussion of an interchange between Fétis and the editor of the *Harmonicon*,
William Ayrton, see Vincent Duckles, "A French Critic's View of the State of Music
in London (1829)" in *Modern Musical Scholarship*, ed. Edward Olleson (London:
Oriel Press Ltd., 1980), 223–37.

[27]Robert Wangermée, "François-Joseph Fétis," *MGG* 4, col. 130.

was referring to the C and B which recur at the end of each stanza, like bells tolling.)"[28]

Fétis had edited Beethoven's first eight symphonies for the publisher Eugène-Théodore Troupenas in the late 1820s, and in his *Mémoires* Berlioz, who did proof-reading for Troupenas before he went to Italy (1831), wrote that Fétis had altered Beethoven's harmonies

> . . . with unbelievable complacency. Opposite the E flat which the clarinet sustains over a chord of the sixth (D flat, F, B flat) in the andante of the C minor symphony, Fétis had naïvely written 'This E-flat must be F. Beethoven could not possibly have made so gross a blunder.' In other words, a man like Beethoven could not possibly fail to be in entire agreement with the harmonic theories of M. Fétis.[29]

After Berlioz threatened to expose the inaccuracies of Fétis' edition, Troupenas removed the "corrections," but Berlioz's anger at Fétis did not subside.[30] Berlioz believed he "avenged Beethoven" with his infamous critique of Fétis in one of the monologues of *Lélio*, the 1832 monodrama sequel to *Symphonie fantastique*, *Le Retour é la vie*:

> These young theorists of eighty, living in the midst of a sea of prejudices and persuaded that the world ends with the shores of their island; these old libertines of every age who demand that music caress and amuse them, never admitting that the chaste muse could have a more noble mission; especially these desecrators who dare to lay hands on original works, subjecting them to horrible mutilations that they call *corrections and perfections*, which, they say, require *considerable taste*. Curses on them! They make a mockery of art! Such are these

---

[28]*A Life of Love and Music: The Memoirs of Hector Berlioz 1803–1865*, trans. and ed. David Cairns (Oxford: The Folio Society, 1987), 202.

[29]Ibid., 166.

[30]In *RM* 5 (1829): 136, Fétis denied there was any substance to the allegation that he had corrected Beethoven's symphonies. Wangermée suggests (*François-Joseph Fétis*, 276–77), since printers' errors in the nineteenth century were legion, Fétis may have believed he was correcting a careless editor and not Beethoven. However, in his *Traité d'harmonie*, Fétis does criticize Beethoven's use of a tonic pedal under dominant harmony in the Sixth Symphony (§ 215, pp. 124–27).

vulgar birds who populate our public gardens, perching arrogantly on the most beautiful statues, and, when they have soiled the brow of Jupiter, Hercules' arm, or the breast of Jupiter, strut and preen as though they have laid a golden egg.[31]

But Fétis may have had the "last word" in this dispute with Berlioz. In 1830, Fétis' *La musique mise a la porte de tout le monde: Exposé succinct de tout ce qui est nécessaire pour juger de cet art* was issued in Paris. *La musique*, which was translated into German, Russian, Spanish, and Italian, may be considered the first significant contribution to what has been called music "appreciation."[32] In 1834, when the second edition of Fétis' *La musique* was issued in Paris, Fétis added a dictionary of terms and a "systematic catalogue" of French books revelant to the art of music. The dictionary of music terms contained an obvious reference to the Berlioz' *Symphonie fantastique* with an entry for *fantastique*: "This word has even slid into music. 'Fantastique' music is composed of instrumental effects with no melodic line and incorrect harmony."[33]

On 2 July 1829 Fétis touched off a furor with an article in the *Revue musicale* in which he said that in the "bizarre opening" of Mozart's quartet KV 465, the composer ". . . appears to have taken pleasure in torturing a delicate ear."[34] Fétis proceeded to "correct" Mozart stating that if Mozart had followed the rules in his *Traité du contrepoint* (p. 75, par. 119)[35] about the distance between imitations, these "inconceivable, purposeless dissonances that are ear-splitting"[36] would never have occurred. On 1 August 1829, one week after the article appeared, F.-L. Perne wrote a letter to the *Revue musicale* stating that Mozart was following the precedents of Bach and

---

[31]For another translation of this passage see Cairns, *Berlioz Memoirs*, 168.

[32]See pages XVII-XIX of Peter Bloom's "Introduction to the Da Capo Edition" of *Music Explained to the World* (New York: Da Capo Press, 1987) for a complete listing of the various editions of *La musique*. Bloom gives a succinct review of the critics' reaction to Fétis' book on pp. IX-XI.

[33]*La musique mise a la portée de tout le monde. Exposé succinct de tout ce qui est nécessaire pour juger de cet art* (Paris: E. Duverger, n.d.), 335.

[34]"Sur un passage singulier d'un quatuor de Mozart," *RM* 5 (1829): 601.

[35]This is par. 123 in the second edition.

[36]Fétis, "Sur un passage," 606.

Handel, and he queried if music that did not conform to Fétis' rules
". . . ought to be rejected as bizarre, shocking, grating, and poor."[37]
Would composers who strove to be innovative incur ". . . unjustly the
censure of the strict conservatives of the scientific purity of known
procedures?"[38] Fétis, defending his critique of Mozart's quartet,
appended a note to Perne's "Polémique" stating that he had made
only a modest alteration and, ". . . had I had the intention of
correcting all that is shocking in the passage, I would have had a
great deal to do."[39]

In 1832 Fétis presented his "Philosophy of Music" course in
Paris, where he set forth his concepts of *tonalité* that "he had begun
to formulate in 1816";[40] he organized and presented the first of the
Concerts historiques, concerts that were dedicated to fifteenth- through
eighteenth-century music.[41] These concerts, which continued
throughout his lifetime, were organized by stylistic periods, genres,

---

[37]F-.L. Perne, "Polémique," *RM* 6 (1830): 25–31.

[38]Ibid., 26.

[39]Fétis, "Note," *RM* 6 (1830): 32. Fétis was not the only one to attempt to "correct"
the opening measures of Mozart's quartet. Gottfried Weber, who offered alterna-
tives to Mozart's opening measures after "a complete *analysis of the entire harmonic
and melodic texture* will . . . account to us *what it is* which seems so strange in these
clashings of sound. . . ," gave a documented summary of the controversy in his
theory text on pages 735–36. (Gottfried Weber, *The Theory of Musical Composition .
. .* ed. John Bishop, 2 vols. [London: R. Cocks and Co., 1851], 2:733–54.) For a
more recent summary of the controversy, see Julie Ann Vertrees, "Mozart's String
Quartet K. 465: The History of a Controversy," *Current Musicology* 17 (1974):
96–114.

[40]Fétis summarized his Philosophy of Music course in a series of eight articles
published in *RM* 12 (1832): 131–33, 139–41, 155–58, 161–64, 169–71, 171–79,
184–87, 196–98. In the preface of his *Traité d'harmonie*, Fétis states (xi–xii) that while
he was walking alone in the Bois de Boulogne, "all at once the truth presented
itself to my mind; questions were posed clearly, shadows dispersed; false doctrines
fell about me piece by piece" (xi) and, after pondering for six hours, he knew that
tonalité was the principle that organizes music. David Lewin ("Concerning the
Inspired Revelation of F.-J. Fétis," Theoria 2 [1987]: 1–12) shows the parallel
between Fétis' revelation and the writings of Rousseau.

[41]Several of these programs are reproduced in Wangermée, *François-Joseph Fétis*,
303–08.

and national origins; they were always accompanied by his lectures on the music being performed. On 20 April 1833, Fétis submitted his resignation to Cherubini as ". . . professor of counterpoint at the Royal Conservatory of Paris, effective 1 May,"[42] to accept an appointment as Director of the Conservatory of Music in Brussels, professor of composition and harmony, and *maître de chapelle* to Leopold I.[43] As the first director of the Conservatory of Music in Brussels, Fétis built an institution that took its place among the best musical conservatories on the continent.[44]

During his tenure in Brussels, Fétis was a teaching administrator.[45] He continued to compose, teach advanced harmony and composition, and conduct the Conservatory orchestra in an annual cycle of four to six public concerts;[46] he wrote textbooks for the students: *Manuel des principes de la musique, à l'usage des professeurs et élèves de toutes les écoles de musique, particulièrement des écoles primaires* (1837); *Traité du chant en choeur, rédigé pour l'usage des directeurs d'écoles de chant, et des chefs de choeurs d'église, de théâtres* . . . (1837); *Manuel des compositeurs, directeurs de musique, chefs d'orchestre et de musique militaire* . . . (1837);

[42]Paris Archives nationales, Fonds du Conservatoire de musique, Dossier Fétis; copy in Bibliothèque royale Albert Ier, Brussels.

[43]On 10 October 1832, during the negotiations between Fétis and the selection committee for a director for the conservatory, Fétis submitted a "Plan d'organisation de la musique dans le royaume de Belgique." Included in this plan were his proposals for "a good conservatory" with preparatory music schools in major cities in Belgium, a reorganization of the theater of Brussels, and the establishment of national music festivals. This plan was quoted extensively by F.-A. Gevaert, *Discours prononcé a l'occasion du centième anniversaire de la naissance de F. J. Fétis* (Gand: C. Annoot-Braeckman, 1884). Wangermée (*François-Joseph Fétis*, 288–99) has reproduced the complete document.

[44]Gevaert, *Discours*, 4. The Conservatory was an outgrowth of several direct predecessors. For a detailed pre-history, see Edouard Mailly, *Les Origines du Conservatoire Royal de Musique de Bruxelles* (Brussels: Hayez, 1879).

[45] In his "Plan d'organization," Fétis stated that the director "must have absolute authority" in musical matters, as well as teach composition (Wangermée, *François-Joseph Fétis*, 295).

[46]Wangermée (*François-Joseph Fétis*, 27) notes that for a long time the Conservatory orchestra, comprised of faculty and students, was the sole ensemble that offered regular concerts for the public in Brussels.

Méthode des méthodes de piano (1837), *Méthode des méthodes de chant* (1837), *Traité complet de la théorie et de la pratique de l'harmonie* (1844), and *Méthode élémentaire de plain-chant, à l'usage des séminaires, des chantres et des organistes* (1843), all of which were published in Paris. For just short of a year (6 August 1833–31 July 1834), Fétis published a separate weekly periodical in Brussels, the *Gazette musicale de la Belgique.*[47] Each issue contained three or four articles, and news and reviews of local and foreign musical events. Perhaps his most monumental undertaking during these years was publishing two editions of his *Biographie universelle des musiciens* (1835–44, 1st ed.; 1860–65, 2d ed.), a work that was begun in Douai and was announced initially in 1827 as a *Dictionnaire historique des musiciens*; it was going to contain biographies of composers, musicians, instrument makers, and an "Introduction historique sur les progrès et les révolutions de toutes les parties de la musique."[48] Although the *Biographie universelle des musiciens* is plagued with errors, it is a valuable source for information about Fétis' contemporaries.[49] Fétis was not trained as a musicologist, yet, as Peter Bloom has noted, Fétis' "methods—combining secondary source materials with archival research, manuscript study, and extensive personal correspondence—were exemplary."[50]

Until his death on 26 March 1871, Fétis held dictatorial authority over the musical life of Brussels as a conductor, teacher, and

[47]On the inside cover of the copy in the library of the Conservatoire Royal de Musique, there is a signed and dated manuscript note (1899) by Alfred Wotquenne: "First year, *absolutely* complete. Unknown to Grégoir (*Recherchés historiques Concernant les Journaux de musique*, etc.) and to Freystätter (*Die musikalischen Zeitschriften* (1884)." Wotquenne was the compiler and editor of the *Catalogue de la bibliothèque du Conservatoire Royal de Bruxelles*, 4 vols. (Brussels: J. J. Coosemans, 1898–1912).

[48]*RM* 1 (1827): 364. Fétis' "Introduction historique" evolved into *Résumé philosophique de l'histoire*, the long preface in the first edition of *BUM* that explains his concept of the development of the musical language.

[49]Many of the articles in *MGG* and *NGrove* use material from *BUM*. Moreover, the *BUM* contains information about earlier musicians, many of whom are not even mentioned in *MGG* or *NGrove*.

[50] "A Review of Fétis's *Revue musicale*," 63–64. Robert Wangermée, Director of Radiodiffusion-Télévision Belge and a Professor at the Université Libre, Brussels, is collecting Fétis' voluminous correspondence for publication (tentatively 1995) by Éditions MARDAGA (Liège).

writer.[51] Few men have had greater influence as an interpreter, teacher, historian, theorist, and critic.

The fame of Fétis rests on his prolific writings on the history, theory, and literature of music. These writings span a lifetime of research and study. When Fétis died, he was writing *Histoire générale de la musique depuis les temps anciens à nos temps* (Paris: Didot, 1869–76); only five volumes of the projected eight were completed. His personal library, which was bequeathed to his sons Edouard and Adolphe, was acquired by the government at the time of his death. Fétis' library, housed in Brussels in the Bibliothque royale Albert Ier, contained more than 7,000 works, including scores.[52]

THEORETICAL CONCEPTS

Fétis' most important theoretical works are the *Esquisse de l'histoire de l'harmonie* (1840), his history of harmonic theory, *Traité du contrepoint et de la fugue* (1824; 2d ed. 1846), and the *Traité complet de la théorie et de la pratique de l'harmonie* (1844). The popularity of the latter, which was translated into Italian, Spanish, and Flemish,[53] extended into the twentieth century; its last printing was in Paris in 1906. Fétis considered his *Traité du contrepoint* and *Traité d'harmonie* ". . . the most original of his works and the most solid of his reputation." Through both of these works there is common thread of organization—tonality. In the preface to the *Traité d'harmonie*, Fétis contends that the efforts of all theorists who have searched for the fundamental principle of harmony in acoustics, mathematics, aggregations of intervals, or classifications of

[51]Robert Wangermée, "François-Joseph Fétis," *MGG* 4, col. 131.

[52]For a complete listing of the holdings, see *Catalogue de la Bibliothèque de F. J. Fétis, acquise par l'État Belge* (Paris: Firmin-Didot et Cie, 1877).

[53]The two Italian editions of *Trattato completo della teoria e della pratica dell' armonia* were done by Albert Mazzucato (Milan: Ricordi, [1845]) and Emanuele Gambale (Milan: F. Lucca, n.d.). Francisco de Asis Gil, a professor at the Madrid Conservatory who had studied with Fétis in Brussels and had dedicated his theory book to Fétis, used the 2d ed. (Paris: Brandus, 1846) for the Spanish translation, *Tratado completo de la teoría y práctica de la armonía.* (Madrid: Salazar, [1850]). The Flemish translation, done by Vanderdoodt, was *Harmonie-Leere ten gebruike der organisten* (Brussels, 1852).

chords have been futile (vii),[54] because tonality is the primary organizing agent of all melodic and harmonic successions. This is the first use of the term "tonality" in music, and the better share of the *Traité d'harmonie* is devoted to explaining his use of the term and how tonality organizes music.[55]

Scales and tonality. Fétis believed that the primary factor in the determination of tonality is the scale: the order of the succession of tones in major and minor, the distances that separate the tones, and the resultant melodic and harmonic affinities (2). Tonality is, then, a governed and conditioned state; it can be described as denoting the congruence to an underlying state—the tonic being the beginning, the end, or an important note of the scale. Twentieth-century theorists, following Fétis' example, have continued to look to the scale in quest of the true basis of music. Schoenberg contended that tonality is ". . . the particular way in which all notes relate to a fundamental tone; . . . and tonality is always comprehended in the sense of a particular scale."[56] Moreover, Schoenberg asserted that scales other than major are "art products," and, because the church modes lack leading tones, ". . . the church modes do not at all conform to the law of tonality."[57] Ernst Křenek proposed that a tone does not become a tonic until ". . . the central triad is built over it"; the position of the tonic note within the scale is completely immaterial.[58] But, Křenek does not explain how the triad achieves a role of centrality. Hindemith, however, took exception to the role of the scale in the determination of tonality:

[54]All subsequent parenthetical page references refer to the *Traité d'harmonie.*

[55]Bryan Simms ("Choron, Fétis, and the Theory of Tonality," *JMT* 19 [Spring 1975]: 119) states that the term "tonalité" can be found in French literature as early as 1810 and was not invented by Fétis. However, Carl Dahlhaus (*Studies on the Origin of Harmonic Tonality*, trans. Robert O. Gjerdingen [Princeton: Princeton University Press, 1990]) asserts that the term "tonality," which was defined by Castil-Blaze in *Dictionnaire de musique moderne* (1821), ". . . was given formal definition by François-Joseph Fétis" (7). Consequently, the term "tonality" is associated with Fétis.

[56]Arnold Schoenberg, *Problems of Harmony*, ed. Merle Armitage, 2d ed. (New York: G. Schirmer, Inc., 1937), 268.

[57]Ibid., 282.

[58]Ernst Křenek, *Music Here and Now*, trans. Barthold Fles (New York: W. W. Norton & Co., 1938), 110.

Scales are undoubtedly an excellent and perhaps even an indispensable aid to theoretical as well as practical music (just as the telephone book is to the use of the telephone) but they are not in themselves the material out of which melodies—and even harmonies—are made.[59]

If one assumes the correctness of Hindemith's refutation of the scale as the guide to tonality, Fétis' quest for tonal coherence in ascending major and minor scales was in vain; scales, which are theoretical abstractions of melodic and harmonic material, are posterior facts rather than musical realities. In and of themselves, scales are totally useless for determining tonality. Scales are cultural manifestations, which Fétis perceived when he said in the *Esquisse* (170) that

... this principle is purely metaphysical. We form this order and the melodic and harmonic phenomena that flow from it as a result of our conformation and education. This is a fact that exists for us by itself, and independently of any extraneous reason for us.[60]

Fétis continues (172),

... it is evident that there remains no other principle for the construction of the scale and tonality than the metaphysical principle; a principle, both subjective and objective, the necessary result of the feeling that perceives the relationship of sounds, and the intelligence that measures them and deduces the results.[61]

Here, the term "metaphysical" means not only the *a priori* character of tonality, but, as Dahlhaus has noted, metaphysical also means "anthropological, because Fétis is using the term in a culturally relative sense."[62] The first note of the scale, the "tonic," is the fundamental note not because of its position as the initial pitch, but by virtue of the musical context from which it has been culled. Hence,

[59]Paul Hindemith, "Methods of Music Theory," *MQ* 30 (1944): 24–25.
[60]Fétis repeats this same statement in the *Traité d'harmonie*, Bk. 4, chap. 5, § 361, p. 249.
[61]Ibid., § 362, p. 251.
[62]Dahlhaus, *Harmonic Tonality*, 8. In the preface to the *Traité d'harmonie*, Fétis rejected an "invariable scale given by nature" and discussed how different cultures selected relationships different from that of "nature's scale" (xx–xxiv). In 1862,

one wastes time analyzing and dissecting scales in search of tonality, because tonality is

> . . . that quality of the musical perception which finds its origin in the organization of a tonal complex about a central point of emphasis. The term 'tonic' achieves a terminological importance since it refers to that tone about which all remaining tones of the complex are grouped.[63]

Tonality existed, therefore, prior to the emergence of major and minor scales; it is not the *result* of the emergence of major and minor scales. Scales are not the arbiter of tonality, as Fétis stated, but the converse. If tonality is a metaphysical principle that manifests itself on the occasion of experience, then modality (*tonalité ancienne*) and tonality (*tonalité moderne*) are not the mutually exclusive properties that Fétis and Schoenberg propound, because modality too defines a particular set of scalar relationships to a fundamental tone: tonic.[64] While Fétis erred by rooting tonality in major and minor scales, he was correct when he stated that tonality can be perceived on the occasion of experience.

Intervals and tonality. In Book 1 of the *Traité d'harmonie*, Fétis broke with the usual taxonomy of intervals in his classification. He defined four kinds of consonances: (1) the perfect consonances, the unison, the perfect fifth, and the perfect octave, which create the

---

Hermann Helmholtz, following Fétis' lead, alleged that tonality was not a "natural law" but a matter of aesthetics. Unlike Fétis, Helmholtz rejected the *a priori* principle of tonality and, contending that "it [tonality] must be tested by its results," embarked upon investigations in acoustics and the physiology of hearing. (Hermann Helmholtz, *On the Sensations of Tone*, trans. Alexander J. Ellis, 2d ed. [New York: Dover Publications, 1954], 249.)

[63]William E. Thomson, "A Clarification of the Tonality Concept" (Ph.D. diss., Indiana University, 1952), 205.

[64]Rosalie Schellhous, who discusses Fétis' use of the metaphysical principle as a hypothesis for music theory ("Fétis's *Tonality* as a Metaphysical Principle: Hypothesis for a New Science," *MTS* 13 [Fall 1991]: 219–40), believes that Fétis' metaphysical theory, which he never really explains in his writings, is derived from Kant, and ". . . is best described as *transcendental* rather than metaphysical" because for Fétis ". . . music itself is never considered to be independent of sensory experience" (229).

feeling of repose. (2) The imperfect consonances, the thirds and sixths, which do not give a feeling of repose, but define the mode. (3) The "mixed" consonance, the perfect fourth, which lacks finality, is not variable in the major and minor modes, and does not demand a resolution as do dissonances; its usage is, however, very limited. (4) The "appellative" consonances, the augmented fourth and diminished fifth, are the intervals that "characterize modern tonality."[65] The remaining intervals, the seconds, ninths, and sevenths, are classified as dissonances because they ". . . are not pleasing by themselves and only satisfy musical sense by their connection with consonances" (8-9).

Recognizing the frailty of his definition of dissonance, Fétis clarified it by stipulating that the dissonant notes must "touch each other, either in a direct way or in an indirect way," i.e., either at the interval of a second (ninth), or a seventh.[66] However, the dissonance created between the fourth and fifth degree of the scale is called "natural," because it is the point of contact between the two tetrachords of the scale (18). This seventh from the fifth degree up to the fourth, one of the constitutive intervals in the "natural" dissonant chord (the dominant seventh chord), did not have to be preceded by consonance, as did all of the other dissonant intervals. Fétis divided the dissonances into two categories: "tonal dissonances" and "dissonances of variable attraction." The first category included the dissonant intervals found within the scale: major and minor seconds, sevenths, and ninths. The "dissonances of variable attraction" are the altered intervals: the augmented second, third, fifth, sixth, and octave; the diminished third, fourth, seventh, and octave. These intervals ". . . have the character of dissonance only because their

[65]Fétis' inclusion of the tritone as a consonance is predicated on the premise that its role in tonality as a tonic-defining interval nullifies its dissonant characteristics. This stance was also taken by Mattheson and Sorge, as well as Catel and Choron (Bryan Simms, "Choron, Fétis and the Theory of Tonality," 122).

[66]This idea of classifying seconds and sevenths as dissonances is not unique to Fétis. In 1764 Abbé Pierre-Joseph Roussier (Traité des accords et de leur succession . . .) stated this same idea on page 6. Furthermore, Bryan Simms (Ibid., 120) has observed that Choron's Principes de composition des écoles d'Italie (1808) indicates that the conjunct intervals of the second, seventh, and ninth are dissonant.

constitutive notes have tendencies toward different tonalities" (10).[67]
These altered intervals were dissonant, not because of their sound,
but their function: they obscured the tonal unity of the scale.

Having completed his classification of intervals, Fétis proceeded
to explain the "laws of tonality," laws that were rooted in the
metaphysical points of repose in a scale. Fétis never defined what
renders the quality of repose to any scale degree; he merely listed
the scale degrees that are imbued with repose. The tonic scale degree
is the only one that has the character of absolute repose; the fourth
and fifth degrees, points of momentary repose, may have the harmony of a fifth or octave. Neither the triads nor the interval of a third
on the fourth and fifth degree may succeed each other because,
". . . having no point of contact between them, [they] present the
aspect of tonal absurdity to the musical sense" (17). Fétis called this
juxtaposition of thirds on the fourth and fifth scale steps *fausses
relations*.

If tonality truly resides in the scale, why exclude the juxtaposition of two of the diatonic intervals contained therein? Fétis was not
referring to his limited concept of dissonance and to the two notes
which, because they separate the two tetrachords, create "natural"
dissonance, since he admitted the progression ii$^6_5$ - V in his har-
monization of the scale with the justification that ". . . the note of this
sixth is at the same time the fifth of the dominant, and that establishes
the contact" (17). If, however, Fétis' objection was to avoid the parallel
fifths that would result from the succession of IV to V, his objection
is unfounded: parallel fifths need not occur in chords that are related
by the root relationship of a second, as he demonstrated so clearly
in the example on page 25 of his *Traité d'harmonie*. In the *Esquisse de
l'histoire de l'harmonie*, Fétis sought refuge for the exclusion of consecutive thirds on the fourth and fifth scale degrees in a rule of Jehan
des Murs (*c*1300-1350)—"we ought to avoid two major thirds by
conjunct motion"—a rule that is not found in des Murs' treatise, *De
Discantu*. However, in 1558 Zarlino stated that consecutive, conjunct

---

[67]The conspicuous omission of the diminished sixth from the category of "dissonances of variable attraction" may be attributed to the fact that the diminished
sixth is enharmonic with the perfect fifth, the interval *par excellence* of repose.
However, Fétis made no comment about it.

major thirds, minor thirds, major sixths, or minor sixths should not be used. For Zarlino, consecutive imperfect consonances

> . . . produce a bitterness in their progression because in the movement of the parts there is missing the interval of the large semitone, in which all the good of music resides. Without this interval every progression of harmony is hard, bitter, and nearly dissonant. This effect also arises from the lack of harmonic relationship between the parts when two major thirds or two minor sixths are heard in succession . . . .[68]

Zarlino continued that since ". . . it is forbidden to place two perfect consonances of the same species consecutively, it is the more forbidden to write two imperfect ones of the same proportion, because these are not so consonant as the perfect."[69] But in *tonalité moderne*, there is absolutely no tonal justification for Fétis' prohibition of consecutive imperfect intervals.

The second, third, and seventh degrees, devoid of tonal repose, could not have root-position triads built on them because the interval of the perfect fifth was the interval of repose. In the preface to the *Traité d'harmonie*, Fétis held that the perfect fifth gained ascendancy as the primary structural interval because the perfect fifth, ". . . as a consonance, produces a feeling of harmonic repose almost as satisfying as the octave" (xxxiii). Theorists writing after Fétis, most recently Hindemith, have concluded that Fétis' assertion about the primacy of the perfect fifth was correct. The reasoning that Fétis used for excluding the perfect fifth on the third degree of the scale could also be used to repudiate his inclusion of the tritone as a consonance, albeit "appellative":

> The reasons for this exclusion [of a perfect fifth on the third degree] are: (1) that the fifth of this note would be formed with the seventh degree, of which the natural attraction toward the tonic

---

[68]Gioseffo Zarlino, *The Art of Counterpoint*, Part Three of *Le Istitutioni harmoniche, 1558*, trans. Guy A. Marco and Claude V. Palisca (New Haven: Yale University Press, 1968), 62.

[69]Ibid., 63.

cannot be satisfying to the conditions of repose; (2) that this same seventh note would establish a false relationship of tonality with the fourth degree, toward which the third itself has an attractive tendency, being separated from it only by a semitone (§ 51, p. 20).

What universal law dictates a false relationship with an adjacent note that is not sounding? Is Fétis implying that the triad on the fourth degree should follow, enabling each note to resolve upward a semitone to its "natural attraction"? This is doubtful in two-voice writing, because the resolution of $\hat{3}$ to $\hat{4}$ and $\hat{7}$ to $\hat{8}$ would create the anathema of "good" counterpoint—parallel fifths. However, the harmonic progression iii - IV is a cliché when it is employed to harmonize scale steps seven and six in a descending major scale.

The sixth degree of the scale caused Fétis some consternation; while he initially excluded it as a point of repose, he nevertheless conceded that it may occasionally be a point of momentary repose and accompanied by a perfect fifth, because the sixth degree is also the tonic of the relative minor, and in the minor mode the sixth scale degree is also the fourth degree of the relative major mode (19). This convoluted reasoning could be applied to any of the remaining scale degrees: the third scale degree in major is the dominant of the relative minor, a point of repose; the second scale degree in major is the fourth scale degree in the relative minor, also a point of repose. Had Fétis failed to identify the sixth degree of the scale as a point of repose, he would have had to deny the viability of the deceptive cadence, the *cadence rompue*, which occurs on the sixth scale degree.

As for the exclusion of the second degree as a point of repose, Fétis stated,

> If sometimes one accompanies it with the fifth, . . . one removes its tonal character and effects a vague change of tonality that opens the way for several endings in different keys; for example:[70]

---

[70]*Traité d'harmonie*, § 51, p. 20.

First of all, the interval of a perfect fifth on the second degree of the scale no more "effects a vague change of tonality" than any other interval or chord unless one wants to modulate via a pivot chord—establish a relationship between two keys through a chord or interval that is mutually identifiable in both. For example, the interval *d-a* in Fétis' example could be replaced with "tonal" intervals and still cadence as Fétis indicated:

For Fétis, the only intervals that could give the second degree of the scale "tonal character" were the sixth and third, or sixth and fourth. Fétis appears to be stating, in his own inimitable way, that the notes of tonal repose are those notes that can be the roots of cadence chords, chords that normally occur in root position; hence, the perfect fifth. This is probably why, in the face of either accepting the sixth degree as an occasional point of repose, or denying the existence of the deceptive cadence, Fétis chose the former path. In spite of his insistence to the contrary, Fétis' theory of tonality was conceived harmonically, because a careful scrutiny of melodic cadence pitches will reveal that *any* note of the scale may be a cadence note, although some notes occur more frequently than others.

This lack of concern for an understanding of the "tonal character" of the second degree of the scale became one of the main theses in *Esquisse de l'histoire de l'harmonie*; Fétis censured every theorist who constructed a triad or seventh chord on the second degree of the scale, and he considered it one of the basic flaws of every harmonic theory until his own.[71]

Chords and tonality. In Book 2, Fétis' notion of points of repose recurred again in his discussion of chords. There was only one consonant chord, that which contained a third and a perfect fifth, and it occurred on the first, fourth, fifth, and sixth scale degrees. The

[71]For Fétis, the seventh chord on the second degree of the scale originates from "modification" by substitution and prolongation of the dominant seventh chord.

consonant chord was called a "perfect chord" because it rendered "the feeling of repose and of conclusion" (23). Root position triads could occur on the other scale degrees only in a nonmodulating sequence, because ". . . the mind, absorbed with the contemplation of a progressive series, momentarily loses the feeling of tonality and regains it only at the final cadence, where normal order is restored" (26).[72] Otherwise, the second, third, and seventh scale degrees may have only first-inversion chords. Since the unstable interval of the fourth, which is ". . . the least satisfying of all the consonant intervals" (35), sets second-inversion chords apart, Fétis, like contemporary theorists, said that one encounters them less frequently than root-position or first-inversion chords. Although six-four chords arise most frequently as double suspensions over the dominant as preparation for the "repose of the perfect chord on the note where it is placed" (35), they can be encountered on the first and second scale degrees as well.

The "natural" dissonant chord, the chord "invented" by Monteverdi, is the dominant seventh; it alone, according to Fétis, determined tonality because it contained the "appellative" consonance.[73] Unquestionably, the dominant seventh chord used in conjunction with the tonic chord clearly defines tonic and establishes a hierarchy of chords based on this relationship to the fundamental chord. However, Fétis' attribution of the "invention" of the dominant seventh chord to Monteverdi cannot be substantiated;[74] this alleged invention was refuted by, among others, François-August Gevaert (1828–1908), Fétis' successor as Director of the Brussels Conservatory

---

[72]Riemann was one of the first theorists to accept and recognize Fétis' definition of a harmonic sequence as a series of nonfunctional chords. (See Dahlhaus, *Harmonic Tonality*, 59.)

[73]As Warren D. Allen has observed, "Eighteenth-century rationalists had extolled early musicians as *inventors*, men who had advanced the art and science of music because of their reasoning powers, and as a result of their conscious efforts. But with the revival of belief in a revealed, rather than an invented, world, historians began to return to supernatural explanations. . . . [and] the history of music began to be written more and more in terms of great names." (Warren Dwight Allen, *Philosophies of Music History* [1939; rpt., New York: Dover Publications, Inc., 1962], 86–87.)

[74]See Shirlaw's comments on this same issue in *Theory of Harmony*, 345–47.

of Music, in the article "Réponse à M. Fétis, sur l'origine de la tonalité moderne" intended for publication in the *Revue et Gazette musicale* on 13 December 1868, but printed privately.[75]

All of the other dissonant chords are "artificial chords," chords that are the result of prolongation (suspension), substitution (which only occurs in the dominant seventh chord or its inversions), alteration, or a combination of these. No chord, aside from the perfect chord and the dominant seventh chord, is an independent structure representing only itself, and every theorist who failed to perceive this was in contradiction "with the true principles of the art and science" (61). Every nondominant seventh chord is the result of suspension; every nondominant seventh chord is simply a triad with an attendant non-chord tone, and any theorist or composer who has placed seventh chords on the other degrees of the scale as structural entities has "forgotten the law of tonality" (66). Fétis' theory of substitution encountered much criticism, which, as Robert S. Nichols has observed, was due ". . . to the refusal of his critics to accept the metaphysical origin of the practices he describes."[76] In editions of the *Traité d'harmonie* subsequent to the first, Fétis appended two notes that responded to the criticisms of Zimmerman, "my friend, professor at the Paris Conservatory, savant musician, and a declared partisan of Catel's theoretical system . . . " (255). "Note A" (255-61) concerns substitution, and "Note B" (261-75) addresses the combination of prolongation and substitution.

The four phases of tonality. The focal point of Book 3 is modulation and its concomitant effect on tonality. The latter is divided into four stages: *unitonique, transitonique, pluritonique,* and *omnitonique. Unitonique,* the first stage of tonality, is, Fétis claimed, the necessary result of plainchant tonality, which consists mostly of consonant triads. Music that was *unitonique* was based on a seven-note diatonic scale that had seven discrete modes, which differed in the placement of tones and semitones (xxvi-xxvii). "In its most extended conception, the tonality of plainchant had fourteen modes or scales, of which

[75]The text of Gevaert's rebuttal to Fétis is contained in Appendix A.
[76]Robert S. Nichols, "François-Joseph Fétis and the Theory of *Tonalité*" (Ph.D. diss., The University of Michigan, 1971), 136.

only twelve have been used" (xlii). For Fétis, modulation using the church modes was impossible, because

> consonant harmony, the only kind that can exist in the tonality of plainchant, furnished no means of introducing *modulation* into music, i.e., of placing the scales in a relationship of affinity to each other; because, conforming to the tonality from which consonant harmony took its principle, it was without tendency, without attraction, and consequently constituted *unitonique* music (xliii).

The "tendency" that was lacking in the church modes was a tritone between the fourth and seventh degrees of the scale to define tonic, and "this lack of tonal determination is precisely the cause for the absence of modulation" (155). This period of tonality, *tonalité ancienne*, existed until the end of the sixteenth century because the composers, ". . . dominated by the nature of the harmonic elements at their disposal, have been unable to escape from the rigorous despotism of this tonal unity" (151). However, as Robert S. Nichols has pointed out, the term *unitonique* does not ". . . preclude one or even several changes of mode within a composition."[77]

Contrary to what Fétis asserted, the composers did "escape from the rigorous despotism" of tonal unity; by the sixteenth century, madrigal composers, following the tenets of Vicentino, were developing pictorial and expressive writing through extensive use of chromaticism and *music ficta*.[78] This trend, which began with Willaert (*c*1490-1562), reached its zenith with Marenzio (1553-99) and Gesualdo (*c*1560-1613). Modulation was effected, not through the tritone, but through common chords and chromatic inflection; modulation and chromaticism were inextricably tied together and a "floating tonality," a tonality that shifts from one tonal region to the next, resulted. Consonant triads—assuming Fétis means root-position triads—were the preferred structure, although, because of the chromat-

---

[77]Ibid., 107.

[78]In the preface of his *Traité d'harmonie*, Fétis contended that Vicentino and his followers failed ". . . to make the synthesis of a chromatic scale in which the semitones have tendencies of resolution with a harmony that, by the nature of its aggregations, is essentially diatonic and deprived of attraction" (xxxviii).

icism, they were often chromatically related, i.e., *E-flat* major to *C* major or *C* major to *C-sharp* minor. The music of the sixteenth century was definitely not *unitonique*, but, on the other hand, it was not "atonal" as Lowinsky propounds.[79] Fétis allowed himself to be deceived by a very limited definition of tonality.

The second phase of tonality, *ordre transitonique*, is the first phase of *tonalité moderne*. *Ordre transitonique* commenced with the "invention" of the dominant seventh chord by Monteverdi, because the relationship of the fourth degree with the leading tone defined tonic.

> With the discovery of the natural dissonant harmony, which is essentially attractive, Monteverdi, having placed the diatonic scales in relation with the chromatic scale, had found the means of transition from one scale to another. *Modulation* existed, and music passed, for this reason, from the *ordre unitonique* into the *ordre transitonique* (xliii).

But the unprepared seventh in the dominant seventh chord did not emerge as a stylistic mannerism until the late seventeenth century. In the late sixteenth and early seventeenth centuries, the seventh of the dominant usually was a passing tone, and modulation was effected through a common chord rather than by "attacking the dominant harmony" of the new key.

While this could be considered a fundamental flaw in his theory of tonality, Anthony J. Kosar maintains that since modulation in the early nineteenth century was a technique for accounting for chromatic events, "secondary dominants, because they do establish references to other keys, are modulations in the nineteenth-century sense."[80] Although the texture of Monteverdi's music is contrapuntal, Fétis treated

---

[79]Edward E. Lowinsky (*Tonality and Atonality in Sixteenth-Century Music* [Berkeley and Los Angeles: University of California Press, 1961], contended that "triadic atonality" arose because the "extreme chromaticism and constant modulation within a triadic context" destroyed tonal stability (39). Dahlhaus (*Harmonic Tonality*, 17–18) points out that by ignoring the historical development of tonality and applying a twentieth-century term to sixteenth-century music, Lowinsky's use of the term ". . . 'atonality' becomes an omnibus and perplexing concept without objective content."

[80]Anthony Jay Kosar, "François-Joseph Fétis' Theory of Chromaticism and Early Nineteenth-Century Music" (Ph.D. diss., The Ohio State University, 1984), 238–39.

the dominant seventh chord in Monteverdi's music as if it arose in a bass-dominated homophonic texture in which the emphasis was on sonorous effect rather than the interweaving of independent lines.

Finally, not only did the "invention" of the dominant seventh chord create modulation, but Fétis contended that ". . . the *cadence*, properly speaking, that is the rhythmic termination of the phrase, did not exist" (152) until there was the harmonic relationship of the leading tone with the fourth scale degree in the dominant seventh chord. The mere appearance of a dominant seventh chord does not create a phrase. A phrase, which consists of harmony, melody, and rhythm, ". . . must be considered in terms of *tension* and *relaxation*, the moment of relaxation being that of the final accent."[81] To produce a cadence, the goal of a phrase, chordal succession must be coupled with, for example, longer note values and changes in harmonic rhythm. Fétis did not distinguish between a structural dominant seventh and a temporary tonicization of a scale degree. With the invention of the dominant seventh chord, ". . . cadences become frequent and regular" (166) and create the ". . . formation of regular rhythm and periodic phrases" (170). Unfortunately, Fétis did not develop any of his concepts of rhythm and periodic phrasing in his *Traité d'harmonie*. He mentioned them for the reader ". . . only to make known that an absolutely new art in music was created with the employment of the natural dissonant harmony" (170). Regular rhythm and periodic phrase structure became a manifestation of late eighteenth-century homophonic music.[82]

Fétis was the first theorist to explore the concept of common tone modulation, a modulation that he identifies as an "intuitive attraction," because ". . . musical sense compensates for this implied harmony at the moment of the tonal change" (180-81). This third phase of tonality was called *ordre pluritonique*. Fétis contended that Mozart was the first

[81]Roger Sessions, *Harmonic Practice* (New York: Harcourt, Brace & World, 1951), 84.

[82]Fétis intended to write a rhythmic treatise, but it never was completed. In the library of the Conservatoire Royale de Musique de Bruxelles, there is a manuscript of the "Oeuvres complètes de F.-J. Fétis concernant la théorie de la musique"; this manuscript contains the plan for Fétis's projected "Traité de rhythme." Wangermée reproduces the manuscript of the "Oeuvres complètes de F.-J. Fétis concernant la théorie de la musique" in *François-Joseph Fétis*, 309-24.

to recognize it as a viable means of expression. Modulation in *ordre pluritonique* is achieved through enharmonic relationships in which one note of a chord is considered the point of contact between different scales. Herein lies the value of the "attractive" dissonances contained in the diminished seventh chord, and the German and Italian augmented sixth chords, because the enharmonic resolutions of each chord afford several different possible key relationships.

The fourth and final period of tonality was *ordre omnitonique*, toward which ". . . the art has been progressing for half a century; it is touching there at this moment" (184). *Ordre omnitonique* results from the alteration of the intervals of natural chords and modification by substitution of notes. The primary problem with extensive alteration and modification by substitution is that the harmonic aggregation reaches a point of saturation when it is impossible to identify the original chord. Fétis gave the following as an example of the dominant four-two chord of G, with substitution of the minor mode (*e-flat* in place of *d*) and alteration of the sixth (*a-flat*):[83]

Regardless of its "origin," this chord defies empirical verification as the dominant seventh chord in G. This is a basic flaw of Fétis' theory of alteration and modification by substitution: he tries to reduce all harmonic structures to one of his "natural" chords—the perfect chord and the dominant seventh. Fétis' theory of chords becomes strictly mechanical; he lacked the vision of Rameau who speculated, and correctly so, that chords evolve through the superposition of thirds. Of this last period of tonality, Fétis said,

> The tendency toward the multiplicity or even the universality of keys in a piece of music is the last term of the development of

[83]*Traité d'harmonie*, 195, ex. 3.

harmony's combinations; beyond that there is nothing more for these combinations (195).

With this definition of tonality, Fétis was prescient: he foresaw the chromaticism of the late nineteenth century and the demise of tonality in the early twentieth century. In 1841, in an article about Liszt (*Revue et Gazette musicale* [8:263]), Fétis wrote that Liszt, who had attended his 1832 lectures, ". . . was struck with the novelty of this idea" of *ordre omnitonique* and wrote some piano music that employed these concepts; in a 17 September 1859 letter to Fétis, Liszt wrote, ". . . I have not ceased to profit from your teachings, especially those from your remarkable lectures on 'ordre omnitonique' . . . ."[84] But this idea of the universality of keys was not accepted by everyone at the time; Riemann wrote (1898) that *ordre omnitonique* was ". . . a harebrained view of the harmonic chaos of continual enharmonic-chromatic modulation."[85] This comment, given Riemann's perspective at the close of a century of changing harmonic and tonal techniques, was wholly unwarranted.

Fétis, unlike his predecessors, turned to music itself for his theories. Despite the weaknesses in his theories, Fétis rejected all extra-musical phenomena (any acoustical-mathematical bias) as organizing principles for music, and he solved the age-old dilemma of whether melody is derived from harmony or vice versa by pointing to their mutual source in the scale. Melody and harmony are products of the same ingredients and are controlled by the same principles. His "points of repose" have as much validity today as they did for Fétis in 1840. Stravinsky employs "points of repose" and "poles of attraction" in his discussion of tonality in *The Poetics of Music*:

---

[84]Cited in Istvan Szelényi, "Der unbekannte Liszt," *Studia musicologica* 5 (1963), 312. Liszt is known to have written a *Prélude omnitonique*, but the work, last seen in a 1904 London exhibition, has been lost. Unfortunately, Searle mistakenly credits the idea of *ordre omnitonique* to Liszt. (Humphrey Searle, *The Music Of Liszt*, 2d rev. ed. [New York: Dover Publications, 1966], 88.)

[85]William C. Mickelsen, trans. and ed., *Hugo Riemann's Theory of Harmony and History of Music, Book III*, (Lincoln and London: University of Nebraska Press, 1977), 186.

... it is no less indispensable to obey, not new idols, but the eternal necessity of affirming the axis of music and to recognize the existence of poles of attraction. Diatonic tonality is only one means of orienting music toward these poles. The function of tonality is completely subordinated to the force of attraction of the pole of sonority. All music is nothing more than a succession of impulses that converge toward a definite point of repose. That is as true of Gregorian chant as of a Bach fugue, as of Brahms' music as of Debussy's.[86]

What Stravinsky and Fétis have said about points of repose has profound meaning in relation to any misunderstanding of the words "tonic" and "tonality," regardless of the age or culture to which one refers. As Rosalie Schellhous has written, "The idea of tonality as a system of relationships among tones of a scale and its harmonies is Fétis's most enduring contribution to musical thought . . . ."[87]

ÉQUISSE DE L'HISTOIRE DE L'HARMONIE

Fétis was a man of strong convictions who was proud of his accomplishments, and the *Esquisse de l'histoire de l'harmonie* is no exception. He referred to it numerous times in his writings, including the preface[88] and Chapter 4 of his *Traité d'harmonie* and "Mon testament musical."[89] Fétis viewed harmony as a musical science that could be codified and systematized; yet his presentation of the history of harmony is not objective: it is permeated with his personal views. Believing in the infallibility of his doctrine of tonality, Fétis injected his personal opinion at every opportunity. Each theorist is analyzed for aspects that further the development of harmonic theory and aspects that hinder that development. Fétis praised the theorists

---

[86]Igor Stravinsky, *Poetics of Music in the Form of Six Lessons*, trans. Arthur Knodel and Ingolf Dahl (1947; rpt. New York: Vintage-Knopf, 1956), 37–38.

[87]"Fétis's *Tonality* as a Metaphysical Principle," 239.

[88]"It would be difficult for me to give a true idea of the inexhaustible source of instruction that I have found in this persevering study [of theory books and scores], the result of which led me to the conviction of the infallibility of my principles. My *Esquisse de l'harmonie de l'histoire, considérée comme art et comme science systématique* has made known to the public the care that I have taken in my research on this subject" [x].

[89]*RGM* 20 (1853): 299, 314.

whose ideas most closely resembled his own, and he castigated those whose ideas ran counter to his, particularly those theorists who searched outside of music for its basis. Virtually no theorist escaped his venom.

As the title indicates, this work is a historical outline rather than an exhaustive study. The *Esquisse*, which must be viewed as a preliminary sketch of the history of the theory of harmony, demonstrates Fétis' thorough mastery of the literature of music theory and his skill in distilling the salient information contained in that literature. Fétis' sole intent in this volume was to provide a succinct record of the facts, errors, and truths of harmony as he perceived them—according to the tenets of his system—so that future theorists would not have to ascertain them and could avoid perpetuating the "errors." Despite a definite slant in many of Fétis' arguments, the *Esquisse* is a polemic couched in a sincere attempt to evaluate and compare the major harmonic systems until 1840 to reveal the "facts, errors, and truths." Herein lies its primary value. Fétis' history of harmony found its summation in his own harmonic theories, because, while "Rameau, Sorge, Schröter, and Catel found the first elements, . . . I have completed the theory by putting it on a solid base";[90] this "solid base" is tonality. Like Riemann would do fifty years later, Fétis attempted to demonstrate that his theory was the result of a long historic development.[91] Perhaps, like Riemann, Fétis should have closed his book with "I hold as highly significant the proof that ideas which contain a truth continually return until they can no longer be kept down. Therefore, this history . . . may be regarded as an account of the origin of my ideas on the theory of music."[92]

The translation. My aim has been to render the meaning of the original accurately in an English translation that is smooth and readable. Fétis' manner of expression is often complex and involved. The temptation to simplify or paraphrase was ever present, particularly in some of the long, intricate sentences. Although a single

---

[90]*Esquisse*, 178; *Traité d'harmonie*, Bk. 4, ch. 5, § 372, p. 254.

[91]Scott Burnham, "Method and Motivation in Hugo Riemann's History of Harmonic Theory," *MTS* (Spring 1992): 1–14.

[92]Mickelsen, *Hugo Riemann's Theory of Harmony*, 223.

sentence is often rendered in two or three English sentences, the flavor of the original has been retained with a fairly literal translation. Occasionally the French text abruptly shifts between the past tenses (mostly "passé simple") and the present tense ("historical present"). Wherever this shift occurred, the English version is usually given in the past tense.

Some textual changes have been made, however. Fétis' spelling of the names of composers, treatises, and musical compositions has been changed from French into the original language or the more usual Latin equivalent, e.g., from Jean Gabrieli to Giovanni Gabrieli; from Gafori to Gaffurius; from *Lucidaire de la musique plaine* to *Lucidarium in arte musicae planae*. Although every effort was made to keep bracketed insertions to a minimum, if the source, author, pages, phrases, or words of a quotation were omitted (either intentionally or accidentally), an ellipsis has been added or the omitted information has been enclosed in brackets. All brackets and ellipses are those of the translator. Since Fétis does not indicate when he has italicized words in the quotations for emphasis, a parenthetical note—[Fétis' italics]—has been added at the close of the quotation by the translator. All musical examples cited by Fétis have been verified, and any discrepancies have been indicated in the notes. Where it was deemed appropriate, another version has been appended. Obvious typographical errors have been corrected without comment.

The notes that have been added by the translator cite modern editions or publications of original sources, bring the content of Fétis' treatise into correspondence with the findings of contemporary scholarship, and attempt to correct erroneous information.[93] To aid the reader in differentiating between Fétis' footnotes and the notes of the translator, all of Fétis' footnotes are enclosed in brackets.

One last problem had to be considered in maintaining the integrity of Fétis' work—terminology. Technical terms (*déchant* or *basso continuo*) have been left in the original language. The names of the scale degrees have not been changed into their present equiv-

---

[93]In *Philosophies of Music History*, Warren Allen asserts it is a ". . . notorious fact that when Fétis could not find a date, he invented or guessed at one" (67n. 11).

alents, because Fétis stated explicitly in his *Traité d'harmonie* (2) that the degrees of the scale are designated by their melodic and harmonic tendencies; hence "third degree," "fourth degree," and "sixth degree" rather than "mediant," "subdominant," and "submediant,"respectively.[94] Finally, because Fétis propounded in his Traité d'harmonie (6) that only the "natural" intervals of major and minor scales can become augmented or diminished through chromatic alteration, the terms "just" fifth (perfect), "major" fourth (augmented), and "minor" fifth (diminished) have been retained.[95]

[94]Fétis said ". . . the first note of any key is called *tonic*, because it gives its name to the key; the second is called *second degree* (and, in the language of some older harmonists, *supertonic*); the third, *third degree* (formerly *mediant*, because it is midway between the first sound and the fifth in the chord called *perfect*); the fourth, *fourth degree* (formerly subdominant); the fifth, *dominant*, because it is found in a great number of combinations of harmony; the sixth, *sixth degree* (formerly *superdominant* [*sus-dominante*]); the seventh, *leading tone*, when it has an ascending tendency toward the tonic, and *seventh degree* in other circumstances" (2).

[95]In rejecting the term "diminished fifth" for the interval between the leading tone and the fourth degree, Fétis wrote, "It must be called *minor fifth*, because there is nothing diminished in an interval whose two notes are in the natural state of the key" (7n.1). Robert S. Nichols ("The Theory of *Tonalité*," 116), points out that this distinction is vital to understanding Fétis' theory of the attractions of scale degrees. However, Nichols translates *quarte majeur* "greater fourth" and *quinte mineur* as "lesser fifth."

Portrait of François-Joseph Fétis. Photograph by Ghémar Frères.
Used with permission, Royal Library, Brussels

FOREWORD

Voluminous histories of music have appeared in Italy, England, Germany, and even in France, where the literature of this art was less cultivated. These histories, rich in erudition with respect to times and facts whose ambiguity has not yet been dispelled because the documents which could remove our doubts have not reached us, have been silent on what in modern art is the most deserving of our interest: I mean *harmony*.

Harmony, considered as art, offers in its history the spectacle of transformations, all the more remarkable as the means and end change at times through the appearance of certain facts which, at first glance, do not seem to have such great importance. Thus through a simple aggregation of tones which we are astonished not to see introduced into art before the end of the sixteenth century, we suddenly see music lose its calm, religious character, acquire the expressive accent that was lacking, and from that time, having become appropriate for the portrayal of passions, give birth to opera, which would not have been able to exist without this accent.

But harmony is not only an art; harmony is also a science which, by the diversity of its elements and the tenuousness of the bonds that bind them together, presents perhaps more difficulties than any other for the formation of a definite theory. What is more worthy of attention than the history of the constant and almost always barren efforts of a vast number of erudite men, philosophers, geometricians, and great musicians for the formation of this theory? Harmony, as a science, touches everything; whence the origin of these systems so contradictory that some have sought its principle in the harmony of the spheres, acoustical phenomena, abstract numbers, the divisions of the monochord, the physical makeup of man, and, finally, in isolated and empirical facts, whose influence has been the greatest obstacle to the science's progress for a long time. Nevertheless, in the midst of multiple errors there appear, occasionally, a few scattered truths, which although misunderstood, remain the foundation stones for the complete edifice.

I believe that the time has come when history ought to set down all the facts, errors and truths; analyze them, search for their origin, and ascertain the actual state of the art and science in order to illuminate the path that remains to be traversed; to spare future theorists the useless efforts of redoing what has already been done, and to avoid the pitfalls already signalled by failures. The volume that I am offering today to a few friends of the science and art is not a history with all its developments; just as the title indicates, this is only the outline of it. It has occurred to me that such a great work could not be released to the public before its attention had been attracted by the indication of the main facts. I am determined to publish the pieces that constitute this outline in a special journal. I am bringing them together in this volume, which is not designated for circulation, only so that my work can be submitted to the criticism of earnest men whose interest it merits with its subject matter.

The Author

Brussels

12 January 1841

CHAPTER I

AN OUTLINE OF THE HISTORY OF HARMONY CONSIDERED AS ART AND AS SCIENCE

[The Creation of a Harmonic System]

From the time simultaneous combinations of sounds began to emerge from the barbaric system of diaphony, i.e., the long successions of fifths or of fourths and octaves, the first elements of harmony present only very crude attempts. When these imperfect successions still recur frequently, when the unison constantly betrays the harmonic objectives of the composition, and in which voice crossing is so frequent, it is difficult to distinguish the melodic line from the accompanying part. These initial attempts were only in two voices. We can see examples in Franco's *Ars cantus mensurabilis*[1] which, in spite of the conflicting opinion of some writers, belongs to the end of the eleventh century, as I have shown in my *Biographie universelle des musiciens*.[2]

---

[1]Although Fétis read Franco's treatise in Martin Gerbert, *Scriptores ecclesiastici de musica sacra potissimum*, 3 vols. (Typis San-Blasianis, 1784), 3:1-17, he was cognizant of the inadequacies of Gerbert's edition. The margins of Fétis' copy contain corrections and, on page 12, the notation, "In a manuscript of fonds de Fontanieu E 30, which is in the Bibliothèque royale de Paris and which contains Franco's treatise [Paris, B.N. lat. 11267, fol. 1-8r], some staves were drawn for an example of the harmony indicated in the text; unfortunately all the manuscript's examples remained blank." A more recent edition of Franco's treatise, with the examples, can be found in Edmond de Coussemaker, *Scriptorum de musica medii aevi* , 4 vols. (Paris: Durand, 1864), 1:117-35.

[2]Reese (*Music in the Middle Ages*, [New York: W. W. Norton & Co., 1940], 289) dates Franco as *fl* c1250-after 1280 and his treatise as "shortly after 1280," but Besseler ("Franco von Köln" in *MGG* 4, cols. 691-92) contends that both of these assessments are too late because the technique that Adam de la Halle demonstrated in his motets (composed between 1262 and 1269) corresponds exactly to the Parisian models of Franco. Besseler asserts that since Adam de la Halle was not innovative technically, de la Halle copied Franco. Thus, Franco's treatise presumably was written c1260. Strunk (*Source Readings in Music History* [New York: W. W. Norton & Co., 1950], 134) accepts the latter date. However, Andrew Hughes (*NGrove*, s.v. "Franco of Cologne") believes that more recent evidence "favors a date of soon after 1230." Fétis' assignment of Franco's treatise to the eleventh century is untenable and its acceptance ". . . would quite upset the theory of a gradual growth of the mensural system towards standardization." (Reese, 289n. 51.) For a discussion and critique of Fétis' BUM article, see Coussemaker, *L'Art harmonique aux xii*[e] *et xiii*[e] *siècles* (Paris: A. Durand and V. Didron, 1865), 22-32.

In this period of the origin of the art, no harmony other than simple intervals of two tones is recognized, although Franco clearly states that there already was three-voice counterpoint at this time. But since he does not furnish an example and since he does not talk about connecting two intervals, there is reason to believe that the third voice was alternatively in unison or at the octave and fifth of one of the other voices. In chapter 11, where he discusses discant or harmony, he divides the intervals into consonances or dissonances, or rather, *concordances* and *discordances*. The concords are divided into three kinds, namely, (1) the perfect concords which are the unison and the octave; (2) the imperfect concords or the major and minor thirds; (3) the mean concords or the fourth and fifth.[3]

Franco also classifies the discords into perfect and imperfect. There are, he says, four perfect discords, namely, the semitone (*semitonus*), the tritone or major fourth (*tritonus*), the major seventh (*ditonus cum diapente*), and the minor seventh (*semiditonus cum diapente*). The imperfect discords are the major sixth (*tonus cum diapente*), and the minor sixth (*semitonus cum diapente*).

It would take too long to examine the principles that led Franco, or rather his contemporaries, to such a classification. But it is evident that these principles were arbitrary and false, because the *tone*, as well as the semitone, is a dissonance, and sixths bring nothing but a sense of concord to the ear and do not imply a necessity for resolution. With respect to the perfect fourth, ranked here among the consonances, we will see in another place that it has given rise to some lively controversies.

Franco gives little information on the use of intervals in the harmony or discant of his time. He only tells us that such harmony could begin with the unison, octave, fifth, *fourth*, major third, and minor third. Here is one of the examples that he gives of the harmony of this time, commencing with a fourth. I have corrected the mistakes

---

[3]The fourth and fifth are intermediary concords—they fall halfway between the perfect and the imperfect concords in aural perception. According to Franco ". . . they produce a concord better than the imperfect, yet not better than perfect." (Coussemaker, *Scriptorum* 1:129.)

of the poor copy by Abbot Gerbert, according to the British Museum's manuscript (*Scriptores ecclesiastici de musica sacra potissimum*, 3:13)[4]

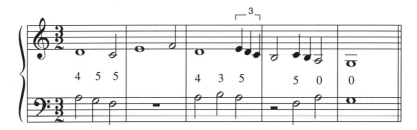

A manuscript from the Bibliothèque royale de Paris shows us the didactics of the art of composition and harmony in a most remarkable state of advancement about the middle of the thirteenth century.[5] Here are some rules, to which I am adding the examples that are lacking in the manuscript:

> Whosoever wishes to discant [to accompany the chant] first ought to know what the octave and the fifth are: the fifth is the fifth note and the octave is the eighth. He ought to examine whether the chant ascends or descends. If the chant ascends, he must take the octave; if the chant descends, he must take the fifth.

> If the chant ascends one note, as *c-d*, one ought to take the upper octave and descend a third, as is shown here:[6]

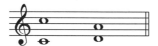

[4]See Coussemaker, *Scriptorum*, 1:131 for a slightly different version of this example.

[5]Coussemaker (*Histoire de l'harmonie du moyen-âge* [Paris: V. Didron, 1852]), who stated that this treatise is found "on the margins of two leafs of Ms. 813, fonds Saint-Victor of the Bibliothèque nationale de Paris, . . . [lat. 15139] fol. 269r and 270r" (244), believed that the treatise was written at either the end of the 11th century or the beginning of the 12th century (34).

[6]Quiconque veult deschanter, il doit premiers savoir qu'est quins et doubles; quins est la quinte note et doubles est la witisme; et doit regarder se li chant monte ou avale. Se il monte, nous devons prendre le double note; se il avale, nous devons prendre la quinte note.
    Se li chans monte d'une note, si comme ut, re, on doit prendre le deschant du double deseure et descendre deux notes, si comme apert:

If the chant ascends two notes, as *c-e*, one ought to take the upper octave and descend one pitch, as in this example:[7]

If the chant ascends three notes, as *c-f*, he must take the octave and retain the same note.[8]

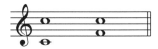

Although these rules and the ones that follow[9] for the accompaniment of various movements of chant appear to have been for the improvised harmony that used to be called *déchant* or *chant sur le livre*, and which the Italians since then have named *contrapunto la mente*, they denote a sensible progress which is not noticed to the same degree in harmonic pieces written in even later times. But, as is seen, it is not a question of concords in this harmony, but solely of two intervals, i.e., the fifth and the octave. We observe as well that regard for intervallic movement constitutes all of the theory of the art, even in this remote time—a strange anomaly in a time when many imperfect movements were being admitted into practice. In the same manuscript where there are rules so consistent with those of a more perfect art, we find examples where the succession of fifths and fourths are numerous even for two parts, but where favorable intervallic movement denotes progression towards a more satisfying harmony. In the three-voice examples, the fifth and octave are used as actual harmony.

---

[7]Se li chans monte deux notes, si comme ut, mi, [mi], sol, nous devons prendre le deschant en witisme note et descendre une note.

[8]Se li chans monte trois notes, ut, fa, nous devons prendre la witisme note et nous tenir ou point.

[9]An English translation of all the rules for *déchant* in this treatise can be found in Hugo Riemann, *History of Music Theory, Books I and II*, trans. Raymond Haggh (Lincoln: University of Nebraska Press, 1962), 81-83.

In the three-voice chanson written at the end of the thirteenth century by Adam de la Halle (which I published in the first volume of *Revue musicale* [1827], as well as several other pieces from the collection where I extracted it),[10] a few examples of complete harmony of the third and fifth, and even of the third and sixth, permit us to see perceptible progress in the sense of harmony.

It is curious to compare this example with the didactic, which we find in the important works of Marchetto da Padova [Marchettus de Padua], an author of the same period. This author, whose fault it is to be obscure by verboseness rather than conciseness, unduly expanded certain parts of the science in which interest is moderate in his *Lucidarium in arte musicae planae*, and does not expand enough on the topic of our actual research.[11] Nevertheless, we notice there (*Tract.* V & VI) that Franco's teaching, with respect to consonances and dissonances, was still in force two centuries after him.[12] Thus Marchetto says (in the second chapter of the sixth treatise) that the fourth is not only a consonance, but a *divine* consonance because it contains in it the sacred quaternary, and because its parts are, with respect to music, those which are in other cases the four seasons of the year, the four evils of the world, the four elements, the four

---

[10]This chanson, "Tant con je vivrai," which was published in the first part of Fétis' article "Découverte de plusieurs Manuscrits intéressants pour l'histoire de la musique" (*RM* 1 [1827]: 3-7), was extracted from the Vallière collection (no. 2736) of the Bibliothèque du Roi, which is now identified as F-*Pn*, fonds française 25566 (*Ha*), f. 34r.

[11]See Gerbert, *Scriptorum* 1:65-121 and Jan W. Herlinger, *The Lucidarium of Marchetto of Padua: A Critical Edition, Translation, and Commentary* (Chicago: University of Chicago Press, 1985).

[12]Fétis' premature dating of Franco's treatise led him to a fallacious conclusion. With the more plausible date of *c*1230-50 for Franco's treatise, his teachings were still in effect nearly one hundred years later. Although the actual date of the *Lucidarium* has not been ascertained, F. Alberto Gallo ("Marchetto da Padova," *NGrove* 11:662) contends the work probably was written between 1309 and 1318, and Oliver Strunk ("The Date of Marchetto da Padova" in *Essays on Music in the Western World* [New York: W. W. Norton & Co., 1974], 41) asserts that it was written between 19 August 1310 and 11 July 1318. However, Jan W. Herlinger (*The Lucidarium of Marchetto of Padua*, 3) has concluded that, since the work is dedicated to Ranieri de Zaccaria, its limiting dates must be between 20 May 1317 and 11 July 1318. Thus the 1275 date given by Gerbert for this treatise is too much too early.

gospels, etc. One must admit that these are strange reasons to make a *divine* consonance out of the worst interval of harmony. The major and minor sixth are a dissonance in Marchetto's theory, as in that of Franco, of whom Marchetto is, in a way, the commentator. In chapter seven of the fifth treatise, Marchetto poses the question: whether the resolution of the *dissonance* of the major sixth to the octave is better than to the fifth, and answers in the affirmative.[13] The examples that he gives of the two types of resolution furnish us some chromatic successions, so much the more strange and remarkable for the time when Marchetto was writing because his work has plainsong, where similar successions would be meaningless, for its goal. Here are a few of his examples:[14]

These successions, and several others where the boldness of Marchetto's imagination appears in a strange way, remained without significance in his time and only had application nearly 300 years

[13]This query of Marchetto occurs in the sixth chapter of the fifth treatise in Herlinger's translation. In chapter 2 of this treatise, Marchetto classified the third, sixth, and tenth as dissonances; and in chapter six, Marchetto argues that the octave (diapason) is more nearly perfect than the fifth (diapente), and that the ". . . dissonance, which is called a sixth, less properly descends to the fifth than to the octave" (Gerbert, *Scriptores* 3:83).

[14]In each of these examples, Fétis erroneously transcribed the treble voice an octave higher than the manuscript indicates. Thus each of the harmonic intervals should be simple rather than compound. The figures have been added by Fétis. These examples have been taken from the second treatise, chapter 6, "On the Diesis," and chapter 8, "On the Chromatic Semitone." Marchetto divided the whole tone into five parts to produce a diesis of one-fifth of the whole tone and a chromatic semitone that is four-fifths of the whole tone. The second example cited by Fétis occurs in both chapters 6 and 8; the first and third examples are found in chapter eight. For two discussions of the types of semitones advocated by Marchetto, see Jan W. Herlinger, "Marchetto's Division of the Whole Tone," *JAMS* 34 (1981): 193-216, and "Fractional Divisions of the Whole Tone," *MTS* 3 (1981): 74-83.

later, because they did not meet any need in the tonality of plain-song.[15] The only one of these things that is found in practice at the close of the thirteenth century is the major sixth accompanied by the third and resolved to the octave. Adam de la Halle furnishes this example of one preceded by a seventh, interpreted as a changed note, with the fourth which was not prepared, because it was regarded as a consonance.[16]

The manuscript of a thirteenth-century music treatise, which, after having been passed on from the library of the Abbot of Tersan into that of Perne, is today in mine, provides me with an example of

[15]Marchetto refers to his *Lucidarium* as "a work by means of which all theorists and performers might rationally understand what they sing in plainchant" in his dedicatory letter (Gerbert, *Scriptores* 3:65). Herlinger (1981) says that the Lucidarium is ". . . for performing musicians, who would have had neither time nor stomach for the laborious computations of Pythagorean arithmetic . . . but who needed some simple index for the sizes of the two semitones . . . ." (76).

[16]Both Coussemaker (*OEuvres complètes du trouvère Adam de la Halle* [Paris, 1872], XV Rondeau, 230-31) and Wilkins (*The Lyric Works of Adam de la Halle* [American Institute of Musicology, 1967], Rondeau No. 15, p. 58) have transcribed this work in triple meter. (See Appendix B, Ex. 1.) In *L'Art harmonique aux xiie et xiiie siècles,* Coussemaker argues that the metric discrepancy, as well as rhythmic errors, renders Fétis' transcription wholly erroneous (pp. vii-viii, 15-16 & 113-19). Fétis fails to indicate the *c-sharp* (m. 2) that, in all likelihood, would have been supplied in performance to eliminate the tritone formed between *c-natural* and *f-sharp*. The resulting cadence, the so-called double-leading-tone cadence, is one of the characteristic closes of the period.

the major sixth with the major third which resolves down.[17] Here is the passage:

I ought to comment in passing that in this treatise the fourth is classified amongst the consonances also, and the major and minor sixths amongst the dissonances. These points of doctrine were, therefore, universally adopted from Franco.

In summing up the facts that arise from the preceding, we see that harmony had made progress very slowly in four hundred years—by the end of the thirteenth century—because it must not be forgotten that some examples of diaphony, or harmony by the succession of fifths, fourths, and octaves, are already found before 900. However, examined for the aims of the art, this progress is immense.

(1) Harmonies of the third and fifth and of the third and sixth are known and employed. This sixth is, as a matter of fact, considered

[17]François-Louis Perne (1772-1832), who had been Fétis' predecessor as librarian at the Paris Conservatory (1819-22), was a French composer, singer, string bass player, and music historian who gained widespread recognition for his work in Greek and medieval music. He authored *Exposition de la séméiographie, ou Notation musicale des Grecs* (Paris: Didot, 1815), "Ancienne musique des chansons du châtelain de Coucy, mise en notation moderne, avec accompagnement de piano" in *Chansons du châtelain de Coucy, Revues sur tous les manuscrits* (Paris: Crapelet, 1830), and numerous articles for the *Revue musicale* (see vols. 2 [1827], 3 [1828], 4 [1828], 5 [1829], and 8 [1830]). Perne's library, which Fétis purchased in 1834 and described as "less remarkable in quantity than in quality" (*BUM*, s.v. "Perne, F.-L."), contained Perne's manuscript copies of polyphonic music and theoretical treatises; these manuscript copies now are part of the Fétis collection in the Bibliothèque royale Albert Ier in Brussels.

as a dissonance, but its use is likened to that of consonances since it is not prepared and resolves up when it is major with the minor third.

(2) Without having disappeared, the successions of fifths, fourths, and octaves have become more rare and are interspersed with contrary motion, elegant and varied.

(3) Finally, with respect to the movement of the parts, there is a didactic of the art which is more advanced than practice and which is expected to prevail in the end over the imperfections of practice. It is in this state that harmony enters into the fourteenth century, where we shall see the art resplendent with new elements.

The earliest document of complete harmony belonging to the fourteenth century which has come to my attention is a three-voice rondeau composed between 1316 and 1327 by Jehannot de l'Escurel [Jehan de Lescurel], and which I published in the thirty-fourth issue of the *Revue musicale* (1832)[18] from a Roman de Fauvel manuscript that is found in the Bibliothèque royale de Paris.[19] This is not the place to examine the worth of this piece of music, with which its author was in advance of his time, either with respect to the melody or the good taste of the ornaments and the art of harmonizing them. But I will point out as remarkable progress the small number of successions of fifths, unisons, and octaves that exists there. The sixth, accompanied by the third, is employed so frequently and in such varied ways that it is evident that this harmony ceased to be considered a dissonance. (See Examples a and b.) For the first time, I also noticed in this piece a succession of two perfect, complete chords with movements as pure as the most proper composer could make them today. (See Example c.)[20]

---

[18]Fétis gives the dates 1314-21 in the *Revue musicale* (12:269) and 1316-21 in the *Biographie universelle* (5:282) for this three-voice rondeau. The date cited above, 1327, is undoubtedly a misprint. In spite of this apparent contradiction, Fétis erred: Jehannot de l'Escurel was executed in 1303 in Paris. (Reese, *Music in the Middle Ages*, 333.) Gilbert Reaney asserts that if 1303 is considered the death year, and *c*1310-16 the origin of the *Roman de Fauvel*, then the secular songs of l'Escurel were written *c*1300. ("Jehannot de l'Escurel," *MGG* 8, col. 666.)

[19]F-*Pn* 145 (*Fauv*), f. 57.

[20]These examples, which were extracted from "A vous débonnaire," use (a) measures 1-2, (b) 15-16, and (c) 6. See Appendix B, Ex. 2 for Wilkins' transcriptions of these measures.

Two three-voice French chansons from the fourteenth century, which I discovered on the parchment of the cover of a register of some archives of Ghent,[21] supply me with one of the oldest examples of a regular progression of sevenths prepared and resolved to a sixth (see Example a), and another of the fourth prepared as a suspension to the third (Example b).

A manuscript music treatise, dated in Paris, 12 January 1375, a copy of which, made by Perne from a manuscript of Roquefort,[22] is in my library, contains a three-voice French chanson that furnishes some

[21]So that no one doubts the age of these chansons, it will suffice to say that they were written in black notation; now, examples of this notation were rare after the first years of the fifteenth century.

[22]Jean-Baptiste-Bonaventure Roquefort-Lamericourt (1777-1833) began his music studies in 1796 after completing military school. To study music history and literature, he bought numerous manuscripts and old editions of books that were gradually sold when he abandoned his musical research in 1808 to study *langue romane*. (*BUM* 7:307-08.)

b.

examples of the same kind (see Examples a and b), but also provides one of a seventh in anticipation of the sixth, and of a suspension to a unison which would be good only if it were at the distance of the ninth (see Example c). This latter fault has been made sometimes by modern musicians, but here it is also compounded by a succession of fifths.

The syncopated harmony that we see established in the fourteenth century, and which became a mannerism amongst the musicians from that time, was an important acquistion of the art. This harmony, I maintain, led to these anticipations which the still unskilled composers confused with suspensions. We can see any number of examples at this time. Francesco Landini, the celebrated mid-fourteenth century composer and organist from Florence, furnishes us with some very remarkable examples, particularly in this passage in an Italian canzonette of which I published the first part in score in the first volume of the *Revue musicale* (1827) from a manuscript in the Bibliothèque royale de Paris.[23]

---

[23]This canzonette, "Non avrà me' pietà," was published in the second part of Fétis' article "Découverte de Manuscrits intéressants pour l'histoire de la musique" (*RM* 1 [1828]: 106-13); measures 2-4 are illustrated. A comparison of the *Revue musicale* copy with this excerpt reveals two misprints in the upper voice: (1) the A4 between mm. 1 and 2 should be tied; and (2) the G4 on the latter half of the third beat in ms. 2 should be E4. Thus, rather than an unstylistic anticipation at the cadence, there is the more characteristic 7-6-1 or "under-third" cadence.

The second measure of this example is regular with respect to the tenor, but not with the intermediary part [upper]. Similar anticipations became more rare when the theory of harmony was grounded on a more solid foundation. These anticipations had disappeared almost entirely in the splendid days of the sixteenth-century Roman school. In modern music anticipations have regained favor; they are considered a simple modification of a natural harmony obvious to the ear. Thus, according to this point of view, the preceding example reduces to consonant harmony as follows:

Since I have cited where the excerpt in question, Landini's canzonette, is found, I ought to warn the reader about the harmonic abhorrences that are found in a complete transcription of this piece inserted in the *Archives curieuses de la musique*: to judge from this example would cause an absolutely false notion about the state of art in the mid-fourteenth century to be formed.[24] In all of the manuscripts

---

[24]Schrade's transcription of this canzonette in *Polyphonic Music of the Fourteenth Century* (4:144) uses a partial signature. (See Appendix B, Ex. 3.)

from the middle ages where there is music, the copyists inserted a multitude of errors and, as Tinctoris remarks in several places in his *Proportionale*, the notational system of this period so frequently confused even the composers that they made numerous proportional errors in notating their works.[25] In the transcriptions that one makes of these early pieces of music, it is necessary, therefore, all the time to make corrections that require as profound a knowledge of the state of the art in the period of each of these pieces as of early notation. Now, no manuscript is distorted by a greater number of mistakes than the one [*cote* 535] where Landini's chanson is found. Some of the symbols are absolutely false; certain things that appertain to one part have been placed in another, and we see there the use of dissonances which never were accepted in the music of the Middle Ages. This is what the transcriber did not understand at all; he has given a wholly false idea of Landini's talent. Landini's superiority over the other musicians of his era could never be doubted and even appears in this work of which I published the first part.

We are indebted to Jehan des Murs [Johannes de Muris] for some valuable information about the didactic of the art of the period in which he wrote, i.e., about 1360.[26] His treatise *De Discantu*, of which I own a manuscript and which can be found in many libraries, contains exact rules on the quality of intervals, their use, and their movement within harmony.[27] Abbot Gerbert has given an extract from the manuscript of the monastery at St. Blaise (*Script. eccles. de*

---

[25]An English translation of this work, "The Proportionale Musices of Johannes Tinctoris," appears in *JMT* 1 (1957): 22-75. Albert Seay's revised translation, *Proportions in Music*, was published by the Colorado College Music Press in 1979. The opening prologue has been translated by Oliver Strunk, *Source Readings*, 193-96.

[26]Lawrence Gushee contends that since "there are no records, however ambiguous, from after 1351 we may be satisfied with a date of *c*1350 for Jehan's death." ("Jehan des Murs," *NGrove* 9:588.)

[27]In his *BUM* (1st ed.; 6:523-24), Fétis stated that he owned this counterpoint treatise, which "is only abridged in most libraries." Although Coussemaker (*Traités inédits sur la musique du moyen âge* [Lille, 1867]) confirms that des Murs probably wrote a counterpoint treatise because later anonymous authors wished to "interpret faithfully des Murs' doctrine," he was annoyed that Fétis had revealed neither the contents of the treatise nor given an analysis of des Murs' precepts (16).

musica, 3:306).[28] There we see that the fourth has disappeared from the group of consonances. As a matter of fact, it is no longer used in the composition that I have cited, with the exception of the chanson of Jehannot de l'Escurel [Jehan de Lescurel], which appeared at the beginning of the fourteenth century. Jehan des Murs acknowledges only the unison, fifth, and octave as consonances. The imperfect consonances are, he says, the major third, the minor third, and the major sixth. Why the minor sixth was not included in this category is unknown. It seems that all of the masters concurred with this part of the doctrine, because the same division is found in a manuscript treatise of Roquefort. However that may be, we see that the ideas towards the major sixth were rectified, and that this interval has taken its natural place among the consonances.

Thus it is in Jehan de Murs' discant treatise that this important rule that has become fundamental in the art of composition is found for the first time: two perfect consonances created by similar movement, whether ascending or descending, must be avoided. Only Jehan des Murs seems to want to weaken the severity of this rule a little, in favor of lack of craftsmanship of the composers of his time, by adding: "in so far as it is possible." Here are his words: "Debemus etiam binas consonantias perfectas seriatim coniunctas ascendendo vel descendendo, prout possumus, evitare."[29] Here the theory was still more advanced than practice, because in the majority of the works of this period that have come down to us, examples of two unisons, two octaves, or two consecutive fifths are still seen, although these faults have become more rare. In this respect, Landini wrote much better than his contemporaries.

Thus, it is in Jehan des Murs' discant treatise that we find for the first time these rules that are still in force in counterpoint: (1) all

[28]While Gerbert's source, the St. Blaise MS, is unknown today, other sources are extant. (Heinrich Besseler, "Johannes de Muris," *MGG* 7, cols. 111-12.) Coussemaker insists that Gerbert's extract is "a fragment of little importance" that has no relationship "with another treatise entitled *De discantu*." (Coussemaker, *Traités inédits*, 15.)

[29]"Also we ought to avoid two perfect consonances in succession, either ascending or descending, as much as possible." (Gerbert, *Scriptores* 3:306.)

counterpoint ought to commence and end on a perfect consonance ("Sciendum est etiam, quod discantus debet habere principium et finem per consonantiam perfectam."). (2) Two major thirds by conjunct motion, ascending and descending, ought to be avoided ("Debemus etiam duos ditonus coniunctos, ascendendo vel descendendo evitare.").[30]

In summarizing what precedes concerning the history of harmony in the fourteenth century, we find there remarkable progress that is summarized here:

(1) The consonances are categorized in their natural order. The fourth ceased to be a perfect consonance; the sixth reentered the category of consonances.

(2) Consonant harmony is, generally speaking, complete. It is composed of the third and fifth, and third and sixth.

(3) Suspensions of consonances, producing harmonies of the fourth and fifth, seventh and third, and even ninth and third, are introduced into the art and produce variety.

(4) The syncopated style is conceived and generally put into practice.

(5) Finally, the usage of four-part harmony commences in this century. But here a strange exception to the rule that forbids the succession of perfect consonances presents itself: these successions were admissible when the concords were complete. Jehan des Murs expresses the exception in this way: "Item possumus ponere . . . duas quintas cum octava et tertia, et duas octavas cum quinta et tertia per ascensum vel descensum tenoris."[31] This rule explains the numerous inac-

---

[30]This alleged quotation about avoiding two major thirds is not contained in des Murs' treatise, *De Discantu*. Fétis has merged des Murs' second rule ("Imperfect consonances ascend or descend stepwise into perfect consonances. . . .") with his fourth rule (consecutive perfect consonances ought to be avoided) to buttress his theory that intervals that possess "a character of tonal repose," as do the thirds on the fourth and fifth degrees, cannot succeed each other because they "present the aspect of tonal absurdity to the musical sense. . . . The name *false relations* is given to the succession of two major thirds . . . , because their quality of repose and mode put into immediate contact tonalities that do not have any relationship." (*Traité d'harmonie*, Bk. 1, § 43, p. 17.)

[31]"Likewise we can place [two fifths with a third in succession, and two octaves in similar fashion and ('duas quintas cum una tertia in rota, et duas octavas simili modo, et')] two fifths with an octave and a third, and two octaves with a fifth and a third, through the ascent or descent of the tenor." (Gerbert, *Scriptores* 3:307.)

curacies of this type that can be observed in Guillaume de Machaut's
four-part Mass, which is believed to have been sung at the coronation
of Charles V, King of France, in 1364. This error was not long in being
rectified. During the first years of the fifteenth century, Guillaume
Dufay, Binchois, and Dunstable professed to write with more elegance.
Dufay, particularly, who was one of the singers of the pontifical chapel
in 1380, appears to have introduced some noteworthy ameliorations
into harmony and the proportional system.[32] Although he may not be
the inventor of white notation as some modern writers have believed,
since some examples of white notation can be found before him, it is
undisputed that he improved it and propagated its usage. It is not
without good reason that writers of the fifteenth century have drawn
attention to Dufay as the greatest musician of his time. Only a
comparison of his compositions with those of musicians who immediately preceded him can give an exact idea of his merit. There we
find the first well-done imitations, and even two-voice canons, which
can be considered as the first attempts at conditional counterpoint.[33]
The fullness of his harmony and the natural stride and melodiousness
of the parts are very remarkable. We can judge this by the opening of
the Kyrie from his four-voice Mass, *Se la face ay pale*.

[32]Dufay was not born until *c*1400. His name appears in the lists of singers in the
Papal Choir on two occasions: (1) from the fall of 1428 until summer 1433; (2)
from June 1435 until May 1437. (Craig Wright, "Dufay at Cambrai," *JAMS* 28
[1975]: 178, 180).

[33]Although canon is not employed extensively as a structural element in sacred
music until after Dufay, canons and imitations are found in Italian trecento music.
Landini's "De! dinmi tu" I (153), a three-part madrigal, has a canon at the fifth
between the two lower voices in the first section and a three-part canon at the
fourth in the ritornello. In the three-voice caccia "Chosi pensoso" 2 (154), the two
upper voices are in canon at the unison. (Schrade, *Polyphonic Music of the Fourteenth
Century*, 4:216-20.) The famous thirteenth-century canon "Sumer is icumen in"
was composed *c*1250. For a concise history of the development of the canon in
western music, see Imogene Horsley, *Fugue: History and Practice* (New York: The
Free Press, 1966), 6-37 .

   In his *Traité du contrepoint et de la fugue* (Paris: Troupenas & Cie, 1825), Bk. 1, §
107, pp. 69-70, Fétis used *contrepoint conditionnel* to describe what the Germans
called *künstlicher Contrapunkt*. Fétis believed that this type of counterpoint, which
is based on consonant harmony, belonged to the tonality of plainchant. ("Mon
testament musical," *RGM* 20 [1853]: 315.) Moreover, Fétis stated that conditional
counterpoint, which preceded the "true fugue," was abused by composers and led
to such puerile conventions as *Contrapunto perfidiato*, *Contrapunto ostinato*, and
Contrapunto alla diritta, all of which Fétis illustrates in his *Traité du contrepoint* using
examples drawn from Angelo Berardi's *Documenti armonici* (Bologne: Monti,
1687).

Having reached this point, the harmony of plainchant tonality truly merits the name art, because in the restrictions of this tonality we would not know how to write consonant harmony any better. A single dissonance left by the leap of a third attracts attention in the third measure. This is what is called *la note changée*, because *f* takes the place of *e*, which would have been the consonant note. This harmonic device was in use until the end of the sixteenth century.

The purity of Dufay's harmony, of which this example is obvious proof and which is found in some pieces by the same composer in a manuscript that belongs to Mr. de Pixérécourt,[34] ought to put us on guard against the transcription of the Kyrie from the *l'Homme armé* Mass of this composer given by Mr. von Kiesewetter (*Geschichte der europäisch-abendländischen oder unsrer heutigen Musik*, Pl. XI).[35] The most flagrant errors abound in this work, and these errors appertain no more to Dufay than to the era in which he lived. There we see a use of dissonances that not only was not customary a long time prior to Dufay, but never even existed, and false relationships there are multiplied. Space is lacking in this outline to make the necessary corrections to this work, undoubtedly taken from an old, faulty copy. But I am unable to refrain from drawing attention to the strange error of the transcriber who has written this piece in the first mode transposed from plainchant, whereas the *l'Homme armé* chanson is in the fifth mode, just as the composition of this chant and the masses of Josquin Desprez [des Près], Pierre de la Rue, and Palestrina composed on the same chanson prove. Thus all the minor harmony of this transcription should be major. I make this observation only to show what false ideas of the history of the art some transcriptions of its monuments, transcriptions made from faulty copies by musicians who do not possess all the necessary knowledge for doing such work, can give.

A regular harmony and one conforming to the tonality of plainchant was composed in Dufay's time and merits to be called art. Nevertheless, a few inaccuracies still appear every now and then in the works of this musician and of his contemporaries or immediate successors: [Gilles de Bins] Binchois, [Petrus de] Domarto, and [J.] Barbingant of whom Tinctoris kept a few fragments.[36] We have seen

---

[34]Only one work in this manuscript is ascribed to Dufay: "Du tout m'estoir abandonée"; "Signeur Leon" has been attributed to Dufay. See Dragan Plamenac, "An Unknown Composition by Dufay?" in *MQ* 40 (1954): 190-200, and "An Edition of the Pixérécourt Manuscript: Paris, Bibliothèque Nationale, Fonds Fr. 15123," Vol. 1, by Edward Joseph Pease (Ph.D. diss., Indiana University, 1959).

[35]For Kiesewetter's transcription of the Kyrie, see Appendix B, Ex. 4.

[36]Tinctoris preserves a fragment from de Domarto's *Missa Spiritus Almus* ("Et in terra") in his *The Art of Counterpoint*, trans. and ed. Albert Seay (American Institute of Musicology, 1961), 126. Examples 50, 58, and 60 in Tinctoris' *Proportionale Musices* are taken from de Domarto's *Missa Spiritus Almus*. (See Seay's transcriptions in *JMT* 1 [1957]: 69, 74.)

aggregations of consonants evolve so as to present complete chords of the third and fifth, and third and sixth. We have seen chord successions become regular, the unison more rare, and unnatural dissonant harmony originate within the system of prolongations. Finally, we have seen direct successions of fifths and octaves disappear, or at least be concealed by means of passing tones. However, a reproach could be addressed to the composers of the perfections then introduced into the art: they did not know how to make the voices sing within narrow ranges without confusing them at each instance by crossings that spoiled the clarity of the harmonic outline. In this respect, the compositions that appeared in the second half of the fifteenth century present a remarkable amelioration. Ockeghem, Busnois, Obrecht, and Tinctoris provide us with examples of harmony as satisfying with the natural placement of the parts as with the fullness of chords and the regularity of their succession.

Here are some of them:

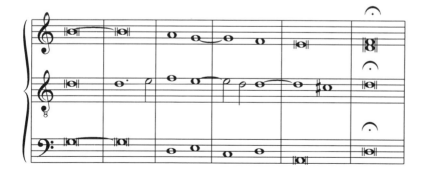

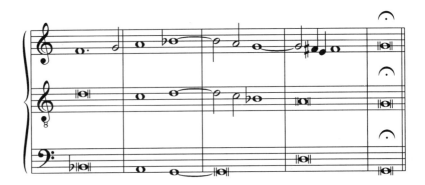

This harmonic fragment, extracted from chapter 18 of Tinctoris' treatise on the various kinds of points in musical notation, offers
several remarkable characteristics.[37] The first is the fullness of the
harmony, although limited to three voices, combined with the
correctness of the successions, and the natural movements of the
voices. Second, one notices that the desire for complete harmony
must have been active at the time that this piece was written (1476),
since the tenor is divided into two parts in the fifth measure (probably
because it was supposed to be sung by a chorus), in order to have the
third, fifth, and octave in the perfect chord. Finally, the 4-3 suspension is used with a great deal of elegance.[38]

The same composer gives us the oldest examples of which I am
aware of the combined prolongations of the fourth and ninth in book
one, chapter five of his *Liber de arte contrapuncti* (see Ex. 1), and of the

---

[37] *Super punctis musicalibus*

[38] The chromatic alterations in this excerpt (mm. 10, 13-15) are not found in
Coussemaker (*Scriptorum*, 4:75) and should be viewed as editorial—those Fétis
believed were applied by the performers at that time according to the rules of
musica ficta or *musica falsa*. A more accurate reading of this example with the
standard 2:1 reduction of values can be found in Albert Seay's edition of *Johannis
Tinctoris Opera Theoretica* (American Institute of Musicology, 1975), 1:195-96. In
modern scholarly editions of early music, editorial chromatics generally are placed
above the note or in brackets to distinguish them from the composer's chromatic
alterations. For more information about musica ficta, see Reese, *Music in the Middle
Ages*, 380-83; Carl Parrish, *The Notation of Medieval Music* (Stuyvesant: Pendragon
Press, 1978), 197-200; Reese, *Music in the Renaissance*, Rev. ed. [New York: W. W.
Norton & Co., 1959], 44-48; *NGrove* 12:802-06, s.v. "Musica ficta, 1. Before *c*1500."

fourth and seventh in the same book, chapter ten (see Ex. 2).[39] This last example has the disadvantage of stating several consecutive and exposed fourths just when the dissonances resolve. To avoid this disagreeable effect, contemporary musicians do not resolve two dissonances simultaneously.

1.

2.

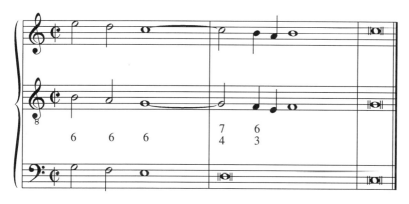

[39]Fétis' predilection for leading tones and his penchant for overediting transcriptions of early music in accordance with his concept of tonality is revealed again here in Ex. 1—there should be no leading tone in the penultimate chord. A careful comparison of Fétis' transcription with Coussemaker's (*Scriptorum* 4:85) reveals two glaring discrepancies: (1) the meter signature in Coussemaker is *tempus perfectum*. (2) The rhythm in the bass line in the first measure should be parallel to the two upper voices; thus there is no double suspension. The 4/3 figure in measure 1 (added by Fétis) should read 9/4. For a modern transcription of ex. 1, see p. 30, mm. 7-8 of Seay's translation of *The Art of Counterpoint*; Ex. 2 (Coussemaker, *Scriptorum* 4:97) occurs in Seay on p. 48, mm. 14-16.

At the time of the history of harmony at which I have arrived, the system of aggregations of consonances and artificial dissonances by prolongation was complete, with the exception of the fourth and sixth, which did not appear as consonant harmony in the works of fifteenth-century musicians. At that time all harmony was contained in chords of the third and fifth, third and sixth, third and octave; and, in four voices, third, fifth, and octave. This harmony is modified by delaying the third, by the suspension of the fourth into the chord of the third and fifth, which produces the fourth and fifth (see Ex. 1); by delaying the octave in the chord of the third and octave, or third, fifth, and octave, which produces the ninth and third, or ninth, third, and fifth (see Ex. 2); by delaying the sixth in the chord of the third and sixth, which produces the third and seventh (see Ex. 3); by delaying the lowest note of this same chord, which produces the second and fifth (see Ex. 4); by delaying both the third and the octave in the consonant chord composed of these intervals, which produces the ninth and fourth, or ninth, fourth, and fifth (see Ex. 5); and finally, by delaying the third and the sixth in the consonant harmony composed of these intervals, which produces the fourth and seventh (Ex. 6).

Such are all of the consonant and dissonant harmonies used by these composers in the second half of the fifteenth century. Until the end of the sixteenth century no others were known, because the tonality of plainchant, the basis of all music until this time, was unable to give rise to anything different. This tonality, which is *unitonique*, i.e., does not modulate, in effect does not contain any harmony other than consonant chords and some suspensions of their natural intervals, producing the artificial dissonances of the second, fourth, seventh, and ninth. Until the death of Palestrina, music was contained within these bounds.

Limited to such a small number of harmonic combinations, it is easy to understand that musicians were destined to search for some elements of interest for their works in a sequence of musical ideas richer in variety. This was what lead them to the discovery of imitations, canons, and contrapuntal fugue. I have said that the earliest traces of these quests can be noticed towards the end of the fourteenth century. These imitations became more frequent in the first half of the next century, and there the earliest attempts at two-voice canon appear.[40] A name was needed to distinguish this new genre of the composition of simple counterpoint; it was given that of *res facta* (completed work).[41] About 1460 Johannes Ockeghem seems to have possessed a quality that was superior to that of all the

---

[40]See n. 33 *supra*.

[41]Tinctoris defines the differences that existed between the composition *res facta*, simple counterpoint, and general counterpoint or *chant sur le livre* in book two, chapter 20 of his *Liber de arte contrapuncti*. Guerson also speaks of it in his treatise entitled *Utilissime musicales regule cunctis summopere necessarie plani cantus, simplicis contrapuncti, rerum factarum* . . . . Lastly, something concerning this composition, but solely with respect to the melodic figures employed there, can be found in the *Rudiments de musique pratique réduits en deux briefs traitez* by Maximilien Guillard (Paris: Nicolas Du Chemin, 1554). [For more recent discussions of *res facta*, see Ernest T. Ferand, "What is *Res Facta*?" *JAMS* 10 (1957): 141-50. Margaret Bent, "*Resfacta* and *Cantare Super Librum*," *JAMS* 36 (1983): 371-91.]

other musicians of his time. It is astonishing to see the degree of perfection to which he brought the treatment of three-voice canons, or, as was said then, of the composition of three voices in one. Here is the beginning of a piece of this genre taken from Glarean (*Dode-cachordon*, p. 454):[42]

[42]The original version was a third higher with a key signature of three flats; I prefer this transposition in order not to use the baritone and mezzo-soprano clefs, which are not very familiar to musicians.

The artist who, as far back as the origin of conditional compositions, demonstrated this perfection of structure truly deserved the
admiration that he inspired not only in his students, but in all of
Europe's musicians. I still find myself obliged to do, at this point, a
critique of the errors that are the pitfalls of music historians, grave
errors that result in a completely false idea of art in past times. The
piece of which I have just stated the beginning was written by the
composer as a single-line enigmatic canon, with these instructions to
serve as the key for the solution of the problem: "Fuga trium vocum
in Epidiatessaron post perfectum tempus," namely, a three-voice
fugue (canon) at the fourth above after a complete measure. Despite
such an explicit instruction, what does Burney do, in his *General
History of Music* (2:475)?[43] He reverses the order of the voices in such
a way that the canon is at the fifth below, and that wherever there
ought to be fifths, there are fourths. Here is his transcription:

---

[43]Vol. 1:729 in the Dover reprint (1957) edited by Frank Mercer.

This ridiculous transcription has been reproduced, nevertheless, by Forkel in the second volume of his *Allgemeine Geschichte der
Musik* [Leipzig, 1801] (p. 530),[44] and by Mr. Kiesewetter in his
prize-winning essay about Dutch musicians (Plates, ex. O).[45]

Once entered upon the path of imitations, canons, and quests
of any genre, musicians regarded these adjuncts of art as the main
object, applied all their faculties to them, and, with very few exceptions where more bold and more original trends appeared, all music,
sacred or secular, continued in this manner until the close of the
sixteenth century, namely, for almost one hundred and eighty years.
Within this long period of time, melody made little progress, because
the themes of popular songs served as the foundation for madrigals
and for all mundane music. And the singing of hymns and antiphons,
or even that of common melodies, was also developed with the
scientific combinations of church music. A small number of compositions, designated by the term *sine nomine*, appeared in the immeas-
urable quantity of works that remain of fifteen- and sixteenth-century musicians.[46] But the themes of these compositions
have so little character, that it is easy to imagine that their composers
attached little value to this part of the art.

---

[44]Fétis apparently did not read Forkel's explanation for the inclusion of Burney's
transcription.   Forkel points out (529-30) that Burney avoided the fault of
Wilphlingseder and Hawkins by correctly transcribing the canon in *tempus perfectum*. But Forkel continues, "On the other hand, Burney side-stepped another of
Ockeghem's instructions, according to which the three voices should follow each
other at the fourth above (*Epidiatessaron*), and wrote it at the fifth below, but
however in the *Epidiapente* instead of the *Epidiatessaron* under the canon. If,
therefore, this canon is to be solved completely according to the composer's
instructions, the upper voice should be changed into the lower, and the lower into
the upper" (533).

[45]*Verhandelingen over de vraag: Welke verdiensten hebben zich de Nederlanders vooral in
de 14e, 15e en 16e eeuw in het vak der toonkunst verworven; en in hoe verre kunnen de
Nederlandsche kunstenaars van dien tijd, die zich naar Italien begeven hebben, invloed gehad
hebben op de muzijkscholen, die zich kort daarna in Italien hebben gevormd? door R. G.
Kiesewetter en F. J. Fétis . . .* (Amsterdam: J. Muller, 1829).

[46]The use of a secular cantus firmus rather than a Gregorian melody was one of
the characteristics of Burgundian polyphony. A *sine nomine* Mass denoted a
composed, as opposed to borrowed, melody serving as the cantus firmus.

With respect to harmony, the tonality of plainchant, which was that of all secular and sacred music, presented no varieties other than those that I indicated previously. Whence it happens that from Ockeghem to the death of Palestrina, i.e., in the space of one hundred and forty years, the chordal combinations remained nearly the same. The well-known composer Palestrina attracted attention to himself in this important aspect of the art only by the perfection that he brought to the voice motion, and by the admirable sense of tonality that shines in his harmonic successions.

The theory of harmony ceased to anticipate the practice of the time when Guillaume Dufay lived. In the second half of the fifteenth century, two men of keen intellect and profound erudition came along to render eminent services to the science, and, with their works, established the situation where it was at that time. The first of these erudite musicians was Johannes Tinctor, or rather Tinctoris, a Belgian priest who was *maître de chapelle* for Ferdinand d'Aragon, King of Sicily and Naples (prior to 1475), and who dedicated his books to this Prince. All of the musical science of this era is contained in his works. *Liber de arte contrapuncti*,[47] i.e., the art of writing, is particularly well set forth by Tinctoris, in the rules concerning the succession of intervals, the sole fault of which is to be too numerous. But one must not search it for an examination of chords taken individually, nor for anything that resembles a system of classification of these chords. The views of musicians were not directed at all towards such considerations; moreover the necessity for systematic classification was not yet understood.[48]

Gaffurius, whose works are a few years later than those of Tinctoris, is, perhaps, inferior to the latter with respect to the lucidity of insights. Nevertheless, he has enjoyed greater renown because his

[47]*Liber de arte contrapuncti* Coussemaker, *Scriptorum* 4:76-153), one of twelve treatises by Tinctoris, is dated 11 October 1477 in the *explicit* of the work. The treatise, which is divided into a prologue and three books, is available in English translation by Albert Seay (see n. 36 *supra*). The preface has been translated by Oliver Strunk in his *Source Readings*, 197-99.

[48]In October 1860, Fétis presented a complete copy of Tinctoris' works to the Bureau de la classe des beaux-arts de l'Académie de Belgique, along with his annotations and a French translation. (*RGM* 28 [1861]: 35-36.)

works have been printed and several editions have been made of them, while those of Tinctoris have remained in manuscript, and copies of them are very rare. Gaffurius has given the rules for the art of writing harmony as well in his treatise *Practica musicae* [Milan, 1496].[49] But in this treatise we find only, as in those of Tinctoris, ideas of intervals and not of chords of three or four tones.

In vain would you search the authors of the sixteenth century to find the science more advanced in these respects. Zarlino himself, this great musician, whose works ought to be considered the code of the art at this time, has nothing that could give us the idea of a synoptic science of chords. Nevertheless, it is in these same works that we find the first notions of double counterpoint, that is, harmony built according to the notion of intervallic inversion of intervals, a notion that was a stroke of enlightenment for Rameau one hundred and sixty years hence, and which led him to the discovery of one of the foundations of the science of harmony. Zarlino dealt with these counterpoints in book 3, chapter 56 of his *Le Istitutioni harmoniche*, the first edition of which appeared in 1558.[50] It is remarkable that inversion at the octave, the results of which are all consistent with tonality, did not occur first to musicians, and that double counterpoint at the tenth and at the twelfth, much less natural, are those of which Zarlino speaks. It is also noteworthy that the examples provided by this celebrated writer of these conditional compositions are the only ones that we know from this era, and that not a single one of them is found in all of those of the masters of the Roman school that reached us prior to the end of the sixteenth century.

I said previously that by the mid-fifteenth century all of the harmonic resources that the tonality of plainchant could produce had been fixed, and that this was a sort of foreboding of the impossibility of introducing any new varieties that threw the musicians into the quest for imitations, canons, and contrapuntal fugues, in which they manifested a singular skill until the end of the sixteenth

[49]*The Practica Musicae of Franchinus Gaffurius*, trans. and ed. with musical transcriptions by Irwin Young (Madison: University of Wisconsin Press, 1969).

[50]Book 3 is in English translation by Guy A. Marco and Claude V. Palisca under the title *The Art of Counterpoint, Part III of Le Istitutioni harmoniche*, 1558, (New Haven: Yale University Press, 1968).

century. The direction taken by all artists during this long interval of more than one hundred and fifty years attracted them so much that not only were they not at all interested in the need to vary the forms of chords, but that melody itself was considered as nothing more than so subsidiary a part to music that they did not even condescend to invent any; and that the most popular cantilenas were taken by twenty different composers for the themes of their works. What is more, so little importance was attached to the signification of words, that they no longer respected either meaning or prosody. The extravagance of the musicians even went so far that in church, while one part of the choir chanted "Credo" or "Miserere," the other musicians said the words of the popular chanson which supplied the theme for the Mass or Psalm, e.g., "Baisez-moi, mon coeur" or else, "Robin, tu m'as toute mouillée."[51]

To be sure, such a degradation of art, a destruction so devoid of common sense, of propriety, is one of the most remarkable facts of its history. Taste, simple and pure sentiment do not have an expression strong enough to denounce such aberrations. However, it is to these outrageous errors that this same art is beholden for the immense mechanical progress that it made then with respect to the purity of the harmonic progressions, the elegance of the movement of the parts, and the magical art of making five or six different voices sing in an easy, natural manner in the most confined space. This art is unknown these days, but was carried to the highest degree of perfection in the sixteenth century, particularly in the Roman school. When Palestrina came, in the second half of that century, he was to refine the taste without impairing the skillfulness of the art of writing, and to give to church music the noblest character, the most worthy of its objectives. While being richer in details and more fruitful in contrapuntal resources than any of his contemporaries or his predecessors, Palestrina imprinted character of ultimate perfection on the music that emanated from the tonality of plainchant. No less superior in the madrigal style, he closed the field. Thus, it became necessary to throw art into new paths, in a word, to transform it. Several men of genius were thrilled by this necessity and made some

[51]"Kiss me, my darling"; "Robin, you got me all wet."

more or less successful attempts. But in the midst of them Monteverdi attracted attention especially with innovations which changed tonality and made it what it is today. Here I request the undivided attention of the reader, because it concerns the most remarkable era of music history and the most fruitful in outcome.

At first simply a violist, later the director of music for the Duke of Mantua, and finally the *maestro di cappella* at St. Mark's in Venice, Monteverdi, born in Cremona about 1565, found fame through a number of inventions that marked a new direction for music.[52] This new direction was in Book 3 of his five-voice madrigals, published in 1598,[53] where his genius showed its boldness by attacking the double and triple suspensions in a manner unknown to his predecessors, principally in the madrigal "Stracciami pur il core," where we notice this passage:[54]

Nothing similar appears in any music that existed prior to the publication of this piece. Some double dissonances are noticed here and there in Palestrina's works, but these instances are rare. Moreover, these dissonances of prolongation are always regularly prepared and resolved in the works of the illustrious master of the Roman school, whereas the passage that we have just seen contains

[52]Monteverdi was born in Cremona on 15 May 1567.

[53]1598 is the date of the third printing. The third book of five-voice madrigals was published initially in 1592 by R. Amadino. (*MGG* 9, col. 518, s.v. "Monteverdi, Claudio.")

[54]Claudio Monteverdi, *Tutte le opere*, ed. G. Francesco Malipiero, 14 vols. (Vienna: Universal, 1926-42), 3:26-32, mm. 73-80.

not only the triple dissonances of the fourth resolved to the third, of the seventh descending to the sixth, and of the ninth resolving to the octave, but the notes suspended by the three upper voices are attacked simultaneously by the tenor in the third, fourth, and fifth measures. This irregularity produces the intolerable dissonances of seconds in the fifth and last measures. On the one hand, Monteverdi enriched harmony with new combinations; on the other hand, he damaged it by rejecting the evidence of the ear which revolts against such harshness.

With respect to the seventh accompanied by the fifth and the major third which is seen in the penultimate measure of the example cited, although it is prepared as a suspension, it is nevertheless an important innovation that must be considered as the origin of modern tonality; because, between the leading tone, which forms the major third, and the seventh, which is the fourth degree of the scale, there is an appellation of cadence, which forms precisely the character of our tonality; whereas these processes of cadence are never necessary in the consonant harmony that results from the tonality of plainchant, nor in the harmony, dissonant with suspensions, that derives from it.[55] If we examine attentively all of the music that preceded the remarkable fact pointed out here, we will see that what gives it the strange character for our ears is the connection of the phrases to each other, without a cadence, which never completes the meaning until the end or some momentary pause. Thus our ear is incessantly frustrated, and searches in vain for a conclusion—the appearance of a phrase before the end of the piece. On the contrary, as soon as the minor seventh with the major third and fifth is utilized, the necessity for the resolution of the two gravitational notes inevitably led to the cadence, determined the resolution that concludes it, and gave a fixed form to the phrases.[56]

---

[55]Fétis, fervently believing that "modern" tonality resides in the tritone, contended that ". . . having no leading tone in the established music of this ancient *unitonique*, since this note acquires it character only by its harmonic relationships with the fourth degree and the dominant in the natural dissonant chords, the *cadence* properly speaking, that is the rhythmic termination of the phrase, did not exist." (Fétis, *Traité d'harmonie*, Bk. 3, § 245, p. 152.)

[56]Fétis asserts that with the advent of the dominant seventh, "cadences become frequent and regular," and periodic phrase structure results. (Ibid, §§ 256-57, pp. 165-66.)

If we are willing to understand how a seventh chord originating from the delay of a sixth chord differs from the seventh chord composed of the major third, just fifth, and minor seventh, such as Monteverdi employed in the example cited, we must notice that when the resolution of the dissonance is made, we have a sixth chord that does not belong to the key because every dominant is, in modern tonality, a note of repose or an intermediary of cadence, which is unable to support the chord of the sixth. This is admissible only in plainchant tonality (see Ex. 1). Moreover, when the seventh chord with a major third is accompanied by the fifth, it is obvious that it does not arise from the delay of a sixth chord, because when the suspension resolves, we would have a harmony of the fifth and sixth (see Ex. 2). Thus it is clear that, according to modern tonality, when the seventh resolves down, the major third ought to move up, which, in the case where the bass is stationary, leads to the six-four harmony (see Ex. 3). It is thus that Monteverdi employed these chords in the example cited.

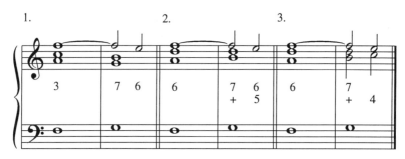

It is correct to say that Marenzio made use of the harmony of the seventh with the major third and fifth in the madrigal "O voi che sospirate" in Book 6 for five voices, published in 1591, namely seven years before Monteverdi had his Book 3 for five voices published.[57] But before long the latter, guided by his instinct, comprehended that the preparation of dissonance was not necessary in dominant harmonies accompanied by the major third, and in this fifth book of

[57]Since Book 6 of Marenzio's five-voice madrigals was published in 1594 in Venice, Marenzio's madrigal "O voi che sospirate" appeared one year after Monteverdi's third book of five-voice madrigals. (*MGG* 8, col. 1638.)

madrigals he attacked, without preparation, not only the seventh but even the ninth of the dominant. Composers have imitated him ever since. The relationship established in these harmonies between the fourth degree and the seventh of the key is the constituent principle of modern tonality. We would search in vain in all the music composed prior to Monteverdi and Marenzio; it does not exist; it could not exist without destroying the tonality of plainchant. The attraction of these two notes, the necessity for the seventh degree to rise while the fourth degree falls, is the peculiar character of the *leading tone*, which received its name from this tendency. Thus, all modern tonality is built on this succession that was unknown to all musicians until the end of the sixteenth century:

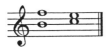

As soon as this succession was admitted into art, it banished the eight church modes from the domain of harmony, and there were only two modes of tonality: major and minor for each note. One or the other of these types was built on each note, with each type constructed in the same way. In both modes the relationship of the fourth degree and the leading tone is the same. As a result of the appellation of these two notes, the final was always the tonic, and the harmonic dominant, namely the note which is heard in the greatest number of chords, was always the fifth degree of the scale.

Another phenomenon was the requisite consequence of the dominant's dissonant harmony. I mean *modulation*, that is to say, the transition from one key to another by the sole act of attacking the harmony of the dominant of the latter without preparation, because this harmony immediately creates the new key with the double appellation of the fourth degree and the leading tone. It is this faculty of liaison between keys that I called *ordre transitonique* in the "Philosophy of Music" course that I taught in Paris in 1832. No counterpart existed in earlier music based on the church modes. Thus it occurred that the efforts of Nicola Vicentino[58] and several other sixteenth-cen-

---

[58]*L'antica musica ridotta alla moderna prattica* (Rome: Barre, 1555), 67.

tury masters to create modulatory music were barren, because never having the need for resolution of consonance and dissonance by prolongation in the earlier tonality, and change of tonic was optional. Actual modulation was never made apparent.[59] Mr. von Winterfeld, who has only a vague notion about all of this, like the other music historians, went astray in his book on Giovanni Gabrieli when he tried to prove the existence of a chromatic genre among the early masters. They did not know this genre, because its existence was impossible in their tonal system.[60]

Who would believe that there was not a word of everything that we have seen regarding such an important era of the change of tonality, with all its consequences, in the general and specialized histories of music? These voluminous compilations abound in non-essential details, but for such a fact no compiler had enough practical knowledge, care, or vision to shed light on this poorly understood matter. All that Burney and Martini saw, copied by Forkel and other routine-minded people, is that Monteverdi added some new chords

---

[59]Fétis believed that the experiments of Vicentino, although sincere, were unsuccessful because they failed in their attempt ". . . to synthesize a chromatic scale in which the semitones have tendencies of resolution with a harmony that, by the nature of its aggregations, is essentially diatonic and devoid of attraction [i.e., comprised of chords of repose]." (*Traité d'harmonie,*" xxxviii.)

Fétis contended that "it is not the same in the new tonality created by the natural dissonant harmony, because, although the form of these scales is diatonic, this tonality is allied with the chromatic scale and borrows from it the means of transforming the tones into semitones (and the semitones into tones) for the uniformity of its scales. The diatonic genre [*tonalité moderne*] also is allied with the chromatic scale in taking each of the semitones of the latter for the first note of its scales. . . . Each of these sounds can be the initial one of a diatonic scale disposed like *c, d, e, f, g, a, b, c*; consequently, there are twenty-one similar scales. On the other hand, each scale having two modes, one major and the other minor, the number of scales or keys is actually forty-two" (xlii–xliii).

[60]The "chromatic genre" may have existed. In *Secret Art in the Netherlands Motet* (New York: Columbia University Press, 1946), Edward E. Lowinsky defined the essential elements of both the technique and the symbolism of "secret" chromaticism, including "secret modulation," in the motets of Clemens non Papa (*c*1510–15; *d* 1555-6), Adrian Willaert (*c*1490–1562), Thomas Crecquillon (*b* between *c*1480-*c*1500; *d* 1557), Nicolas Gombert (*c*1495-*c*1560), Hubert Waelrant (*c*1516–17; *d*1595), and Adrianus Petit Coclico (1499/1500-after Sept. 1562).

to those that had been used before him; as for the results of these new harmonies, no one questioned them.

Notice, however, that these results were not confined to those that I have made known earlier, because as soon as there was means for modulation and cadential action, phrases were shaped rhythmically—they had closes. In their succession, they had as a goal to move successively from one key into another, then to return to the original key in order to vary the feelings which, previously, were built on another foundation. Now, in the first half of the seventeenth century the direction of all music in a system of alternative modulation led to the abandonment of canonic and imitative counterpoint, which then existed only as an object of study, and produced the substitution of real and tonal fugue, the technique of which consists of a system of regular modulation by means of a principal phrase called the *subject*. The true fugue, then, dates only from this epoch, although the name was known much earlier.[61] But the name misled the erudites in music, who, without a solid knowledge of the art, confused all these things. Imperceptibly the dissonant harmony of the unprepared dominant settled into the fugue, as in all other music. The free introduction of this harmony into similar learned pieces was slow because the change of tonic was not perceived, and because the actual principles of this tonal change were still a mystery to the musicians. The rigorous conditions of early counterpoint, the necessary consequence of plainchant tonality, restrained the masters and created indecision amongst students. Even today, when students of composition schools leave the study of simple counterpoint to take up that of fugue, their professors have a great deal of difficulty explaining the reasons for the free employment of natural dissonances in the

---

[61]For Zarlino's followers the word "fugue" had a very precise meaning. In *The Art of Counterpoint*, Zarlino points out (126-34) that there are two types of fugues: strict (*legate*), or what is now recognized as canon, and free (*sciolte*), in which "the imitating voice duplicates the other in fugue or consequence [answer] only up to a point; beyond that point it is free to proceed independently" (127). In both types of fugue, the consequence, which had to be exact, occurred "by direct or contrary motion" at the unison, fourth, fifth, or octave. Imitations, on the other hand, while also classified as strict or free, could occur at any interval: the generic classification was retained, but the specific quality of the interval could vary (135-41).

fugue since the free employment of natural dissonances was forbidden in counterpoint. It [the free employment of natural dissonances] results in a kind of trial and error the first few times. However, I have explained all of this in the second half of my *Traité du contrepoint et de la fugue*, which was published sixteen years ago.[62] But a great deal of time is necessary to make apparent to everyone the facts in an art-science where the considerations are as multifarious as in music, and when the art-science is capable of numerous transformations.

In creating the fugue, the new tonality created double counterpoint at the octave, because the necessity of alternatively passing the subject and the countersubjects, which served as an accompaniment, to the lower and treble voices obliges the musicians to turn their attention to the consideration of intervallic inversion at the octave, from which the rules of double counterpoint arose. From this we understand that these rules are the prolegomena of the fugue. We can evaluate the lack of criticism and clear thinking that led Berardi,[63] Tevo,[64] Fux,[65] Marpurg,[66] and Albrechtsberger[67] to deal with double counterpoint only after the fugue, which would not exist without double counterpoint. I have restored the rational order of these studies in my *Traité du contrepoint et de la fugue*. Several works, published since then on the same subject, have followed this order.[68] With regard to double counterpoint, I still ought to cite an additional

---

[62]Book 4 of Fétis' *Traité du contrepoint et de la fugue* deals with fugue.

[63][Angelo Berardi], *Documenti armonici* (Bologna: Giacomo Monti, 1687).

[64][Zaccaria Tevo], *Il musico testore* (Venice: Antonio Bortoli, 1706).

[65][Johann Joseph Fux], *Gradus ad Parnassum, sive manuductio ad compositionem musicae regularem, methodo nova* (Vienna: [van Ghelen], 1725).

[66][Friedrich Wilhelm Marpurg], *Traité de la fugue* (Berlin: [A. Haude & J. C. Spener], 1756). [Fétis has given the publication facts for the French translation. The German edition, *Abhandlung von der Fuge nach dem Grundsätzen und Exampeln der besten deutschen und ausländischen Meister*, was published in 2 vols. in Berlin by A. Haude und J. C. Spener in 1753-54.]

[67][Johann Georg Albrechtsberger], *Gründliche Anweisung zur Komposition* (Leipzig: Breitkopf, 1790).

[68]In "Choron, Fétis and the Theory of Tonality" (*JMT* 19 [1975]: 112-38), Bryan R. Simms points out that "Choron—not Fétis—was the one who restored this more logical order" (118) in his *Principes de composition des écoles d'Italie* (1804), a book that predates Fétis' treatise by twenty years.

proof that the history of the art in general, and of harmony in particular, is ill-known, even by the most educated men; much more is made of some curiosities of little importance than of those that have real value.

In the first months of 1830, Mr. de Vos Willemenz, a member of the *Institut des Pays-Bas* and secretary of the fourth class of this erudite society, wrote to me, enclosing the volume that contained the report of Mr. Kiesewetter and myself on Netherlandish musicians: "You will read with interest that Mr. Kiesewetter has demonstrated that the Netherlanders are the inventors of double counterpoint." As a matter of fact, the second part of Mr. Kiesewetter's report has the title *L'Invention du contrepoint artificiel, nommé par les modernes CONTREPOINT DOUBLE, peut-elle être attribuée aux Néerlandais?*[69] Now, in examining this subject, Mr. Kiesewetter assumes that double counterpoint is only a division of the part of the art that he designated with the general expression *contrepoint artificiel* and the invention of which he attributes to the musicians of the Netherlands School. From this we are expected to conclude that he considered the fifteenth-century musicians the inventors of this type of counterpoint. Seeing his error on this subject, I wrote to Mr. Kandler, my corresponding member in Vienna and friend of Mr. Kiesewetter, and showed him that double counterpoint did not arise prior to the second half of the sixteenth century. Mr. Kandler communicated my letter to his friend, who wrote to me on 27 July 1830 from the Baden spa near Vienna:

> I am indebted to you for a very ingenious observation, one worthy of a professor of counterpoint as well as a scholar in historical fact of the musical art; an observation that truly was never so clearly presented to me. It is that the old masters were not yet aware of this type of counterpoint that the academy of our day calls *contrepoint double*,[70] and

[69]*Kann den Niederländern die Erfindung des künstlichen, oder von den Neuren also genannten doppelten Contrapunktes zugeschrieben werden?* [pp. 13-22].

[70]Why "of our day"? Didn't [Lodovico] Zacconi deal with *De' Contrappanti doppii* in the second part of his *Prattica di musica*, published in 1622? Isn't it also the same for L[odovico] Penna in Book 2 of his *Primi albori musicali*, published in 1656 [1672]? for [Giovanni Maria] Bononcini in the second part of his *Musico prattico* (1673)? for [Angelo] Berardi in his *Documenti armonici* (1687), and for twenty other seventeenth-century writers?

of which the first traces are found towards the end of the fifteenth century. I acknowledge that immediately I went through one hundred scores from my collection, and I am convinced of the accuracy of your assertion, because everything that I have been able to find of the same kind was actually only simple imitation. If there was a short passage that seemed to announce the outline of inversion, the latter was not followed, and immediately I noticed that it was suggested only by accident and not intentionally in the forms. [Fétis' italics.]

In rendering justice to the sincerity of Mr. Kiesewetter, who acknowledged an important error with so much candor, we cannot help regretting that the study he carried out after having read my letter had not preceded his work.[71] Nonetheless, this error remains published in a book whose influence is much greater because it has been awarded a prize by an academy.[72] And it is precisely this authority that compels me to stress the fact that the natural harmony of the dominant created modern harmony; that the latter led to the destruction of imitative counterpoint in the tonality of plainchant and to the creation of the fugue; finally, that the inseparable conditions of the fugue gave birth to double counterpoint at the octave. All of this is connected but, once again, the philosophy of music history has been unknown until today.

[71]Fétis, who was no admirer of Kiesewetter, wrote a very acerbic critique of Kiesewetter and his work in 1853 in "Mon testament musical" (*RGM* 20:364).

[72]For their memoirs, Kiesewetter received a gold medal and Fétis a silver medal from the Quatrième classe de l'Institut des sciences, de littérature et des beaux-arts du Royaume des Pays-Bas. The commission published both works (see n. 45 *supra*) because although "Mr. Kiesewetter's *mémoire* gives a more general view of the history of the art, Fétis' is more complete in the information that he provides about the artists; this is a good ensemble . . . ." (Wilhelm de Vos Willemenz, as quoted in *Document historique sur la priorité des Néerlandais sous le rapport de la science musicale à l'époque de la Renaissance* [1855], 2). In the first edition of *BUM* (1:xxii), Fétis acknowledged that he had profited from the work that his "savant competitor" had done. By the time the second edition of his *BUM* appeared (1860-65), Fétis conceded that "unexpected circumstances obligated him to undertake some works for which he was unprepared," including his 1828 memoir (232). Although Fétis' study is considerably shorter (54 pages) than Kiesewetter's (115 pages of text plus 73 pages of musical examples), Fétis does show a connection from Dufay and Binchois through Obrecht, Ockeghem, Tinctoris, Josquin, de La Rue, and Gombert to Willaert and Lassus. For a discussion of each of the respective memoirs, see Wangermée, *François-Joseph Fétis*, 123-39.

Because the expressive accent, which is composed of the appellation of the resolution of the leading tone in conjunction with either the fourth degree of the two modes or with the sixth degree of the minor mode, was contained in the natural dissonant harmony, music assumed a dramatic character with the birth of this harmony. All the new forms which transformed the art—true opera, the cantata, the air with instrumental accompaniment, the recitative—all arrived at almost the same time.

But everything in an art that is being transformed is not won. The boldness of the genius who discovered the new harmony and all its consequences was unable to accommodate the rigorous rules of the art of writing to which the composers of the old schools were indebted for the admirable purity of style which renders their works imperishable, and which made them models of disheartening perfection. Inaccuracies of every kind began to be profuse in the works of the musicians of Venice and Naples. Rome alone resisted and preserved some excellent traditions that more than two centuries have been unable to destroy completely. Proud of its success, the new school did not delay invading the church. The dramatic style was introduced into religious music and took the place of the staid, solemn, and pious tone of Palestrina's works. Then the absurdity of this secular expression began to be applied to holy things: the "Gloria," "Credo," "Sequences," and "Psalms" became dramas instead of prayers and professions of faith. The symbols of the suffering of the Savior were transformed into a representation of carnal agony, and one went to church to experience emotions rather than to go there to pray with meditation.

This is not all. Choirs of instruments had become necessary since choirs of voices had ceased to constitute every type of music. Thus, instruments assumed the same importance in the church as in the theater and became indispensable especially for the accompaniment of motets for solo voice or two voices that were published in tremendous quantity in the first half of the seventeenth century. The *concerto* style succeeded the simple (*osservato*) style of older sacred music. From that time the genres were merged and, as Abbot Baini said, church music was destroyed. Since then some beautiful works have been written for church music in the system of expression: the

Psalms [1724] of [Benedetto] Marcello, the *Miserere* of Jomelli,[73] some of the compositions of Alessandro Scarlatti, [Leonardo] Leo, [Giovanni] Pergolesi, and, in more recent times, the masses of [Luigi] Cherubini offered some models of perfection in this genre. But the genre itself is an abasement of the primary object of art in worship. The degradation was so heartfelt that even Rossini, this leading propagator of brilliant art, frequently told me that the only profound and lasting impression of a sacred nature in church music that he had experienced was made by the works of Palestrina, which he had heard twenty-five years before in Rome. For worldly people, and even for musicians who only hear a mediocre performance of this music in Paris concerts, undoubtedly there is more than some exaggeration in the words of the composer of *Guillaume Tell*. But for anyone who has made a serious study of immortal works, objects of his admiration, there is a conviction that true church music ceased to exist with the appearance of theater music, and that one lost on the one side what was being gained on the other side. Thus, it was not for lack of motive that Artusi attacked Monteverdi and the other innovators in his book against the imperfections of modern music.[74] Only he did not understand that instead of the older art, which they had ruined, they had fashioned a new art whose existence was immense.

With music for solo voice, accompanied by the organ or other instruments, the bass, which was called the *continuo* to distinguish it from the interrupted bass of older choral music, was born. Before long this bass instrument and *continuo* led to the need for certain signs to indicate to the accompanist the chords with which he was supposed to support the voice. Thus the systematic science of har-

---

[73]Nicolò [Niccolò] Jommelli [Jomelli] (1714-74) wrote at least seven choral works called "Miserere"; only three of them are dated—1751, 1759, and 1774. (See *NGrove* 9:695.)

[74]Fétis is referring to a two-volume work of Giovanni Artusi. The first volume, *L'Artusi, overo delle Imperfettioni della musica moderna*, appeared in 1600 and was followed in 1603 with a second volume entitled *Considerazioni musicali*. Monteverdi replies to the attacks of Artusi in the foreword to his Fifth Book of madrigals. For an English version of the "Foreword with the 'Declaration' of His Brother G. C. Monteverdi," see Strunk, *Source Readings*, 405-12.

mony commenced, the last consequence of Monteverdi's inventions and of tonal change. Therefore it was in the early years of the seventeenth century that this science, the investigation of which is about to concern me, commenced.

Among the generally accepted uncertainties about the most important facts of music history, there are few which would be more difficult to dispel than those that have enveloped the origin of *basso continuo*. Lodovico Viadana, a minorite friar and *maestro di cappella* of the Mantua Cathedral in the early years of the seventeenth century, generally is looked upon as the inventor of this bass. Nevertheless, his rights to this invention have been disputed recently with the appearance of so much evidence that it is necessary to examine thoroughly this historic question. I will try to satisfy the doubts on this subject, and to restore to each one the glory that belongs to him in the creation of the early foundations of harmonic science.[75]

We know that the name *basso continuo* specifies an accompanimental bass that is different from the vocal bass of older compositions. The bass of the latter frequently was interrupted, whereas the other is continuous. The continuous bass probably arose as soon as there were some songs for solo voice supported by the accompaniment of an instrument. According to [Giovanni Battista] Doni (*Trattato della musica scenica in opere*, 2:23),[76] the first attempt at this genre of music was the episode of Count Ugolin set to music about 1580 by Vincenzo Galilei for solo voice with viol accompaniment. Although we no longer have this piece, we are able to get an idea of its structure from

---

[75]With the words "primary foundations of harmonic science," Fétis is referring to the contributions of figured bass to the development of the harmonic sciences. John W. Mitchell ("A History of Theories of Functional Harmonic Progress" [Ph.D. diss., Indiana University, 1963]) summarizes these contributions as (1) the continuation and expansion of the triad as the basic unit; (2) the triad governed by a major or minor scale basis; (3) the concept of the succession of vertical structures; (4) the importance of chordal placement—a budding concept of harmonic function; (5) the fusion of theory and practice—combining the techniques of composition, accompaniment, and improvisation; (6) counterpoint and harmony bound together—the linear viewed as part of the vertical successions (32-35).

[76]*Trattato della musica scenica* is the first work in volume 2 (*De' trattati di musica*) of *Lyra Barberina amphichordos*, ed. by A. F. Gori and Giovanni Batista Passeri, 2 vols. (Florence, 1763).

the recitative in Jacopo Peri's *Euridice*, and in the dramas of Emilio de' Cavalieri, works that preceded the invention attributed to Viadana by a few years.

Nevertheless, the bass accompaniment of these early attempts at dramatic music do not correspond precisely to this invention, because it did not seem to have been destined to serve as a guide for the accompaniment of the right hand on the harpsichord, namely, to be the bass for a series of chords. There is reason to believe that originally this bass, which served as the accompaniment for the recitative, was played alone. It is pertinent to state that Alessandro Guidotti, editor of Emilio de' Cavalieri's musical drama *La Rappresentazione di Anima, e di Corpo* which was published in 1600 in Rome, said, in the preface that preceded this work, that the figures placed under the bass notes represented the consonances and dissonances, and that the sharp and flat placed before or below the figures indicated the major or minor nature of the intervals.[77] But the particulars that Viadana himself provides prove that he had used *basso continuo* for organ and harpsichord accompaniment prior to the publication of Emilio de' Cavalieri's work; that this invention dates back to 1596 or 1597, and that it originated in Rome where Guidotti could have become acquainted with it. In 1603 Viadana published a collection of motets entitled *Cento Concerti Ecclesiastici, a Una, a Due, a Tre e a Quattro Voci con il Basso continuo per sonar nell' Organo Nova inventione commoda per ogni sorte de Cantore, e per gli Organisti*, 5 vols. in quarto (Venice: Giacomo Vincenti, 1603).[78] Volume five contains the *basso continuo* part: *Basso per sonar nell' organo*. In the preface to the reader, after he had reviewed the motives that had led him to write sacred music for every genre of solo voice with an accompaniment part for the organ, he adds that he conceived them about six years

---

[77]"Li numeri piccoli posti sopra le note del Basso continuato per suonare, significano la Consonanza, ò Dissonanza di tal numero: come il 3. terza: il 4. quarta: & cosi di mano in mano.

Quando il diesis è posto avanti, ouero sotto di un numero, tal consonanza sarà sostentata: & in tal modo il b molle fa il suo effetto proprio" [n.p.].

[78]1603 was the date of the 2d printing of Viadana's work. The op. 12 motets were published initially in 1602. (Federico Mompellio, "Viadana, Lodovico" *MGG* 13, col. 1575.)

earlier (1597) in Rome, and he decided to publish these compositions in a genre of which he is the inventor, because this invention has been favorably received, and because he has since found many imitators.[79] (See the identical words of Viadana in the article "Basso continuo" in Lichenthal's *Dizionario e bibliografia della musica*.) No objection has been raised against Viadana's assertions.

The *basso continuo* part of this composer's motets has no figures for chords, and he says nothing about the subject in the instructions in the preface. Neither is there any mention of the classification of chords into consonant and dissonant. The purpose of the instructions, as much for the singers as the organist, is the manner for performing the different pieces contained in the work. For the organist, Viadana recommends: (1) play the score simply; (2) do not cover the singer when he embellishes the cadences; (3) glance at the whole piece before performing; (4) never accompany the treble voices too high nor the bass voices too low; (5) play *tasto solo*, i.e., without chords, the fugal entrances, etc.[80] In 1609 a new Italian edition, enlarged with several works, was published by Vincenti in Venice. To the rules prescribed in the preface of the previous edition, information about the use of figures above the *basso continuo*, which appears to have been borrowed from Guidotti, was added. In the same year another edition of the work in Latin, Italian, and German appeared with this title: *Opera omnia sacrorum concentuum, Cum basso continuo et generali, Organo adplicato*, . . . (Frankfurt am Main: Emmelius, 1609). The same printer produced other similar editions in 1613, 1620, and 1626.

I ought not to neglect to say that an English musician, Richard Dering, had published a work of five-voice motets with *basso continuo* under the title *Cantiones sacrae quinque vocum, cum basso ad organum* (Antwerp: Pierre Phalèse, 1597). But at this time this musician had just arrived from Italy; undoubtedly he was one of the imitators of

[79]The preface has been translated into English in F. T. Arnold, *The Art of Accompaniment from a Thorough-Bass*, 1 (1931; rpt. New York: Dover Publications, Inc., 1965): 2-4n. 3. Another translation appears in Strunk, *Source Readings*, 419-23.

[80]An annotated translation of Viadana's rules can be found in Arnold, *Art of Accompaniment*, 1:9-20; the Italian version is appended on 20-21.

whom Viadana spoke. It is improbable that this Englishman had had anything to do with the invention of the new genre of music, which, moreover, he did not usurp.[81]

Crüger, a contemporary of Viadana, appears to me to be the oldest author who said positively that this musician was the inventor of *basso continuo* in his *Appendix De Basso Generali, seu continuo*, in the course of his book entitled *Synopsis musica* (Berlin, 1624). Here are his words: "Bassus Generalis seu continuus, So von fürtrefflichen Italienischen Musico Ludovico Viadana erstlich erfunden."[82] If my memory is correct, more evidence in favor of Viadana, closer to the time of the invention, exists in the preface that Gaspar Vincenz, organist at Speyer, placed at the beginning of Abraham Schad's *Promptuarium musicum* (1611); but I do not have this collection near at hand. After Crüger, Printz expressed himself on this subject in a no less positive manner in his history of music.[83] Brossard appears to have drawn his information on that account from the latter's book, but I do not know from which authority he said, in the article "Basso continuo" in his *Dictionaire de musique*, that Viadana published a treatise on *basso continuo*. J. J. Rousseau copied Brossard and, without examination, cited this alleged *basso continuo* treatise.[84]

Abbot Baini, who had no knowledge at all of Crüger's passage[85] and who had not seen the 1603 collection of motets where Viadana

[81]The existence of this purported 1597 edition has been disproven by Sir Frederick Bridge in *Twelve Good Musicians: From John Bull to Henry Purcell* (London: Kegan Paul, Trench, Trubner and Co., Ltd., [1920]), 50-62. Bridge believes that the date 1597 is a misprint for 1617; Fétis probably secured the erroneous date either from Hawkins (*A General History of the Science and Practice of Music*, 2:577) or Burney (*A General History of Music*, 2:292). The discovery of additional facts and the subsequent reassessment of the existing information about Dering's (Dearing, Deering, Diringus) career reveals that he was not in Italy in 1597. He probably made his first trip to Italy between 1610 and 1612. See Peter Platt, "Dering's Life and Training," *Music and Letters* 33 (January 1952): 41-49.

[82]"*Basso generale* or *continuo* was invented first by the excellent Italian musician Lodovico Viadana" (213).

[83][Wolfgang Kaspar Printz.] *Historische Beschreibung der edeln Sing-und Kling-kunst* (Dresden, 1690), chap. 12, § 11, [132-33].

[84]Neither Brossard nor Rousseau gives a title to this alleged treatise.

[85]Giuseppe Baini did have knowledge of both Brossard's and Rousseau's articles, as he states on page 149 of the *Memorie-storico-critiche* . . . .

reported his invention and the time when it was known in Rome, established in several places in his *Memorie storico-critiche della vita e delle opere di Giovanni Pierluigi da Palestrina*, namely volume 1, pages 149-50, note 238, that before Viadana's birth, about the middle of the sixteenth century, (1) a counterpoint was improvised with instruments on the bass of vocal compositions; (2) in order to avoid the dissonances that could arise from this mixture of counterpoint by improvised instruments and written vocal parts, some figures and symbols that indicated the nature of intervals were marked above the bass; (3) Viadana's contemporaries, particularly Banchieri in his *Moderna prattica della musica* (1613), do not cite him as the inventor of *basso continuo*, but as one of the first and best didactic authors on this subject. The authorities cited by the learned Baini do not, to my mind, prove his first two assertions. With the multitude of published compositions in the second half of the sixteenth century with the words *da cantare e suonare*, I am certain that the instruments performed the same parts as the voice. As to the figures and symbols placed above the bass, we do not notice them at all prior to 1600. The idea must be credited either to Emilio de' Cavalieri or to Guidotti. As for Viadana's invention, Mr. Baini's error results from knowing neither the passage where this musician speaks nor the testimony of Crüger.

From all of the preceding, it follows that (1) about 1580 the initial idea of a continuous bass accompaniment arose from the first attempts of solo voice songs accompanied by an instrument; (2) this bass, becoming more animated and varied in its forms, was applied to the organ for vocal accompaniment by Viadana, and from him received the name *basso continuo* about 1596;[86] (3) about the same time the usage of figures and symbols for raising and lowering notes above the bass was introduced either by Emilio de' Cavalieri, his editor Guidotti, or perhaps by some other unknown musician. Soon afterward, many sacred works with figured *basso continuo* were published. From that moment the madrigal-like genre, namely unac-

---

[86]Arnold stated that "The term was first brought into general notice owing to the large and immediate circulation of Viadana's *Concerti*, 1602, though the term *Basso continuato* was used by Guidotti in 1600." (Arnold, *Art of Accompaniment*, 1:6n. 2.)

companied music for several voices and in an imitative style, ceased
to be in vogue in order to make way for what the artists themselves
called the *nuove musiche*.

We would be deceiving ourselves if we believe that the formation of a harmonic system was the immediate consequence of the
double invention of *basso continuo* and figures intended to denote its
accompaniment: things did not move so quickly. The slowness of the
scientific progress in this respect is likewise one of the remarkable
facts of music history. Some direction that appeared in the first half
of the seventeenth century concerning the art of figured bass accompaniment only contained observations of detail, which showed no
consideration at all for the generation of a chord. At last, a fact of
some importance appeared twenty-five years after the publication of
Viadana's work; in this fact the first elements of a science of harmony
are found. It merits all our attention. [Agostino] Agazzari from Siena,
a contemporary of Viadana, had developed Guidotti's instructions
of the use of figures and had extended the application in his *Del
Sonare sopra'l Basso con tutti li stromenti e dell'uso loro nel conserto*, placed
at the front of the fifth book of his motets, which were published in
1607. He did not indicate the nature of the chords that ought to be
connected with such and such scale degree. Galeazzo Sabbatini,
maestro di cappella to the Duke of Mirandola, went farther in the small
work entitled *Regola facile e breve per sonare sopra il Basso continuo
nell'Organo, Manacordo, ò altro Simile Stromento* (Venice, 1628; 30 p. in
quarto); because he gave the first rule of the octave that is known,
namely, the harmonic formula indicating the proper chord for each
note of the scale.[87] It is of this formula that Sabbatini wishes to speak

---

[87]In the rule of the octave, each degree of the ascending and descending major or
minor scale was given a fixed harmony that was employed in unfigured basses.
Since François Campion (*Traité d'accompagnement et de composition, selon la régle des
octaves* [1716; rpt. Geneva: Minkoff, 1976]) was the first French theorist to publish
complete bass octaves in this form, "the *règle de l'octave* was associated in the moinds
of most eighteenth-century musicians with the name of Campion."(Thomas
Christensen, "*The Régle de l'Octave* in Thorough-Bass Theory and Practice" (*Acta
Musicologica*, 64 [1992]: 100).

when he said that he is the inventor of its method. But the ambiguity of his words leads one to believe that this musician was the first who had an accompaniment treatise. This is an unmistakable error.

It does not seem that Sabbatini's method had much success in its newness,[88] because Lorenzo Penna, who had a treatise on *basso continuo* and the manner of accompaniment, said not one word about the rule of the octave in book 2, chapter 23 of his *Li primi albori musicali* (Bologna [Monti], 1656).[89] Most of his rules are arbitrary; he does not go into the formation of chords at all. Things remained in this state in Italy with respect to harmonic theory until the end of the seventeenth century. But the practice of accompaniment made considerable progress, particularly in the schools of Pasquini in Rome and of Alessandro Scarlatti in Naples. For their students, these great masters wrote numerous figured basses, to which the name *partimenti* was given. Instead of striking chords, following the French and German usage, these masters demanded that the accompanist have all the accompaniment parts sing in an elegant manner.[90] In this connection, the Italians maintained an incontestable superiority in the art of accompanying for a long time.

The book of Francesco Gasparini, *maestro di cappella* in Venice, made progress in the method of exposition, although the book ought not to be regarded as a systematic treatise of the science. This book,

[88]In his discussion of this treatise, Arnold (*Art of Accompaniment*, 1:110-26) concluded that "The work is of very great interest from the point of view of the antiquarian, but of little practical value . . . because the examples, dealing as they do with strings of triads, rarely represent anything likely to be encountered in actual practice" (126).

[89]Lorenzo Penna's (1613-93) 3-volume composition treatise was published in 1672. Subsequent editions appeared in 1674, 1679, 1684, 1690, and 1696 (*MGG* 10, col. 1016, 73 s.v. "Penna, Lorenzo"). A facsimile of the 4th ed. (1684) was reprinted in Bologna by Forni in 1969. Penna was one of the earliest theorists to discuss unfigured basses in volume 3, and Arnold (*Art of Accompaniment*, 1:133-54) examines some of the precepts.

[90]Most likely Fétis is referring to the style of *basso continuo* accompaniment that Peter Williams called the "Scarlatti cantata style [which] consisted of fairly smooth melodic lines, often imitative, [and] usually in few parts." (*Figured Bass Accompaniment*, 2 vols. [Edinburgh: Edinburgh University Press, 1970], 1:75.)

L'armonico pratico al cimbalo, appeared for the first time in 1701.[91] In a very few pages, it gives the proper principles for the accompaniment of various bass movements, progressions, and especially for major and minor scales. It is in this last part that Sabbatini's rule of the octave is found again. This rule, different in several respects from the usage established in the French and German schools, offers this peculiarity: the fourth degree of the ascending minor scale is accompanied by a perfect chord, while the same note in the major mode is accompanied by the six-five chord.[92] Gasparini's book, frequently reprinted, has remained the *vade mecum* of all the Italian schools during the entire century, and has been favorably replaced by Fenaroli's harmonic treatise, about which I will speak later. The systematic works of Tartini, which emerged about fifty years after *L'armonico pratico*, exercised no influence on the practice of the Italian schools. I shall say later what these works were.

I have cited Crüger as the author of a method on the accompaniment of *basso continuo* which was published as a supplement to the second edition of his book *Synopsis musica* (Berlin, 1634). This method is important because for the first time the isolated construction of isolated consonant chords, described by the author as *trias harmonica*, is found there; the name was retained by his successors.[93] It does not seem that Crüger understood the formation of the natural

[91]Martin Ruhnke (*MGG* 4, col. 1415) states that the first edition of Gasparini's treatise was published in 1708 in Venice by Bortoli; the sixth and last edition was released in 1802, nearly a century after the initial printing. In his *Biographie universelle* (3:414-15), Fétis gives 1683 for the first edition and 1708 for the second edition. Gasparini was only fifteen years old in 1683.

[92]Although Gasparini stated (69) that the fourth degree in minor, whether approached by step or by leap, must always be accompanied by a minor third, he neither stated nor consistently illustrated this scalar degree with a "perfect chord," i.e., a minor chord in root position. Occasionally he used six-three or six-five-three. Likewise, the chord that was found on the fourth scale degree in major varied inconsistently between the perfect chord, the six-three, and the six-five-three. See the scalar patterns in Francesco Gasparini, *The Practical Harmonist at the Harpsichord*, trans. Frank S. Stillings and ed. David L. Burrows (New Haven: Yale University Press, 1968), 74-75.

[93]The term *trias harmonica* is not unique to Crüger. It appears to have been coined in 1610 by Johannes Lippius in his *Disputatio musica tertia* (Wittenberg: Johan. Gormani, 1610). (See Benito Rivera, *German Music Theory in the Early 17th Century: The Treatises of Johannes Lippius* [Ann Arbor: UMI Research Press, 1980], chap. 6.)

dissonant chords—at least he says nothing about them—although they were already known in his time.[94] The other German writers of the same period who have *basso continuo* treatises at the close of the seventeen century and the beginning of the eighteenth century, particularly Printz[95] and Werckmeister,[96] added a few changes to the chordal successions in the examples furnished by Crüger, but did not try, any more than their predecessors, to form a synoptic classification of these harmonic groups.

The theoretical science of harmony made progress in the hands of Friedrich Erhard Niedt, a German musician who was a notary in Jena at first, then settled in Copenhagen where he died in 1717.[97] A poor writer, he frequently tires the reader with his diffuse style, but it cannot be denied that he imparted a salutary impulse to harmonic

[94]A "natural dissonant chord" is one in which the seventh and ninth are unprepared. Fétis placed the dominant seventh and dominant ninth chords into this classification.

[95]Wolfgang Caspar Printz (1641-1717), *Phrynis oder Satyrischer Componist* (Quedlinburg: Okel, 1676-77). This is "Printz's most important work" because "it is one of the most extensive summaries of music theory written in Getmany in the 17th century" (George J. Buelow, "Printz, Wolfgang Caspar" *NGrove* 15:274). However, in 1678 *Refutation des Satyrischen Componistens oder so genannten Phrynis*, . . . was published anonymously, and in 1674 Printz replied with *Declaration oder Weiter Erklärung der Refutation des Satyrischen Componistens*. Both the *Refutation* and *Declaration* are included in the 2d printing of *Phrynis Mitilenaeus, oder Satyrischer Componist* (Dresden and Leipzig: J. C. Mieth and J. C. Zimmermann, 1696).

[96]Andreas Werckmeister (1645-1706), *Die nothwendigsten Anmerckungen und Regeln wie der Bassus continuus, oder General-Baß wol könne tractiret werden* . . . (Aschersleben: G. E. Strunze, n.d.; 2d ed. 1715). An overview of Werckmeister's basso continuo treatise, including his eight short rules [Ibid., §§ 122-24, pp. 60-61], can be found in Arnold (*Art of Accompaniment*), 1:202-13. Arnold observed that Werckmeister's "directions for the treatment of a figured Bass are of a purely elementary character" (205).

[97]Niedt, who referred to himself as "Imperial Notary Public in Jena" on the title page of the first printing of *Musikalische Handleitung* (Hamburg: Nicholaus Spieringk, 1700), died in Copenhagen in April 1708. Since Mattheson wrote in the preface that part 3 was the "last work" that Niedt "drew up shortly before his death," Fétis erroneously assumed that Niedt died the year that part 3 was published, 1717.

theory with the first two parts of his book on this science. The first, *Guide musical*,[98] contained a *basso continuo* treatise. It contains the formulas for harmonic cadences that are still in use today, the way to realize them, and the theory of the passing notes [*Durchläuffer*] that can be substituted for struck chords.[99] The natural dissonant chords of the seventh and ninth are presented there in their true character, i.e., as able to be attacked without preparation. But the ninth chapter, with reference to these chords, gives a false ascending resolution of the seventh in several examples. This fault recurs in several places. It is remarkable that Mattheson, to whom we owe a second edition of the second part of Niedt's book, said nothing about this irregularity. The last chapter of the first part also attracts attention with the formulas for harmonic modulations which no author had shown previously.[100]

In the second part of his *Musicalische Handleitung*, Neidt presents many variations of simple bass movements, with rules for ornamenting the harmony in the upper voices. Mattheson issued a second, enlarged and improved edition of the second part (Hamburg, 1721), to which he added the disposition of sixty of the best German organs. The third part of *Musicalische Handleitung* relates to counterpoint.[101]

The development given by Niedt to the science of harmony and accompaniment does not go so far as to search for the normal generation of chords; the idea of such a generation had not occurred to any theorist before Rameau conceived it. Thus we ought not to expect to find more progress in this connection in the few books

---

[98]*Musikalische Handleitung, oder Gründlicher Unterricht. Vermittelst welchen ein Liebhaber der Edlen Music in kurzer Zeit sich so weit perfectioniren kan, . . .* (Hamburg: B. Schiller, 1710).

[99]See Chapter 8, "On the Figured Thorough-bass."

[100]Chapter 11 contains the harmonic progressions for modulation. There are *twelve* chapters in the first part.

[101]English translation by Pamela L. Poulin and Irmgard C. Taylor under the title *The Musical Guide: Parts I (1700/1710), 2 (1721), and 3 (1717)* (Oxford: Clarendon Press, 1989). Niedt's introduction, a brief discussion of each of the "twelve short chapters" and a summary are published in Arnold (*Art of Accompaniment*), 1:213-39. Strunk's translation of Niedt's Foreword, "a short satiric novel," can be found in *Source Readings*, 454-70.

published in Germany after Neidt's work. But the method of exposition and the natural classification of the principal variation of harmony received considerable improvements in the *basso continuo* treatises that *maestri di cappella* Heinichen and Mattheson revealed soon afterwards. Heinichen published the first essay on his method in 1711 in Hamburg in a book entitled *Instruction fondamentale et nouvellement inventée qui, par une méthode certaine et profitable, peut conduire un amateur de musique la connaissance complète de la basse continue.*[102] This work is divided into two parts, each of which contains five chapters. In the first part the author arranges all the true chords into two classes, consonant and dissonant. The perfect chords—major, minor, and the chord of the sixth—are the only ones admitted into the first classification by Heinichen. The six-four chord does not appear in the exercises that he gives for the use of consonant harmony, because he does not accept an unprepared fourth. In the second classification, all of the dissonant harmonies are listed according to the prolongation of intervals. In this classification, Heinichen confused those of the dominant harmony that exist by themselves, independent of every circumstance of prolongation. In this respect he is less advanced than Niedt, his predecessor. The third chapter deals with passing notes and the way to distinguish them from the actual notes by means of the beat of each genre of *Tacten*. Heinichen manifests a great sagacity in this matter and presents some delicate considerations that have been very neglected by moderns. In the following chapter we find the application of all the rules that concern chords, figures, and passing notes in all the keys. The last chapter contains exercises for accompaniment.

In the second part of the book we find some rules for the accompaniment of an unfigured *basso continuo*,[103] a very good chapter

---

[102]*Neu erfundene und gründliche Anweisung, wie ein Music-liebender auff gewisse vortheilhafftige Arth könne zu vollkommener Erlernung des General-Basses . . .* , 284 p. in quarto.

[103]Heinichen, who expanded upon Sabbatini's rule of the octave, focused upon the role of chords in a musical context.

on recitative accompaniment, another on modulation, and some general exercises for accompaniment.

Seventeen years after the publication of this book, the author produced a new edition, which seemed more like an entirely new work on the framework of the first. An immense encyclopedia on the art of accompaniment at the beginning of the eighteenth century, Heinichen's new work, which forms a volume of over 1,000 pages,[104] appeared under the title *La basse continue dans la composition, ou instruction nouvelle et fondamentale*, etc.[105] I have just said that this book is realized on the same plan as the first, although the material is developed with a great deal more depth.[106] Nevertheless, Heinichen's ideas had been modified with respect to the dominant seventh, because he presents some examples of it as a natural dissonant chord (pp. 145-146).

Mattheson, whose name dominates music literature in Germany during all of the first half of the eighteenth century, benefitted from the work of Niedt and Heinichen for the composition of his book, *Examplarische Organisten-Probe im Artikel vom General-Bass* . . . (*Exemplaire de l'examen de l'organiste en ce qui concerne la basse continue. . .*), published in Hamburg in 1719 in quarto. Just as the title indicates, the principal part of the work is composed of figured basses or *partimenti*, accompanied by analyses of various harmonic circumstances which are encountered there. A theoretical introduction precedes these exercises; it offers some rather vague harmonic principles, mixed with

---

[104]This work has fewer than 1,000 pages—there are 960 pages of text plus an introduction, an index, and the errata for a total of 986 pages.

[105]*Der General-Bass in der Composition, oder: Neue und gründliche Anweisung, wie ein Musik-Liebender mit besondern Vortheil, durch die Principia der Composition,* . . . (Dresden: The Author, 1728). The errors are so numerous in this volume, that he had to make 10 pages of *errata* in small print.

[106]George J. Buelow has made a comparative study of the two editions, first in his dissertation: "Johann David Heinichen, *Der Generalbass in der Composition*: A Critical Study with Annotated Translation of Selected Chapters" (New York University, 1961), chap. 2, and then in *Thorough-Bass Accompaniment according to Johann David Heinichen* (Berkeley and Los Angeles: University of California Press, 1966), 261-79. Buelow contends that "Heinichen's account of the art of accompanying [is] the most comprehensive in the entire Baroque literature" (*Thorough-Bass Accompaniment*, 17).

calculations of the numerical proportions of intervals. Although approaching Heinichen in the details of analysis, Mattheson's book is absolutely different from that of the former as to plan, because no chord classification can be seen there. As in most of Mattheson's books, in this one we encounter a multitude of things foreign to the subject, or which have no direct bearing on it. The second edition of this book, *Grosse General-Baß-Schule*, is no more methodical than the first, although much more developed.

In his *Petite école de la basse continue (Kleine General-Baß-Schule)*, an absolutely different work from the one that preceded, Mattheson created a truly methodical harmonic treatise, preceded by the principles of music.[107] He goes farther than Heinichen in the division of chords into different classes,[108] and examines with much more care the harmonic circumstances of the preparation and resolution of dissonant chords. Nevertheless, it can be said that this book, published thirteen years after Rameau's *Traité d'harmonie*, is not on the level to which this great man had just raised the science.[109] In all his work, Mattheson observes profound silence on the theory of chord generation conceived by the French theorist. Moreover, with the analysis that he gave of the *Traité d'harmonie* in his *Critica Musica* (2:7-11), it is evident that he understood neither this work nor the theory of chord inversions discovered by Rameau.

[107]The book, published by Kiszner (Hamburg, 1735), is divided into four "classes": (1) lowest, (2) ascending, (3) higher, and (4) upper. Each class is divided into seven lessons (*Aufgaben*), and on occasion the lesson is subdivided into smaller units called *Abtheilungen*.

[108]Mattheson's division of chords into classes is based solely upon the frequency of occurrence of each chord. Mattheson ordered the chords into three distinct groups: (1) common or most harmonious, (2) less common, and (3) uncommon. While the first class of chords professed to deal solely with consonances, this classification included the diminished triad, the augmented triad, the dominant six-five, the supertonic six-five, and the augmented sixth chords. Mattheson considered the latter two groups of chords—the less common and uncommon—dissonant.

[109]In his review of *Kleine General-Baß-Schule*, Arnold (Art of Accompaniment) found ". . . extraordinarily slovenly and incorrect progressions which the author occasionally permits himself in the examples" (1:281). Arnold pointed out examples of poor voice leading, including parallel fifths and octaves, and crossed voices; and he censured Mattheson for his low ". . . standard of correctness in the employment of 4-part harmony" (1:283).

Several treatises on accompaniment and *basso continuo* were published in France before Rameau entertained his theory of chords and of fundamental bass; the main ones were those of Saint-Lambert, Boyvin, Couperin, and Dandrieu.[110] All are written in the same spirit, namely, without criticism and with a unique view of accompanimental practice. In order to have an idea of the usefulness that could be drawn out of these works, it suffices to glance at the division of harmony that Boyvin placed in his *Traité [abrégé] de l'accompagnement* (Paris: Ballard, 1700). There are, he said, three kinds of chords, namely, perfect, imperfect, and dissonant. The perfect chord is composed of the third, fifth, and octave; the imperfect chord contains the fourth and the sixths; the dissonant chord includes the second, seventh, etc. "*Although ordinary usage demands that dissonance be preceded by consonance, one may dispense with this rule now and then and create some that are not preceded by consonance; this is recognized by good usage and good taste.*"[111] [Fétis' italics.] Thus, this poor Boyvin knew no other way to distinguish natural dissonances than by "good usage and good taste"! Such was the state of the science when Rameau gave it a real existence. Presently I will expose the creations of this man of genius, and the results which they produced in all Europe.

---

[110]Monsieur Saint-Lambert, *Nouveau traité de l'accompagnement du clavecin, de l'orgue et de quelques autres instruments* (Paris: Ballard, 1707). (*A New Treatise on Accompaniment With the Harpsichord, the Organ, and With Other Instruments*. Trans. and ed. John S. Powell [Bloomington and Indianapolis: Indiana University Press, 1991]). Jacques Boyvin, *Traité abrégé de l'accompagnement pour l'orgue et pour le clavessin* (Paris: Ballard, 1700). François Couperin, *Règles pour l'accompagnement* (c1698) in his *Oeuvres complète* (Paris: Éditions de l'Oiseau Lyre, 1933), 1:13-17. Jean-François Dandrieu, *Principes de l'acompagnement [sic] du clavecin* (Paris: The Author, 1719).

Saint-Lambert was the first theorist to advocate the addition of another flat to the key signatures of flat keys in the minor mode to reflect the status of the sixth scale degree (e.g., *c* minor with three flats rather than two). Saint-Lambert's treatise, one of the most comprehensive of the early eighteenth-century, French, thorough-bass treatises, is discussed in Arnold (*Art of Accompaniment*), 1:172-202. Given Fétis' general dislike of German theorists, it is odd that he did not comment about Heinichen's references to both Boyvin and Saint-Lambert in *Der General-Bass in der Composition* (see pages 93, 135 and 938).

[111]Jacques Boyvin in *Archives des Maîtres de l'Orgue des xvie, xviie, xviiie Siècles*, 6:75.

While the science was stationary, art was enriched by various types of new effects. Thus, composers had introduced some momentary alterations of natural notes into chords, and with this means had established ascending and descending tendencies, which multiplied the expressive accents. The chords affected by these alterations assumed a new appearance. Moreover, as well as substituting the sixth degree for the dominant in the dominant seventh chord and its derivatives,[112] they had given rise to some new dissonant chords that were attacked without preparation, like those from which they originated. The substitution in the seventh chord had produced the chords commonly called the "major dominant ninth" in the major mode, and the "minor ninth" in the minor mode.[113] The same substitution in the first derivative of the seventh chord had created the leading-tone seventh in the major mode, and that of the diminished seventh in the minor.[114] Lastly, each of the derivatives of the seventh chord had undergone a double transformation consistent with the mode in which it was to be employed. The result of the substitutions of minor mode and the ascending alteration of the natural notes of the perfect chord and its derivatives had been to create the *transition*, i.e., the optional modulation that can be resolved into several keys and leaves the ear irresolute until the completion of the resolution.[115]

---

[112]A "derivative" is an inversion. It is "derived" by transposing, for example, the dominant (root) note to an upper octave. The resultant structure, a dominant six-five chord, is the second combination of a dissonant chord (Fétis, *Traité d'harmonie*, Bk. 2, chap. 4, pp. 40-44).

[113]To obtain a complete triad on the resolution of a dominant seventh in four voices, Fétis propounded that the root of the dominant seventh be doubled and the fifth omitted. The substitution of the sixth degree for the doubled note created the dominant ninth. "The substitution of the sixth degree for the dominant is always a melodic accent placed, for this reason, in the upper voice . . . ." (Ibid., § 120, pp. 47-48.)

[114]In each inversion of the dominant seventh in which substitution will occur, the substituted note must be in the soprano. Fétis explains, "The sixth scale degree is a melodic accent in the inversions as in the fundamental chord, and consequently it is always placed in the upper voice and is found at the distance of a seventh from the leading tone . . . ." (Ibid., § 121, p. 48.)

[115]Having no discernible root, the diminished-seventh chord can easily adapt into any key because the listener is wholly dependent upon context for the harmonic role of this chord. The German and Italian augmented sixth chords share, to a

It is from this new order of facts that the emotion of surprise, so frequently called forth, arose, and in that way is weakened in modern music! One must not believe that those who found these novelties were passionately fond of them. They employed them only very guardedly, and their appearance in compositions was so unusual until the era when Mozart took possession of them, that they were considered, as it were, only as exceptional licenses.

Such was the situation of the art and science when Rameau undertook to join together the harmonic elements in order to give them a systematic foundation. Born in Dijon in 1683 of a father who had more inclination for music than knowledge of its theory and practice, he had no other teacher for composition; a few clavecin lessons that he received from an organist, a family friend, constituted all of his elementary education.[116] Later he visited northern Italy, but it seems that the sojourn that he made to Milan was of such little profit to his education, that he was more than thirty years old before he learned the rule of the octave from an obscure musician named Lacroix in Montpellier.[117] It is from that moment that his meditations on harmony date. Going to Paris in 1717, but being unable to locate

---

lesser extent, this same ambiguity: their identity as an augmented sixth or as a dominant seventh can be ascertained only within a musical context. This is what Fétis is referring to here when he says "completion of the resolution," and upon which he elaborates in Bk. 3, chap. 3 of his *Traité d'harmonie.*

[116]There is no evidence to substantiate Fétis' assertion that Rameau had only a few clavecin lessons from a family friend. Jean-Philippe's father, a musician and organist, instructed each of his eleven children in music. Of this instruction, Hugues Maret (*Eloge historique de Mr Rameau* [Dijon: Causse, 1766], 43) states, "He taught them music even before they had learned to read; the rewards, suitable to what they desired, were given to those who knew their lessons well, and a lack of attention or slothfulness was severely punished."

[117]When Rameau actually learned the rule of the octave cannot be ascertained; nothing about his early years was written during his lifetime. Sister Michaela Maria Keane, S.N.J.N., suggests that during his return home from his short sojourn in Italy ". . . he may have met M. de la Croix who was to teach him at the age of 20, the then popular rule of the octave." (*The Theoretical Writings of Jean-Philippe Rameau* [Washington, D.C.: The Catholic University of America Press, 1961], 10.)

there suitably, he was obliged to retire to a province, and for four years he fulfilled the duties of organist at the Cathedral of Clermont in Auvergne.[118] These four years were spent perusing the books of Mersenne, Kircher, Zarlino; some treatises on accompaniment, and drafting his *Traité de l'harmonie*, which he completed at the age of thirty-nine and published in Paris in 1722.[119]

This book created little sensation when it appeared; the novelty of the material and the obscure and verbose style of the author made it intelligible to only a few readers. It is even permissible to say that people did not exactly understand its importance. This was the creation of a new science that merited the attention of educated musicians. But where could the latter be found in a time when education for artists was lacking, and when all their learning was restricted to a knowledge of the contemporary practices of their art? If they had been able to understand that Rameau's work did no less than lay the foundations of a philosophic science of harmony, the idea would have seemed so ridiculous to them that it certainly would have been the object of their taunts. There was a great distance between this frame of mind to that which would have been necessary to welcome the *Traité de l'harmonie* with the interest that it was worthy of inspiring.

At last I am getting to the analysis of the theory, so new then, set forth in this book.

[118]Cuthbert Girdlestone (*Jean-Philippe Rameau: His Life and Work* [London: Cassell & Co., Ltd., 1958], 5) insists that when Rameau arrived in Clermont and how long he stayed is unknown. Sister Michaela Maria contends (*The Theoretical Writings*, 14) that Rameau was in Clermont for a period of six years, probably 1716-22.

[119]Book 3 was translated into English in London for J. French as *A Treatise of Musick, containing the Principles of Composition* (n.d.). In 1752, Robert Brown reprinted this translation in a larger format "For the Proprietor, And Sold by John Walsh, in *Catherine Street* in the *Strand,* and all the other Musick Shops in Town." Neither book identifies the translator and both identify Rameau as "Principal Composer to his Most Christian Majesty, and to the Opera at *Paris.*" In the late eighteenth century, Griffith Jones, "Organist of the French Chapel, Soho," translated Book 4 as *A Treatise on Harmony in which the Principles of Accompaniment are fully explained, and Illustrated by a variety of Examples* (London: Longman & Broderip, n.d.). 250 years were to elapse between the first publication of Rameau's treatise and a complete English translation by Philip Gossett (with an introduction and notes): Jean-Philippe Rameau, *Treatise on Harmony,* (New York: Dover Publications, 1971).

Zarlino, Mersenne, and Descartes introduced Rameau to the cognizance of applying numbers to the science of sounds. His ardent soul was enthused by this science that revealed the possibility of giving a positive foundation to music theory.[120] From that time the regular divisions of the monochord appeared to him to be the point of departure for a harmonic system, and all his attention was turned towards the development of the logical consequences of the facts revealed by these divisions. In the beginning of his book, he established that the identity of the results of the science of numbers makes evident the utility and infallibility of this science in its connections with music, whether it is applied to the divisions of a single string, or whether it has for its objective the length of strings corresponding to these divisions, the dimensions of the tubes of wind instruments, or the rate of vibrations. His efforts have, then, for a goal to show that the sound of a string in its entire length, represented by 1, is identical to the ear with the divisions of the same chord corresponding to the numbers 2, 4, 8, which produce the octaves of this entire string. This identity of octaves, to which he returns later in his other works, notably in a pamphlet of which it is the particular object,[121] seemed to him rightly the foundation of the system of fundamental bass that he wanted to establish, and of which he will speak later.

On the other hand, a statement from Descartes' *Compendium musicae* became the criterion for the generation of chords for him. It is stated in this way: "I can still divide the line A B [the monochord] into 4, 5, or 6 parts, but not further, because the ear is unable to distinguish any further the differences of pitch without considerable effort."[122] Now the numbers 1, 2, 3, 4, 5, 6 give the

---

[120]In the preface to the *Traité*, Rameau wrote, "Music is a science that should have definite rules; these rules should be drawn from an evident principle, and this principle cannot be known to us without the help of mathematics." (Rameau, *Traité de l'harmonie réduite à ses principes naturels, divisé en quatre livres* [Paris: Ballard, 1722], n.p.)

[121]*Extrait d'une réponse de M. Rameau à M. Euler, sur l'identité des octaves, d'ou résultent des vérités d'autant plus curieuses qu'elles n'ont pas encore été soupçonnées* (Paris: Durand, 1753), 41 p. in octavo.

[122]Rursus possum dividere lineam A B in 4^{or}. partes vel in 5e. vel in 6, nec ulterius fit divisio: quia, scilicet, aurium imbecillitas sine labore majores sonorum differentias non posset distinguere. (*Compendium musicae* [Trajecti ad Rhenum, 1650], 12-13.)

perfect chord, with the intervals doubled and arranged on the monochord in the following way:[123]

c		c	g	c	e	g		c
1		2	3	4	5	6		8
		octave		double octave				triple octave

After having developed at great length the demonstration of this principle of the existence of the perfect chord in the laws of numbers applied to the division of a resonant string, Rameau envisions a theory from which all the other chords are generated by a supposition or superposition of a certain number of major or minor thirds,[124] or derived by the inversion[125] of these original aggregations of thirds.[126]

One difficulty arises, however, in the outcome of the division of the monochord taken as the basis for consonant harmony: it gives only the perfect major chord. Rameau understood that it was grave

---

[123]With the exception of the number eight which Rameau added, this arithmetical series represents Zarlino's *numero senario*, in which all of the primary consonances can be expressed using only the numbers 1 to 6, although Zarlino did step outside of his *senario* to generate the minor sixth with the ratio 8:5. Zarlino identified 8 as the cube of 2. (See Shirlaw, *Theory of Harmony*, 40-42.) Rameau, like Zarlino, omitted the number seven from his arithmetic series, because he was trying to confine his theory to the consonance of the major triad as it is expressed in the *senario*. However, Rameau was not the first person to add the number 8 to the series. As Benito V. Rivera has written, Johannes Lippius explicitly stated in his treatises of 1610 (*Disputatio musicae tertia*) and 1612 (*Synopsis musicae novae*) that ". . . the choral arrangement *par excellence* is that which mirrors the numerical series 1, 2, 3, 4, 5, 6, 8 . . . ." (Benito V. Rivera, "The Seventeenth-Century Theory of Triadic Generation and Invertibility and Its Application in Contemporaneous Rules of Composition," *SMT* 6 (1984): 65).

[124]*Traité de l'harmonie*, 33.

[125]Otto Siegfried Harnish (c1568-1623) was the first theorist to recognize the relation-ship between root-position and inverted triads in his *Artis musicae* (Frankfurt, 1608). (See Joel Lester, "Root-Position and Inverted Triads in Theory Around 1600," *JAMS* 27 [1974]: 110-19.) However, the attribution of triadic generation and inversion belongs to Johannes Lippius, because he was the first to both generate the triad and explain inversions. This milestone in harmonic theory, which prefigures that of Rameau, was established in Lippius' writings of 1610 and 1612. (Benito Rivera, "Seventeenth-Century Theory," *SMT* 6 [1984]: 63-64.)

[126]Ibid., 34ff.

enough to reverse his system if he stuck to this general result. He dodged it by only drawing upon the proportions of the major third (4:5) and the minor third (5:6), given by the notes *c*, *e* and *e*, *g*, in order to form all of his combinations of thirds. This combination became his point of departure. He says,

> As a matter of fact, in order to form the *perfect chord*, one *third* must be added to the other, and to form all the *dissonant chords*, three or four *thirds* must be added to one another. The difference among these dissonant chords only arises from the different position of these *thirds*. This is the reason we can attribute to them all the power of harmony by reducing it to its first degrees. One may prove it by adding a proportional *fourth* to each *perfect chord*, from which two *seventh chords* arise. By adding a proportional *fifth* to one of these *seventh chords*, a *ninth chord*, which will contain within itself the four preceding chords, will arise.[127]

From this theory, Rameau established that there are two perfect chords, one major, the other minor, and that each of these chords generates, by inversion, a sixth chord and a six-four chord.[128] To the perfect major chord that he transposes, no one knows why, he adds a minor third and forms a dominant seventh (*g, b, d, f*) which, by inversion, gives the chords of the *false fifth* (minor fifth and sixth), *small sixth* (leading-tone sixth), and the *tritone*.[129]

By the addition[130] of a minor third to the perfect minor chord (*a, c, e*), he forms the minor seventh chord (*a, c, e, g*), which has for derivatives, by inversion, the chords of the *large sixth* (six-five), *small sixth* (four-three) and the second.[131]

The addition of a major third to the perfect major chord provides the *major seventh* chord (*c, e, g, b*) for Rameau.[132]

---

[127]*Traité de l'harmonie*, 33.

[128]Ibid., 34ff.

[129]Ibid., 37.

[130]This paragraph as well as some of the following were extracted from my *Revue musicale*, 14:114.

[131]*Traité de l'harmonie*, 39.

[132]Ibid., 40.

A minor third added below the perfect minor chord (*g, b-flat, d*) produces that of the seventh with the minor fifth that we designate by the name *leading-tone seventh* (*e, g, b-flat, d*), and its derivatives by inversion.[133]

The aggregation of two minor thirds gives Rameau the *false fifth* chord (minor third and minor fifth or perfect diminished chord), and that of two major thirds gives the *augmented fifth* chord, as well as their derivatives by inversion.

Rameau finds the origin of the diminished seventh chord (*c-sharp, e, g, b-flat*) with the addition of a minor third below the *false fifth* chord (*e, g, b-flat*).[134]

He calls *chords by supposition* those which are created, according to him, with the addition of one or more thirds under any seventh chord. It is thus that he explains the origin of *ninth* and *eleventh* chords, which we now consider as the retardation of the octave by a ninth and of the third by a fourth. With the ignorance that he had of the technique of prolongation, he demonstrates a rare sagacity in finding a reasonable explanation for the difference of this *dissonant fourth*, an object of so much embarrassment for former theorists.[135]

If we were to put ourselves into the situation where Rameau found himself, namely, in complete absence of any harmonic system at the time when he was writing, we could not help but admire the powerful mind that created all that he invented, and of which I have just stated a summary, although the system is essentially false. Fascinated by certain properties of combinations that the intervals employed in the construction of chords possessed, this genius of a man seized hold of them to form the foundation of his theory. When he published his *Traité de l'harmonie*, he had not yet focused his attention on the phenomenon of the production of harmonics in the resonance of a sonorous body,[136] which subsequently made him modify his ideas,

---

[133]Ibid., 41.

[134]*Traité de l'harmonie*, 42.

[135]*Traité de l'harmonie*, 73.

[136]A "sonorous body" is the acoustical phenomenon in which the fundamental tone is accompanied by its overtones in a harmonic ratio. This acoustical principle was the theoretical basis for Rameau's 1737 treatise, *Génération harmonique*.

and which, successively, gave rise to the publication of his *Nouveau système de musique théorique* and his other works.[137] This was still only the principle of the superposition and supposition of thirds that guided him in his system when his first harmony book appeared. Now, in order to make the application of this principle to all chords, he found himself obliged to abandon the whole idea of tonality, because he did not always find the thirds disposed as he wanted them in his system for each dissonant chord, on the notes where these chords are placed following the tonal principle. For example, the minor seventh chord with a minor third, the eternal stumbling block of all false harmonic systems, this chord, I say, which is commonly called the *seventh chord on the second degree* because it is formed on the second note of the major scale (*d, f, a, c*), could not arise from the perfect minor chord of this second note, because he knew very well that in the system of modern tonality this chord does not occur on the note from which it is set in motion. Thus, for the origin of this *minor seventh chord with a minor third,* he was obligated to take the perfect minor chord of the sixth degree (*a, c, e*), so that his seventh chord (*a, c, e, g*) seems to be connected to this last note.

By operating in this manner for most of the dissonant chords, Rameau was obliged to consider these chords as isolated occurrences, and to discard all the rules of succession and tonal resolutions established in previous treatises of accompaniment and composition. Because these rules, consistent with the natural laws of tonality,

[137]*Nouveau système de musique théorique, où l'on découvre le principe de toutes les règles nécessaires à la pratique, pour servir d'introduction au traité d'harmonie* (Paris: Ballard, 1726) [B. Glenn Chandler, "Rameau's *Nouveau système de musique théorique*: An Annotated Translation with Commentary" (Ph.D. diss., Indiana University, 1975)].

Génération harmonique, ou Traité de musique théorique et pratique (Paris: Prault, 1737) [Deborah Hayes, "Rameau's Theory of Harmonic Generation: An Annotated Translation and Commentary of *Génération harmonique*" (Ph.D. diss., Stanford University, 1968)].

Démonstration du principe de l'harmonie, servant de base à tout l'art musical théorique et pratique (Paris: Durand, 1750).

Nouvelles réflexions de M. Rameau sur la Démonstration du principe de l'harmonie, servant de base à tout l'art musical théorique et pratique (Paris: Durand, 1752) [Roger Lee Briscoe, "Rameau's *Démonstration du principe de l'harmonie* and *Nouvelles réflexions de M. Rameau sur sa démonstration du principe de l'harmonie*: An Annotated Translation of Two Treatises by Jean-Phillipe Rameau" (Ph.D. diss., Indiana University, 1975)].

assign certain positions to the chords, they were incompatible with the doctrine of the generation of chords by the superposition or supposition of thirds. Such, then, was the radical vice of the harmonic system conceived by Rameau. It consisted of destroying the rules of sequence based on aural impression, although it might qualify as *arbitrary*, in order to substitute a certain order of generation, fascinating for its regular aspect, but the effect of which was to leave all the harmonic groups isolated and without connection.

Too good a musician not to understand that after having rejected the rules of the succession and resolution of chords incompatible with his system, he had to supply some new rules which would not be contrary, Rameau conceived his theory of *fundamental bass*, the system of which he set forth in the second article of chapter 18 in his *Traité de l'harmonie*. This article was captioned "The way to compose a Fundamental Bass underneath any kind of Music."[138]

The fundamental bass in Rameau's system is only a means of verifying harmonic regularity, and not an actual bass. This is why he pointed out[139] that one ought not to stop writing successions of consecutive octaves or fifths.[140] The principal rules of this bass are (1) to form harmony with the other parts, there can be perfect chords only on the tonic, fourth degree, dominant, and the sixth degree; and seventh chords on the dominant and the second degree. However certain successions of the fundamental bass sometimes made it necessary to restore cadential action to this bass with a six-five chord on the fourth degree to the tonic. This difficulty led Rameau to consider this chord as a perfect chord on the fourth degree, to which the sixth can be optionally added; he gave it the name *added sixth*. But, given the perfect identity of this chord with that of the six-five derived from the minor seventh on the second degree, which he designated as the *large sixth*, he gave the former the name *chord of*

---

[138]*Traité de l'harmonie*, 134.

[139]Ibid., 135, no. 7.

[140]According to Rameau, the fundamental bass of a chord is the tone corresponding to the string length that, when divided harmonically, will produce all the tones of the chord. Consequently, successive fifths and octaves are permissible in the fundamental bass, because they are not occurring between composed voices.

double employment, and supposed that until it resolved on the perfect chord of the dominant, it is the *large sixth* chord and is derived from the minor seventh chord.

Until it is followed by cadential action towards the tonic, it is the added sixth and fundamental chord.

Now, it is evident that this so-called fundamental chord, which we could not compose of *superimposed* or *supposed thirds*, destroys the economy of Rameau's system from top to bottom. But such is the result of prejudice, when the inventor of the system of fundamental bass deceived himself on this capital shortcoming, and when his partisans did not even perceive it.

The other rules for the verification of harmony with the fundamental bass were.[141] (3) in every perfect tonic or dominant chord, at least one of the notes that composes the chord should be found in the preceding chord. (4) The dissonance of the dominant seventh chord ought to have been heard in the preceding chord as well. (5) In the six-five or *added sixth* chord, the bass, its third or its fifth must have been prepared in the preceding chord, *but the dissonance formed by the sixth against the fifth is free in its movement.* (6)

---

[141]Here Fétis is summarizing Rameau's rules. For some unknown reason, (2) is omitted.

Every time that the dominant is found as the fundamental bass, it ought to descend a fifth or rise a fourth. (7) When the fourth degree is the fundamental bass, it ought to rise a fifth or descend a fourth.

These rules, given by Rameau for the formation of a bass different from the actual bass of the music and for the verification of good employment of chords, could have been established by him only in an arbitrary manner: it would have been impossible for him to state a rational theory based on the very nature of harmony. Moreover, they have several essential defects that all the inventor's sagacity was unable to rectify. One was the inadequacy of these rules for a number of circumstances, an inadequacy that has become much more apparent since numerous harmonic combinations unknown in Rameau's time have been introduced into music. But it is not only for their inadequacy that the fundamental bass rules fall short; it is also in their contradistinction to tonal gravities and to the judgement of the ear in most of the successions. According to this doctrine, several of these successions were rejected, in spite of musical instinct and the laws of tonality. Thus, according to the fourth rule, the dissonance of the dominant seventh chord or of its derivatives ought to have been prepared in the preceding chord, whereas what distinguishes these natural dissonant chords from dissonances of prolongation is precisely that they could be attacked without preparation. Following the fifth rule, the bass, the third, or the fifth ought to be prepared, while the sixth is free in its attack. Now, in this chord it is not at all the sixth that is the dissonance, but the fifth, and the peculiarity of this dissonant fifth is precisely of being able to be employed only with preparation, while the bass and the third are free. Moreover, the specified succession of this six-five to the perfect tonic chord is not good, and although it has been employed in these times by Beethoven and some other German musicians, it is, nevertheless, a harmonic absurdity since the dissonance has no resolution.

The fundamental bass doctrine was, in the origin of Rameau's ideas, only an accessory, or, if you will, a complement of his harmonic system. In the sequel, when this great musician became enthusiastic about the phenomenon of the production of the perfect chord in the resonance of a sonorous body of large dimension,[142] he felt somewhat embarrassed about the subject of the perfect minor chord when the experiments did not find the product in this phenomenon. A little self-satisfaction for his theory of fundamental bass made him contrive the *double employment* of the six-five chord. A condescension analogous to his new ideas made him discover[143] some quivering of aliquot parts[144] of the sonorous body that produced to a weaker degree this perfect minor chord which he needed.[145] As a matter of fact, he would have been able to find many other resonances and quiverings in a sonorous body of certain shapes and dimensions, but I will demonstrate elsewhere that these phenomena have no coincidence with the real system of harmony. However that may be, we noticed that from that time on Rameau insisted less than he formerly had on his doctrine

---

[142]Père Louis-Bertrand Castel, a close friend of Rameau, drew Rameau's attention to the writings of Joseph Sauveur in Castel's extensive 1722 review of Rameau's *Traité de l'harmonie* for the Jesuit *Journal de Trévoux*. (This sixty-six-page review is reprinted in Jean-Philippe Rameau [1683-1874], *Complete Theoretical Writings*, ed. Erwin R. Jacobi, 6 vols. [American Institute of Musicology, 1967], 1:xxviii-xlix.) Rameau appears to have studied the acoustical theories of Sauveur and Mersenne before writing the 1726 sequel, since he mentioned both authors in *Nouveau système de musique théorique* (17). Moreover, as Thomas Christensen has observed, the title of Rameau's 1726 treatise was taken from Bernard de Fontenelle's 1701 report on Sauveur's research to the *Académie royale des sciences*, "Sur un nouveau système de musique." (Thomas Christensen, "Eighteenth-Century Science and the *Corps Sonore*: The Scientific Background to Rameau's Principle of Harmony," *JMT* 31 [1987]: 25-26.)

[143]*Démonstration du principe de l'harmonie*, [64 ff].

[144]An "aliquot part" is that part of any quantity that will measure the whole without a remainder—an exact (integral) divisor. Thus, 4 is an aliquot of either 12 or 16, whereas 5 would be an "aliquant" of 12 or 16.

[145]Rameau's explanation is rather confusing. He said,

"The *minor third* then of necessity will be generated from the difference of the effect between it and the *major*.

"The ear also indicates clearly the operations of the principal generator, *C* in this circumstance; it chooses there, itself, a fundamental *sound*, which becomes subordinate to it . . . .

"In forming the *minor third* of this new fundamental *sound*, that one judges must be the *sound A*, the principal *C* still gives its major third for a fifth . . . . This new fundamental *sound* that one can regard in this case as a generator of its *mode* is not a generator except by subordination. It is forced to follow, in all points, the law of the first generator, which cedes to it its place only in this creation, in order to occupy there that which is the most important." (*Démonstration*, 70-71.) (cont.)

of the generation of chords by the combination of thirds, while his system of fundamental bass pleased him more each day. Therefore it was this part of what he called "his discoveries" that were most successful. Many people who did not understand the theory of the generation of chords in the *Traité de l'harmonie* were enthused over fundamental bass, by means of which they believed they learned "composition," thanks to some short formulas.

One observation that has escaped all the critics who spoke about the fundamental bass system is that, even in admitting his rules as infallible and conforming to what we call the laws of tonality and our musical consciousness, they would not have been able to take the place of older practical rules, because the application of the latter ones gave immediate results, whereas the fundamental bass was only a means of verifying errors that had been made.[146]

Notwithstanding the radical shortcomings of various parts of Rameau's system, it is nonetheless true that this system could only have been the work of a superior man, and that it will always be noteworthy in the history of art as a genius' work. Moreover, in the system there is an idea that alone would immortalize its author, might he otherwise not have any titles to fame: I wish to speak of the consideration for the inversion of chords which belongs to him, and which is fruitful in favorable results. Without it, no system of harmony is possible; it is a general idea that can be applied to all good theory and can be considered the premier foundation of the science.

According to James W. Krehbiel ("Harmonic Principles of Jean-Philippe Rameau and his Contemporaries" [Ph. D. diss., Indiana University, 1964], 51-52), the fundamental C is using one of its overtones to produce an interval that is foreign to the original fundamental. However, Rameau does not explain how A becomes a generator, even a "subordinate" generator. Is the implication an arithmetic derivation of the generator A from E?

[146]In "Mon testament musical" (*RGM* 20 [1853]: 298), Fétis stated that Rameau's fundamental bass was ". . . an infallible guide for mediocre musicians and for ignorant amateurs."

CHAPTER II
THE RESULTS OF THE CREATION OF A
HARMONIC SYSTEM

Each era has its tendencies in every matter. We observe that the need to search for a theoretical base for harmonic practice was a preoccupation of eighteenth-century musicians and scholars, and that this general tendency became more pronounced immediately after the publication of Rameau's *Nouveau système de musique théorique* in 1726. The first who rushed into this research was the illustrious geometrician Euler. If it is true, as Forkel says and as I have repeated on his authority, that a first edition of Euler's *Essai d'une nouvelle Théorie de la musique*[1] was published in 1729 in St. Petersburg, he was only fifteen years old when this book appeared.[2] I know only the edition that he put out in 1739. Even then he was considered one of Europe's greatest mathematicians, and his admirable intellectual proficiency had shown in several academic essays and in his *Mécanique analytique*. Using as a point of departure the principle expressed by Leibnitz, that music is a secret arithmetic of sound relations that man makes without realization,[3] he concluded that the most simple ratios are those that ought to please more because they are more easily understood. He formulated some tables of degrees of suavity of the harmonic relations of sounds based on the numbers that serve to express these relations. Trying to prove visually what happens when two tones are heard, he established that the sensation of the unison, expressed by the ratio 1:1, produces the aural effect of perfect order

---

[1][Leonhard Euler], *Tentamen novae musicae ex certissimis harmoniae principiis dilucidae expositae* (St. Petersburg, 1739).

[2]Charles Smith refuted the existence of this alleged edition. He contended that "Euler had almost completed the *Tenamen* in 1731, about eight years before publication. This information plus a succinct statement of purpose is contained in a letter (pa) May, 1731 to Daniel Bernoulli . . ." ("Leonhard Euler, *Tentamen novae theoriae musicae*, trans. and commentary" by Charles Samuel Smith [Ph.D. diss., Indiana University, 1960], 8.)

[3]"Music charms us, although its beauty consists only in the harmonies [*convenances*] of numbers and in counting (of which we are unconscious but which nevertheless the soul does make) of the beats or vibrations of sounding bodies, which beats or vibrations come together at definite intervals." (Leibnitz, *The Monadology and Other Philosophical Writings*, Robert Latta [1898; rpt. London: Lowe & Brydone, Printers, Ltd., 1951], 422.)

because the vibrations of two sounds that give this impression to our perception occur in our mind as two lines of dots corresponding perfectly.

1 . . . .   ratio of the unison
1 . . . .

The ratios of the simple octave, of the double, triple, etc., octave, also strike the mind with a feeling of order, but not that of identity, because the vibrations of a sound located at the octave above the other are double in number, and they increase in the same proportion from octave to octave, so that the sensation produced in the ear by these octaves is in proportion to what strikes the eyes from the sight of these figures:

2 . . . .   first octave
1 .   .   .   .

4 . . . .   second octave
1 .   .   .   .   .

The ratios 2:1, 4:1, etc., thus constitute, following Euler's doctrine, the second and third degrees of suavity of the harmonic relations of sounds because of the proportional facility that the mind has to comprehend these ratios.

This facility diminishes progressively as the ratios become complicated. The complication is as great as the first numbers that express this ratios rise further. For example, the ratio 3:2, which is that of the fifth, already expresses a disorder of vibration where the identity is restored only at each third vibration on one hand, and at each fourth vibration on the other hand. For the eyes, the effect corresponds to lines of dots disposed in this order:

3 . . . . ratio of the fifth
2 .   .   .   .

This ratio is the one that Euler places in the fourth degree of harmonic suavity.

The identity becomes more infrequent and the ratio more difficult to grasp if the ratio is 4:3, i.e., if the two tones form the interval of the fourth. Euler likens the sensation that results from this interval to that which produces two lines of dots disposed in this way for the eyes:

4 . . . . ratio of the fourth
3 . . . .

Euler places this ratio in the fifth degree of harmonic suavity.

The ratio of the major third (5:4), placed by Euler in the seventh degree of suavity, ought, according to him, to give the ear a sensation analogous to that which would produce the ratio of two lines of dots disposed in this order for the eyes:

5 . . . . ratio of the
4 . . . . major third

Here, there arises a difficulty that seems radical and destructive to the theory of the suavity of the union of tones based on the simplicity of numerical ratios and that clearly shows the theory clashes with the rules of the art. Every musician whose ear will be consulted will declare that the major third, and even the minor, of which the ratio is 6:5 and which occupies the eighth degree of suavity in Euler's system, give him a much more agreeable sensation than the fourth. From that come the rules that, in counterpoint or simple two-voice composition, admit thirds among the best unions of two tones and banish the fourth.

This is not the only anomaly found in the classification of the union of two tones by degrees of suavity based on the numerical ratios, because Euler ranks not only the minor third, expressed by the ratio 6:5 in the eighth degree, but the major second (9:8) which, as one knows, is a dissonance, and the minor sixth (8:5). Euler foresaw the objections that would be raised against his system in this regard. He believed that he refuted them with the following paragraphs:

I have already said that the designation of chords includes those that are commonly called *consonances* and *dissonances*. With the help of our method, we will be able to assign, to a certain extent, the bounds that separate these two categories of chords, because the

dissonances belong to the highest degrees of suavity and we consider
as consonances the chords that belong to the lower degrees. Thus,
the tone [major second], created from two tones having the 8:9 ratio
and belonging to the eighth degree, is included among the dissonances, while the *ditone* or major third, with a 4:5 ratio and which
appears in the seventh degree, is considered a consonance. However,
it does not follow that dissonances ought to be thought of as starting
from the eighth degree, because in this same degree are included the
ratios 5:6 and 5:8, which are not considered dissonances.

   If this matter is examined attentively, one will recognize that the
difference between consonances and dissonances lies not only in the
ease of perception of the sought-for ratio, but that the difference
ought to be considered in the whole process of the composition. The
chords whose use is less advantageous in music are called dissonances,
even though they are easier to perceive than some others classified
among the consonances. This is why the tone 8:9 is included among
the dissonances, and some other chords of a proportion are considered consonances. This is the same way that one explains why the
fourth, with a 3:4 ratio, is taken by musicians as a dissonance,
although there is no doubt that it can be perceived easily.[4] [Fétis'
italics.]

---

[4]"Iam monui, me hic sub consonantiae nomine tam consonantias, quam dissonantias vulgo sic dictas complecti. Ex tabula autem apposita et methodo nostras limites
quodammodo definiri posse videntur. Dissonantiae enim ad altiores pertinent
gradus, et pro consonantiis habentur, quae ad inferiores gradus pertinent. Ita
tonus, qui constat sonis rationem 8:9 habentibus, et ad octavum gradum est relatus,
dissonantiis annumeratur, ditonus vero seu tertia maior ratione 4:5 contentus, qui
ad septimum gradum pertinent, consonantiis. Neque tamen ex his octavus gradus
initum potest constitui dissonantiarum; nam in eodem continentur rationes 5:6,
et 5:8, quae dissonantiis non accensentur.

   "Hanc rem antem attentius perpendenti constabit dissonantiarum et consonantiarum rationem non in sola perceptionis facilitate esse quaerendam, sed etiam ad
totam componendi rationem spectari debere. Quae enim consonantiae in concentibus minus commode adhiberi possunt, eae dissonantiarum nomine sunt appellatae, etiamsi forte facilius percipiantur, quam aliae, quae ad consonantias
referuntur. Atque haec est ratio, cur tonus 8:9 dissonantiis annumeretur, et aliae
multo magis compositae consonantiae pro consonantiis habeantur. Simili modo
ex hoc explicandum est, cur quarta seu diatessaron sonis rationem 3:4 habentibus
constans a musicis ad dissonantias potius quam ad consonantias referatur, cum
tamen nullum sit dubium, quin ea admodum facile percipi queat." (Euler, *Tentamen novae theoriae musicae*, chap. 4, pars. 14-15, pp. 62-63.)

The weakness of the illustrious geometrician's reasoning here is obvious. One of two things is true: either the criterion of his theory is general, or it is not. Only in the first case would it have real value, but the criterion destroys it when it contradicts itself after the introduction of the system. What more flagrant contradiction of the principle of harmonic suavity based on the simplicity of the ratio of sounds than to see the harsh dissonance of the major second, the minor third (consonance of repose), and the minor sixth (suspensive consonance of conclusion) put into the same degree? In vain, Euler pretends to explain this anomaly by saying that the chords whose use in music is less advantageous ("quae enim consonantiae in concentibus minus commode adhiberi possunt") are called dissonances ("eae dissonantiarum nomine sunt appellatae"), even though they are easier to perceive than others that are classified among the consonances ("etiamsi forte facilius percipiantur, quam aliae, quae ad consonantias referuntur"). This opposition of experience with principle is the condemnation. Moreover, notice that the statement of Euler's theory is in such absolute terms that even he is unable to deal with this result. This is how he expresses it:

> Several simple sounds heard together constitute the composite sound we call the *accord* . . . .

> To find the suavity in a chord, it is imperative that the relation that exists between the simple sounds that compose it be perceived. And here since one is not concerned with the duration of the sounds, the pleasure will consist solely in the perception of their differences with respect to lowness and highness. Now, since the lowness and highness of sounds are measured by the number of vibrations produced simultaneously, it is evident that those who are conscious of the mutual relationship of these numbers will also perceive the suavity of the chord.

> We have established previously that sounds can be represented by the number of vibrations produced by each in the specified time, i.e., that their quantity, determined by the degree of highness or lowness, is measured by these numbers. For a pleasing chord, it is necessary that the ratio that occurs between the quantities of simple sounds, or among the sounds themselves [(for we may consider sounds as

quantities)], be perceived as numbers. In this way, we reduce the perception to the cognition of numbers . . . .

By applying these precepts, it will be easy to assign to the perception of each chord a certain degree of suavity, which will be known with how much ease or difficulty the chord can be comprehended. . . .[5]

I do not believe I need to show what contradiction exists between these paragraphs and those that have been cited previously. I will continue the analysis of the system set forth in *Tentamen novae theoriae musicae*:

The classification of chords of three or more sounds, following their degrees of suavity, can be done in the same manner as those chords of two sounds; thus it is superfluous to give new explanations on this subject. Only it is advisable to note that the simplest chord of three sounds belongs in the third degree of suavity, which is composed of the tones 1:2:4, and its exponent[6] is 4. It is apparent from this that the more sounds of which a chord is composed, the higher

---

[5]"Plures soni simplices simul sonantes constituunt sonum compositum, quen hic consonantiam appellabimus . . . .

"Quo igitur huiusmodi consonantia placeat, oportet, ut ratio, quam soni simplices eam constituentes inter se tenent, percipiatur. Quia autem hic duratio sonorum non spectatur, sola varietatis, quae in sonorum gravitate et acumine inest, perceptio istam suavitatem continebit. Quamobrem, cum gravitas et acumen sonorum ex pulsuum eodem tempore editorum numero sint mensuranda, perspicuum est, qui horum numerorum mutuam relationem comprehendat, eundem suavitatem consonantiae sentire debere.

"Supra autem iam constituimus ipsos sonos per pulsuum, quos dato tempore conficiunt, numeros exprimere, ex hocque sonorum quantitatem seu tenorem, qui gravitatis et acuminis ratione continetur, metiri. Quo itaque proposita consonantia placeat, necesse est ut ratio, quam sonorum simplicium quantitates, seu ipsi soni (sonos enim tanquam quantitates consideramus) inter se tenent, percipiatur. Hoc igitur modo consonantiarum perceptionem ad numerorum contemplationem revocamus . . . .

"Facile igitur erit consonantiae cuiusvis perceptionem ad certum suavitatis gradum reducere, ex quo apparebit, utrum facile an difficile et insuper quo gradu proposita consonantia meute comprehendatur. . . ." (Ibid., chap. 4, pars. 1-4, [pp. 56-58].)

[6]An exponent is the smallest integer into which all of these numbers can be divided equally. Thus it is the least common multiple.

the degree of suavity of the chord [i.e., the more the suavity decreases], even if it is the simplest genre of sound.[7]

If there is nothing in the contents of this paragraph to which to object with respect to the mathematical principle, since it is apparent that each added tone complicates the comparison of ratios, it is nonetheless true that, as a result of this same paragraph, there is new proof that the principle is in opposition with, under the ratio of suavity, what experience demonstrates; because in a chord composed of consonances, for example, the doubling of all the tones in various octaves, from the lowest to the highest, is one of the most fascinating and most powerful harmonic effects. The least experienced amateur musician is sensitive to this effect.

Nothing is more difficult for a musician than to explain what Euler proposed in what follows the above paragraph:

> I will not concern myself any further with the division of chords that have just been discussed, because I am going to make use of another, both more suitable and useful, namely, their division into *complete* and *incomplete*. I call a chord *complete* if no other tone can be added without raising its degree of suavity [i.e., without the suavity decreasing], or without its exponent becoming larger. Such is the chord composed of the sounds 1:2:3:6, which has 6 as an exponent; with the addition of the any new tone, the exponent will become greater. On the other hand, a chord is *incomplete* when, to the tones that compose it, one or more can be added without increasing the exponent. For example, the chord 1:2:3 does not raise its exponent even if the sound 6 is added.[8]

---

[7]"Trisonarum et multisonarum consonantiarum secundum suavitatis gradus enumeratio simili modo perficietur, quo bisonarum, ita ut superfluum esset tam abunde de iis explicare. Id tantum animadverti convenit simplicissimam consonantiam trisonam ad gradum suavitatis tertium pertinere sonisque 1:2:4 constare, cuius exponens est 4. Ex quo intelligitur, ex quo pluribus sonis consonantia sit composita, eam ad eo altiorem quoque suavitatis gradum pertinere, etiamsi sit in suo genere simplicissima." (Ibid., chap. 4, [par. 20], p. 65.)

[8]"Eo autem magis hanc consonantiarum divisionem ulterius non persequor, cum aliam multo aptiorem et utiliorem divisionem sim allaturus, quae fit incompletas consonantias. Voco autem consonantiam completam, ad quam nullus sonus superaddi potest, quin simul ipsa consonantia ad altiorum gradum sit referenda; seu eius exponens fiat magis compositus: huiusmodi est consonantia sonis 1:2:3:6

What Euler calls a "complete chord" is composed of a fundamental sound, the octave, the fifth and the octave, and the doubling of this fifth, because these are the sounds that correspond to 1:2:3:6; whereas the chord can be complete in the meaning attached to this expression in music only by adding the third to these sounds. But it is evident that the chord called "perfect" by musicians is, according to the celebrated geometrician's theory, placed in a degree a long way from the point of absolute suavity, which is found only in the 1:1 ratio. Let us imagine a chord composed of *c, e, g, c*, and we will find combined there (1) the ratio 2:1 which is that of the octave; (2) 3:2 for the fifth *c, g*; (3) 4:3 for the fourth *g, c*; (4) 5:4 for the major third *c, e*; (5) 6:5 for the minor third *e, g*; (6) and finally 8:5 for the minor sixth *e, c*. And if by chance the chord has its third doubled, as in *c, e, g, c, e*, it will be necessary to add to all of the preceding ratios that of 5:3 for the major sixth *g, e*. Now it is precisely to retain the simplest ratios possible that Euler composed his chord in this combination, 1:2:3:6, in lieu of 1:2:3:4:6.[9] Because he wanted to have the greatest suavity possible, he avoided the complication of the 4:3 ratio, which is that of the fourth *g, c*. Let us imagine, according to this, the excessive complication of all the combined ratios and the remoteness of the perfect chord, composed of all of its intervals and their doublings, from the first degree of suavity!

Such is the inevitable result of the suavity of harmony founded on the simplicity of numerical ratios. Fascinating at first sight because it seems to have something philosophical, the initial idea of this theory does not support the development of its consequences. But

---

constans, cuius exponens ets 6. Superaddito enim quocunque novo sono exponens fiet maior. Consonantia contra incompleta mihi ets, ad quam unum vel plures sonos adiicere licet, citra exponentis multiplicationem: ut huius consonantiae 1:2:3 exponens non fit maior, etiamsi sonus 6 addatur, quamobrem eam incompletam voco." (Ibid., chap. 4, [par. 21], p. 65.)

[9]The inclusion of 4 raises the exponent to 24, and, hence, to the sixth degree of suavity, as opposed to the fourth degree. The inclusion of 5 would raise the exponent to 60 and move the chord into the seventh degree of suavity.

before an opinion about the worth of Euler's system is set forth, it is necessary to consider it in its other applications. I am going to proceed to this examination, and I will continue to restrict myself to pointing out that this system is the most complete negation imaginable of the reality of Rameau's [system], which as we saw (*Gazette musicale*, no. 40), was finally summed up in the production of the harmonic intervals of the perfect chord through the resonance of the large sonorous bodies. According to Rameau, the objective fact in harmony is identical with the subjective conscience, while, according to Euler's doctrine, the aggregations of sounds are nothing but fortuitous formations which we perceive only as numerical ratios; and the feeling of the harmonic ratio of sounds grows weaker in the same proportion that these ratios become complicated and lose their simplicity.

It is this prevailing idea, the premise of all his system, that did not permit him to approach the construction of truly complete chords, according to musical sense, in the chapter of his book devoted precisely to this subject. His scale of degrees of suavity is already so high with simple harmonies of two tones admitted by the ear with pleasure, that the construction of harmonies of three and four distinct tones for him must have seemed a source of intolerable confusion for hearing as well as embarrassing for the mind. I admit that I am unable to explain why this circumstance did not enlighten him about the shortcoming of his principle if, as his son-in-law and biographer Mr. Fuss said, music was one of Euler's main pastimes.[10] It is true that he adds that when cultivating music, Euler brought all his geometric mind to it. It is very likely this mind, which imagined nothing if it was not in the form of a calculation, which absorbed the

---

[10]Nicolaus (Nikolai Ivanovich) Fuss (Fus) (1755-1826) was a Swiss mathematician who was recommended by Daniel Bernoulli to become Euler's secretary in 1772. Fuss, who wrote his first papers under Euler's direct guidance in 1774 and 1776, had more than one hundred papers in several branches of mathematics (spherical geometry, integration of differential equations, the theory of series, etc.) published by the St. Petersburg Academy of Sciences. The bulk of Fuss' writings contains solutions to problems raised in Euler's works. (*Dictionary of Scientific Biography* s.v. "Fuss, Nicolaus.")

pure feeling of harmony for Euler, put his intelligence at variance with his ear.

In spite of the insurmountable difficulties that he encountered for his construction of chords by subjecting them to his scale of suavity, he dares to treat the laws of the succession of two chords in the fifth chapter of his book. The incisiveness, the precision of his mind, made him see that the succession of harmonies ought to be one of the causes of pleasure that it procures, as well as the composition of chords. In this he saw farther than Rameau, whose views had embraced only combinations of isolated chords.

> The order that we follow demands that we now investigate what the nature of two tones or of two chords which succeed one another will be, so that the condition of pleasure is fulfilled. To obtain an agreeable succession of sounds or chords for the ear, it is not sufficient that each of them please individually. It is also necessary that they have a certain relationship to each other that can be defined best by calling in an *affinity*. [Fétis' italics.][11]

Nothing is more true or more thought-provoking than this passage. To see it separately, we would believe that the writer had preceded his century in the theory of music, and that he had penetrated its secret. But before long disenchantment occurs. And at first, instead of beginning to examine the succession of the two sounds of which he spoke and to build the scale of these sounds, namely the scale or rather the scales, he enters into the subject with chords. If he speaks about the isolated sounds of which they are composed, it is only to consider the particular numbers to establish the ratio of succession. In order to know with what facility a succession can be appreciated, it is necessary to express the simple sounds that comprise it with the numbers that represent them and form the smallest multiple in it; then to find this multiple in his table of

---

[11]"Hoc igitur capite ordo requirit, ut investigemus, cuiusmodi esse debeant duo soni vel duae consonantiae, quae se invicem sequentes atque successive sonantes suaves sint perceptu. Non enim ad suavitatem successionis sufficit, ut utraque consonantia seorsim sit grata; sed praeterea quandam affectionem mutuam habere debent, quo etiam ipsa successio aures permulceat, sensuique auditus placeat." (Ibid., chap. 5, [par. 1], p. 76.)

degrees of suavity; that degree to which it will correspond will make known how much ability is necessary to perceive the proposed succession. After having said (chap. 5, par. 2) that in order to know with what facility a succession can be evaluated, it is necessary to express the simple sounds that make a part of it with the numbers that represent them, and to form the smallest multiple of them. Next, to find this multiple in his table of degrees of suavity, and that degree to which it will correspond will make known how much ability is necessary to perceive the proposed succession. He arrives (par. 3) at this necessary, but monstrous for a musician's intelligence, conclusion in his system:

> Therefore, the two chords that compose the succession ought to be considered *as if they sound together*. The exponent of the composite chord that arises from this hypothesis will indicate the degree of suavity to which the succession itself is raised.[12] [Fétis' italics.]

Leaving aside that such a conclusion contains impossibilities musically, Euler's problem becomes evident in realizing the inevitable consequences of his system, because he contradicts himself twice on the same page. As a matter of fact, it is easy to understand that if the calculation of ratios becomes complicated with respect to a single chord, it is more so in the combination of ratios in two chords. This consideration leads the great geometrician to express himself thusly:

> Just as the most simple chord of three tones is more difficult to perceive than the most simple *bisona*, so the difficulty of perceiving any chord, be it the simplest of its kind, will be increased with the number of tones that compose it. *Nonetheless, the suavity of multi-tone chords will not only be equal to, but will surpass those of a simple tone or that of a chord that would be created from two tones.*[13] [Fétis' italics.]

[12]"Ambae igitur consonantiae successionis tanquam simul sonantes considerari debebunt, huiusque consonantiae compositae exponens declarabit, quam suavis et perceptu facilis sit ipsa consonantiarum successio." (Ibid., par. 3, [p. 77].) [The second sentence was slightly distorted in the translation to French. It should read: "The exponent of the composite chord will indicate with what suavity and facility of perception the succession of sonorities is endowed."]

[13]"Quemadmodum enim simplicissima consonantia trisona magis est composita, quam simplicissima bisona; ita ex quo pluribus sonis constet consonantia, magis etiam erit composita, etiamsi sit simplicissima in suo genere. Hoc tamen non

And a little farther on (par. 7) these words are found: "However it cannot be denied that the simpler the exponent of a succession of two chords, the easier it is to comprehend the order that governs it."[14] Now since the fundamental principle of all Euler's system was that the pleasure that results from harmony is in proportion to the simplicity of ratios, this last passage is a flagrant contradiction with the preceding.

I will not examine the laws of the succession of chords according to this theory any further. What we have seen will suffice to make clear to what results it is bound to lead. I still have to expose the formation, from this same theory, of what Euler calls "genres of music." The eighth chapter of *Tentamen novae theoriae musicae*, where he has dealt with this subject, is one of the work's most curious.

Euler calls "genres of music" a system of composition where one would make use of only a certain number of predetermined chords. Thus the first genre, according to him, contains no harmony other than the octave but, owing to its simplicity, it is not employed. Music's second genre is that which contains only the tones 1, 3, and their multiples, i.e., the fifth, octave, and their doublings. "By representing the lowest tone with 3, the form of the harmony will be 3:4:6 [*g, c, g*], where the lower interval is the fourth and the upper interval is the fifth."[15] He adds that this genre is still too simple, and that it has never been used. But in this he is mistaken, because the *diaphony* of the tenth and eleventh centuries was nothing else.

---

obstante suavitas non solum eadem, sed etiam maior percipitur ex consonantiis multisonis, quae ex sono simplici, vel consonantiis duobus tantem sonis constantibus." [Ibid., chap. 5, par. 5, pp. 77-78]. [Again, the second sentence was distorted in the translation to French. It should read: "This, therefore, will not only obviate the suavity of the same, but also may be perceived as having greater suavity than those of a simple tone or that of a chord that would be created from two tones."]

[14]"Iterim tamen negari non potest, quo simplicior fuerit successionis duarum consonantiarum exponens, eo facilius etiam ipsam successionem et ordinem, qui in ea inest percipi"[p. 78].

[15]"Forma etiam huius octavae, infimum sonum ponendo 3, ita potest repraesentari 3:4:6, ubi interuallum inferius est quarta, superius vero quinta." (Euler, *Tentamen novae*, chap. 8, § 14.)

The third genre is that in which the sound 5, i.e., the major third, is introduced into harmony but without preserving the sound 3, which is the fifth, so that the chords there are composed of only the third and octave. Apropos of this new harmonic element, Euler makes this remark: "Until our day, we have admitted into music only chords whose exponents are composed of the prime numbers 2, 3, 5. In fact, in the formation of chords musicians have not gone beyond the number 5."[16] A century before Euler, Descartes said in his *Compendium musicae*: "Rursus possum dividere lineam A B in quatuor partes vel in quinque vel in sex, nec ulterius fit divisio: quia, scilicet, aurium imbecillitas sine labore majores sonorum differentias non posset distinguere."[17] This principle, which is still held by many geometric theoreticians, was refuted by Euler himself about thirty years after the publication of his *Tentamen novae theoriae musicae* in his *Mémoire* entitled "Conjecture sur la raison de quelques dissonances généralement reçues dans la musique," inserted into the anthology of the Academy of Berlin (1764). This *Mémoire* purported to discover the principles of the rational construction of the dominant seventh (g, b, d, f) and of the six-five (f, a, c, d). After having remarked that the character of the chord g, d, f is contained in the ratio of b, expressed by the number 45, with f represented by the number 64, he points out that the latter number undergoes a modification through the attractive affinity of the interval. He adds (par. 13) that the ear substitutes 63 for 64, so that all the numbers of the chord are divisible by 9, in such a way (par. 14) that for the audition of the tones g, b, d, f, expressed by the numbers 36, 45, 54, and 64, we think we hear 36, 45, 54, and 63, which, reduced to simplest terms, gives 4, 5, 6, 7.[18] Euler concludes his *Mémoire* with this outstanding paragraph:

[16]"In Musica ad hunc usque diem aliae consonantiae non sunt receptae, nisi quarum exponentes constent numeris primis dolis 2, 3 et 5, adeo ut musici ultra quinarium in formandis consonantiis non processerint." (Ibid., §15.)

[17]Descartes, pp. 12-13. ["The line A B may be divided into four, five, or six parts, but it may not be further divided: for, it will be admitted, the ear is unable to distinquish greater differences of sounds without effort."]

[18]Euler, believing that the ear is not capable of perceiving complicated proportions (e.g., 36:45:54:64 or $2^6 \times 3^3 \times 5$), found his justification for alteration in equal-tempered tuning: "In equal temperament, which makes all 12 intervals of an octave equal, there are no exact consonances except the octaves; there the fifth is expressed by the irrational proportion of $1 : \sqrt[12]{27}$, which is somewhat different

It is commonly contended that only the proportions composed of the three prime factors 2, 3, and 5 are employed in music. The great Leibnitz has already remarked that in music we still have not learned to count beyond 5, a remark that is unquestionably just for string instruments following the principles of harmony. But if my conjecture is founded, we can say that today in composition we count up to 7, and that the ear is already accustomed to it: *it is a new genre of music that is being employed and that was unknown to the ancients.* In this genre the chord 4, 5, 6, 7 is the most complete harmony, since it includes the numbers 2, 3, 5, and 7. But it is also more complex than the perfect chord in the common genre, which contains only the numbers 2, 3, and 5. . . . [Fétis' italics.][19]

Euler returned to the same subject in his *Mémoire,* "Du véritable caractère de la musique moderne" (Academy of Berlin, 1764), and confirmed his conjecture with some exhaustive theoretical developments.[20] It is necessary to render justice to this great man. If the fascinating but false hypothesis on which he built his system led him astray, and if his weak sense of harmony caused him to construct some intolerable aggregations of tones in his chapter on genres of music, the philosophy of this art is nonetheless indebted to him for the discovery of a truth as irrefragable as new in the paragraphs of the *Mémoire* that I have just cited. He was the first who saw that the character of modern music resides in the dominant seventh chord, and that its determining ratio lies in the number 7. But until today his words have not been understood. This ratio constitutes the genre

---

from that of 3:2. Nevertheless, when an instrument is tuned according to this temperament, the ear is not jarred by this irrational proportion, and, hearing the interval *C:G*, it does not fail to perceive a fifth or the proportion 3:2." ("Conjecture sur la raison de quelques dissonances generalement recues dans la musique," in *Mémoires de l'Académie Berlin,* 20 [1764]: 168.)

[19]Ibid., 173.

[20]To recognize seventh chords, particularly the dominant seventh, as more consonant and to give seventh chords a lower ratio, Euler used the seventh partial as well as the second, third, and fifth partials to derive scales. Beginning on *F* and using the formula $2^n \times 3^3 \times 5^2 \times 7$, Euler derived a 24-tone chromatic scale. He called the 12 new tones in the octave *tons étrangers.*

that I have called *transitonique*. I will show in my *Philosophie de la musique* that the *ordre pluritonique*, which is that of current music, has raised its exponent to the prime number 11, and that the last limits will be attained in *ordre omnitonique*, where the exponent will be raised to 15. I have already indicated this in some of my articles on this philosophy, particularly in the plan of my work (*Gazette musicale*, 1840, p. 4) in paragraph four of the second book.

I will not begin the examination of the bizarre and inadmissible combinations of various genres of music set forth by Euler in his *Tentamen novae theoriae musicae*, because all of these things are really incompatible with true art. But I will remark that before having found the important truth of which I have just spoken (in relation to the numerical expression of the dominant seventh chord), it was impossible for him to give the exact formation of the diatonic-chromatic genre, the eighteenth of his table, which he rightly considered as characteristic of modern tonality.

Here I ought to stop the analysis of this system, the first that was produced after that of Rameau. In spite of the illustrious name of its author, it has remained unrecognized, and I think I can affirm that until today no musician, not even one of those who has made the theory of art the object of his studies, has either known or understood it, although copies are not scarce.[21] Only d'Alembert expressed a not very favorable opinion of this system in a note placed among his mathematical works. It is probably of this note that Mr. Fuss (Euler's biographer), erudite geometrician and president of the Imperial Academy in St Petersburg, wished to speak when he put it this way:

> This principle [the one of agreeableness procured by the harmony in proportion to the simplicity of numerical ratios] has been called inadequate. But since no mathematician is able to subordinate the relative qualities of emotion to the rigor of his calculations, it is difficult to prove the solidity of it. If this principle is conceded, we will

[21]Fuss claimed that Euler's *Tentamen novae theoriae musicae* "had no great success, apparently because it contained too much geometry for the musician, and too much music for the geometer." ("Éloge de Léonard Euler, prononcé en français, par Nicolas Fuss" in Leonard Euler, *Oeuvres complètes en française* [Brussels, 1839], 1:xii.

be obliged to acknowledge that it is impossible to make better use of
it, nor to reason with more solidity and penetration. Moreover, all
the objections to this principle are not likely to harm the actual work.
They could only lead one to consider it as a perfect edifice in all its
parts, but built on shifting terrain. While admiring the skill of the
architect, one would pity him for not having been able to construct
it on more solid ground.[22]

This conclusion is precisely that one at which we arrive after an
attentive and intelligent study of Euler's work. The complete disap-
pointment of so great a mind that had mastered so many other
difficult subjects offers a serious subject for reflections on the use of
mathematics in music theory.[23]

Once the thought of the possibility of an exact and complete
theory of harmony occurred, we saw systems of every kind, presented
as the realization of this thought, rapidly follow one another. After
those of Rameau and Euler came the one the celebrated violinist
Tartini set forth in a book titled *Trattato di musica secondo la vera scienza
dell' armonica* (Padua: [Stamperia del Seminario (Giovanni Manfrè)],
1754, 175 p. in quarto). This book is divided into six chapters, the
contents of which follow: (1) "On the Harmonic Phenomena, Their
Nature and Their Use"; (2) "On the Circle, Its Nature and Its Use";
(3) "On the Musical System, Consonances and Dissonances, Their
Nature and Definition"; (4) "On the Diatonic Scale, On Musical
Practice Genre: Its Origin, Its Use, and Its Consequences"; (5) "On
the Modes and Ancient and Modern Keys"; (6) "On Intervals and on
Modulations of Modern Music."

One of the most remarkable phenomena of the human mind's
lack of consistency comes in this book, because there we see a man

---

[22]Ibid., xiii.

[23]Helmholtz believed that the fundamental problem in Euler's theory was his
failure to express how the mind ". . . contrives to perceive the numerical ratios of
two combined tones." Helmholtz endeavored to rectify this deficiency in his
investigations of the physiological processes, and concluded that the human mind
". . . perceives *only the physical effect* of these ratios, namely the continuous or
intermittent sensation of the auditory nerves." (Herman Helmholtz, *On the Sensations of Tone*, trans. Alexander J. Ellis [2d ed.; New York: Dover Publications, 1954],
231.)

acquainted with all the secrets of his art search outside of the structure of this art for the principles that are to be used for the base,[24] wear himself out in barren efforts to draw the principles from a dubious body of physics and from calculations about whose mechanics he knew nothing. Repelled by the obscurity that prevails in the whole work, critics reproached Tartini for not having presented his ideas in a clear enough manner, and attributed the lack of clarity that they observed to his writing style.[25] With more attention, they would have seen that the obscurity is in the ideas themselves, and that if ingenious insights are not lacking in the system that the author endeavored to coordinate, rigorous liaison among them does not exist; finally, they would have seen that the results that he draws from them are unsound.[26] But let us not anticipate, and let us say only that since Tartini's system exercised no influence on the formation of a harmonic system, it will suffice to give a succinct analysis of it here.

The first chapter of the *Trattato di musica* contains an account of various phenomena of harmonic resonance as they had been observed by his time. He accepts those of the production of harmonics forming the octave of the fifth and the double octave of the third of the principal sound of a deep sonorous body, and does not reject the resonance of octaves and double octaves of this sound to the weakest degrees. But he does not immediately draw any conclusion from this fact. Moving ahead to the examination of natural tones produced by the horn and trumpet at the harmonic points of the division of their

[24]Fétis is referring to Tartini's physical-mathematical system as evidenced by his use of harmonic, arithmetic, and geometric proportions.

[25]Recognizing that ". . . there are many parts of the original very complicated and difficult to comprehend," Tartini's follower, Benjamin Stillingfleet, attempted to explain these principles "in a more easy way" (iii) in *Principles and Power of Harmony* (London: J. and H. Hughs, 1771).

[26]In his remarks about Fétis' critique of Tartini, Rubelli states, "If Fétis maintains that not only Tartini's manner of presentation, but also his ideas are obscure and unclear, he certainly is not wrong. But it is severely exaggerated when he accuses Tartini of not having correctly understood his own methods of calculation, because the computations that are contained in the *Trattato* are almost without exception correct." (Giuseppe Tartini, *Traktat über die Musik gemäss der wahren Wissenschaft von der Harmonie*, übersetzt und erläutert von Alfred Rubeli [Düsseldorf: Im Verlag der Gesellschaft zur Förderung der systematischen Musikwissenschaft e. V., 1966], 28.)

tubes, he devotes himself to some confused reasoning, and to some hazardous conjectures in order to explain the conflicting results given by the production of harmonics in the resonance of deep sonorous bodies and the progression generated by these tubes. Moreover, neither does he draw any fundamental conclusion from this fact, and he goes rapidly to the examination of harmonics produced by the monochord called the *tromba marina*. He radically deludes himself in this examination when he affirms that by lightly touching the point that cuts this string in half, its harmonic cannot be produced.[27] If he did the experiment, some extraordinary circumstance must have prevented the production of this harmonic, the existence of which other tests have proved. All the reasoning that he sets upon this fact thus fall wrongly. In addition, here he commences to hint at his system according to which it would not be the fundamental sound that would generate the harmonics, but the combination of the latter, from which the fundamental sound would result. And to prove it, he took the organ stop called the *fourniture*, where on each touch a series of pipes tuned in a harmonic manner produce the perfect major chord with various doubling of their intervals because of the number of pipes of which they are composed, and which produce only the feeling of a single sound to the ear. But this demonstration is deceptive, because the harmonics of the *fourniture* are absorbed into the feeling of a single tone only by adding some large low-pitched stops such as the bourdon or the eight-foot open flute; so that here, as in everything, it is not the harmonics that generate the low sound, but the latter that contains the harmonics.

[27]Rubeli disagrees with this statement that Fétis attributes to Tartini. Rubeli says, "Such an assertion, however, appears nowhere in the entire first chapter, although it would fit later theoretical statements. Here Fétis has obviously carelessly read a passage that contains, indeed, a significant misobservation of the system. For Tartini maintains (p. 12 of the first chapter), that if a string were touched at the point 2/5 (thus not at the point 1/2), then no higher tone would arise, as is the case with contact on the point 1/5, but only an 'ambiguous hum' ('um certo tal qual ronzamento'). In reality there appears on all points that delineate a divisible distance through 1/5 of the total string length, . . . the fifth overtone that corresponds to the basic sound of the string." (Ibid., 29.)

Tartini likens to the phenomenon of the plain organ stop the one that had been pointed out previously by Serre from Geneva,[28] and by Romieu from Montpellier.[29] "We have discovered," he said, "a new harmonic phenomenon that admirably proves the same thing, and indeed a great deal more."[30] This phenomenon, assigned the name "third tone," is the product of an experience in which two treble sounds forming a harmonic interval between them produce, when they resonant loudly and with perfect justness, a third low-pitched sound that is the fundamental of these harmonics, although it is its product in experience.[31] This phenomenon is the irrefragable proof for Tartini that harmony reduces itself to unity, represented by the fundamental sound of every chord, and, in his enthusiasm for this discovery, he exclaims, "Therefore unity, considered in all its ratios, is inseparable from the harmonic system. The harmonic system itself enters into unity as into its principle."[32]

From the preceding it is evident that Tartini's point of departure for the formation of a harmonic system is exactly the antitheses of Rameau's.[33] From the following we will see that this point of

[28]Jean-Adam Serre (1704-?) deals with difference tones in intervals only in *Essais sur les principes de l'harmonie, où l'on traite de la Théorie de l'Harmonie en général,* . . . (Paris: Prault fils, 1753). Krehbiel ("Harmonic Principles of J.-P. Rameau") discusses Serre's findings on pages 116-29.

[29]Jean-Baptiste Romieu (1732-66) explained difference tones in an article entitled "Nouvelle découverte des sons harmoniques graves, dont la résonnance est très sensible dans les accords des instruments à vent" published in the *Mémoires de la Société des Sciences de Montpellier,* 1752. (Fétis, *BUM* 7:304-05.)

[30]"Si è poi scoperto un nuovo fenomeno armonico, che prova mirabilmente lo stesso, e moito di più." (*Trattato de musica secondo la vera scienza dell' armonica,* 13.)

[31]As a general rule, Tartini was mistaken in the placement of the difference tones: they are an octave too high for first-order difference tones. Serre was one of the first critics to point out this error in his *Observations sur les principes de l'harmonie, occasionnées Par quelques écrits modernes sur le sujet,* . . . , (Geneva: H. A. Gosse and J. Gosse, 1763), pt. 2, pp. 83-84, 119.

[32]"Dunque dal sistemo armonica è inseparabile la unità considerata in qualunque rispetto, anzi il sistema armonico si resolve nella unità, come in suo principio." (Tartini, *Trattato,* 13.)

[33]Shirlaw denies this, asserting that through mathematical and scientific principles Tartini attempts to demonstrate the correctness of Rameau's theories. (Matthew Shirlaw, *Theory of Harmony* 293.)

departure leads him to some less complete and much less satisfying results that those of the illustrious French musician's theory.

The aim of the second chapter of Tartini's book is to exploit the properties of the circle, and particularly of the circle taken as inscribed in a square, for the theory of harmony. The idea of the application of these properties to music was not new, because Ptolemy devoted himself to examining this question in the second and ninth chapters of the third book of his *Harmonics*;[34] the same subject has been discussed in great depth by Othon Gibel in his *Introductio musicae theoriticae didacticae* (pp. 125ff). The obscurity in this chapter is more profound than in all the rest of Tartini's work, and one can see in the rash propositions, uniquely founded on arbitrary ratios that the author himself did not understand, that he had so little confidence in the results that his pursuits had produced that he ended by declaring that these speculations were not necessary to comprehend his system.[35] Here are his words: "Però mi son dilatato, e ho divagato di molto in questo secondo Capitolo per cose non affatto necessarie al sistema Musicale" (p. 47). Thus it would be fruitless to follow him in his "divagations" on this subject. However, perhaps it is not fruitless to give an example, taken from this same chapter, of the lack of soundness of this celebrated artist's argument; we will find it in the following paragraph.

Tartini recognized that he has demonstrated algebraically and by the most detailed arithmetical method that the three terms 1, 2, x were supposed to form a harmonic ratio (x designates an infinite

---

[34]Pages 229, 252ff of the Wallis edition (Oxford, 1682), or Vol. 3, pages 129 and 141 of the mathematical works of the latter.

[35]Rubeli takes exception to this paragraph: ". . . Fétis' derogatory criticism about the second chapter of the *Trattato* is unjustified. Although Tartini often makes it difficult for the reader, one must still grant him that he arranges the content clearly. The added mathematical examples at the end of the second chapter—and this intention is expressed clearly in the text many times—were to persuade the mathematicians of the correctness of his new harmonic way of thinking. Undoubtedly this manner of thinking is absurd in itself, but it is a gross misunderstanding if one believes he himself doubted his proofs; it is wholly misleading to believe he himself did not quite trust these proofs, and that for this reason, he explained, that they [the proofs] were not absolutely necessary for the comprehension of this system." (Tartini, *Traktat*, 29).

size in relation to the first two terms). He adds that the circle proves it, because, he says, the radius represents the first term, 1; the diameter the second term, 2; and the circumference expresses the third, x. In the enthusiasm that this discovery inspires, he exclaims, "Oh! what will the results of such a conspectus be, if it is true!"[36] Farther on he is obliged to recognize that it would be absurd to pretend that the circumference of the circle is, in this circumstance, a size equal to x, i.e., a definite size.[37] To summarize the long garrulousness of this chapter, which d'Alembert himself found to be impenetrably obscure and which fills twenty-eight pages in quarto size, has no aim other than to establish the similarity and relationship of harmonic unity with the unity of a circle in which all arcs and their angles converge for its formation, as harmonics tend to resolve into the fundamental tone. He does not doubt that there would be a demonstration of his proposition, if the problem of the quadrature of the circle had been resolved. Supposing, for an instance, the reality of these relations, we cannot understand why Tartini had thought to rush into this research without possessing the most rudimentary elements of analysis.[38]

The result of Tartini's harmonic unity is precisely contrary to that of the phenomenon of the sonorous body adopted by Rameau as the basis of his system, because the former departs from the harmonics to return to the low tone, while the latter follows an inverted course.[39] Whence it follows that Tartini's system lacks *criterion* for the generation of chords; it cannot match the beautiful

[36]"Oh quali, e quante consequenze da tal vista, s' è vera"! (27).

[37]Moreover, Serre had shown that this is not at all the circumference of the circle, but the hyperbola, viewed between its asymptotes, which included precisely the conditions Tartini needed.

[38]Some of Tartini's arithmetic premises are discussed and analyzed by Alejandro E. Planchart, "A Study of the Theories of Giuseppe Tartini," *JMT* 4 (April, 1960): 32-61, and D. P. Walker, "The Musical Theories of Giuseppe Tartini" in *Modern Musical Scholarship* (London: Oriel Press Ltd., 1980), 93-111.

[39]While Rameau emphasized the multiplicity of sound with the sonorous body, Tartini ". . . considers multiplicity a function of unity and regards the division of unity into multiplicity and the resolution of multiplicity into unity as parts of a complete cycle." (Planchart, 36). Thus Tartini and Rameau are not, as Fétis would lead one to believe, in direct opposition to one another.

theory of inversion discovered by Rameau. This consideration alone
demonstrates the superiority of the French musician's work, with
respect to the practical didactic, and the barrenness of the principle
of unity so highly spoken of by the Paduan violinist. This radical
flaw was noticed neither by J. J. Rousseau in the erroneous analysis
that he did of Tartini's theory in the article "Système" in his
Dictionnaire de musique, nor by d'Alembert in his Encyclopédie article
"Fondamental," nor even by Suremain-Myssery, who wrote a special
report on this subject, and who grasped the question much better
than d'Alembert and Rousseau.[40] Tartini so completely lacks a point
of junction between his principle of unity and the facts of the practice
of the art that in the third chapter of his book, having come to the
musical deductions of his speculations, he finds nothing but some
arbitrary rules of which some are insignificant, and of which the
others are contrary to the known rules of the art of writing.[41] He
cannot form a complete table of the chords recognized in harmony,
and in those that he cites, he falls into some gross errors with respect
to constituent intervals.

   Tartini has nine practical rules. With the first he recommends
that the chord tones be arranged so as to form, as much as possible,
a harmonic proportion, i.e., that they be arranged in this order: 1,
1/2, 1/3, 1/4, 1/5, etc. This can be good for the perfect chord in which
the octave actually can be placed close to the bass, then the fifth, and
finally the third in the top part. But this is not always practical in the
other chords, and, besides, it would be in obvious opposition with
the considerations of succession, considerations upon which the
whole art of writing rests.[42]

---

[40]Antoine Suremain de Missery, *Théorie acoustico-musicale, ou De la doctrine des sons
rapportée aux principes de leur combinaison* (Paris: Didot, 1793).

[41]Frederic Johnson ("Tartini's *Trattato di musica seconda la vera scienza dell' harmonica*: An Annotated Translation with Commentary" [Ph.D. diss., Indiana University,
1985]) alleges that Tartini had no interest in providing rules for writing. "Tartini's
purpose was to delve into the physical laws of acoustics . . . . His writing is of less
value to practicing musicians, because it is directed toward the student of philosophy" (vi).

[42]Fétis has misconstrued the intent of this rule which is to preserve the *spacing* of
the harmonic proportion and not the ordering.

Tartini's second rule is that a perfect chord ought not to double the principle tone at the double octave by following this progression: 1, 1/2, 1/3, 1/4, 1/5, etc., namely, by composing the chord *c, c, g, c, e,* etc.

The reason for this bizarre rule, absolutely contrary to practice and which would make all harmonic music impossible, is explained only with much effort and in an almost unintelligible manner by Tartini. But a patient study of his obscure sentences discloses that the rule intends to avoid the fourth that is found between the two terms 1/3, 1/4, i.e., between *g, c,* and constitutes the proportion 4:3 which, according to Tartini, is a basic element of dissonance.[43] This false theory classifies the fourth among the dissonances, as if the intervals could not be generated by the inversion of intervals of the same kind, and as if the fourth was not, in this respect, the product of the fifth, which is a consonance. I say this theory has no consideration other than the dissonant aspect when the fourth occurs, when through the result of prolongation the fourth strikes the fifth at the second. But in this case it is not as a fourth that the note that forms the interval is dissonant, but as a second. This is a fundamental principle that has been recognized by none of the authors of harmonic systems.

Having not perceived, or rather not being able to admit the theory of inversion[44] since his principle of unity makes him follow a contrary route, and yet understanding the necessity of harmonies

---

[43]This is a complete distortion of the rule set forth by Tartini, which he expresses thusly: "Tones that are in proportion as 1:1/2:1/4 ought not to be employed as harmony, although they are contained in the harmonic sextuple 1, 1/2, 1/3, 1/4, 1/5, 1/6 . . . . The tones 1, 1/2, 1/4 contain merely the possibility of a harmonic chord, but they still form no definable harmony, as for example the chord 1, 1/3, 1/4 [C2-G3-C4], or 1/2, 1/5, 1/6 [C3-E4-G4], or 1/3, 1/4, 1/5 [G3-C4-E4], and therefore they also produce no satisfactory chord. Moreover, 1, 1/2, 1/4 is a geometric progression, and we will see later that the geometric progressions are at the base of the dissonant chords." (Tartini, *Traktat,* 167.) While the geometric progression 1, 1/2, 1/4 is not dissonant, the geometric progression 1:3:9 [*c-g-d*] is dissonant. (A geometric progression is a series of numbers that progress by multiplying each preceding term by a fixed number called the "common ratio," e.g., the common ratio of 2, 8, 32, 128 is 4.)

[44]To the contrary; Tartini recognized the theory of inversion, but he employed the word "position" instead. (Planchart, "Theories of Giuseppe Tartini," 51.)

derived from fundamental chords, Tartini could not present a regular system of the generation of chords. But he compensated for it with his third rule, which permits all the tones that are part of the chord to be carried in an arbitrary way, either the low-pitched or the high-pitched.[45] But fruitlessly Tartini took a great deal of trouble to shroud this rule with the appearance of abstruseness, which he knows how to put everywhere. It is no less true that after having taken an opposite direction to that of inversion for the construction of his system of unity, he was obliged to enter into the veritable order of generation, without which there would be no possibility of harmonic variety.

But here is a much more striking contradiction.[46] After having forbidden the doubling of the octave (1/4) in his second rule because of the fourth that it forms with the third term of the progression (1/3), Tartini establishes in his fourth rule or musical law:

> The intervals of the octave, fifth, fourth, major third, and minor third, as essential parts of the system or of harmonic resonance, which forms the most perfect and complete consonance, are all consonances because they are all of the same nature or of integral unity, which is the sextuple harmonic progression.[47]

Thus here the fourth, which was dissonant, becomes the consonance it actually is. But notice that the major sixth, about which he does not speak, is also included in the harmonic progression 1, 1/2, 1/3, 1/4, 1/5, 1/6 since it is found between g, the third term of this progression, and e, the fifth term. As for the minor sixth, it could not be found in the six terms of his progression.

---

[45]The third rule has nothing to do with voice-leading. Tartini said, "But it would contradict the mathematical and physical facts of my system, if one were to add notes that cannot be brought to unity with a note of the sextuple through transposition by one or more octaves. . . . Rule three: The tones of the harmonic sextuple may be transposed by one or more octaves." (Tartini, *Traktat*, 168.)

[46]Fétis' unfounded interpretation of Tartini's second rule led to this seemingly "striking contradiction."

[47]"Che gl' intervalli di ottava, quinta, quarta, terza maggiore, e terza minore, come parti integranti del sestuplo armonico sistema, ch' è la perfettissima consonanza integrale, sono tutti consonanti, perchè sono della natura del suo tutto, o sia della sua unità integrale, ch' è la sestupla armonica." (Tartini, *Trattato di Musica*, 65.)

Notice further, that the sixth term would be useless (since it is only the doubling at the octave of the third term) if it did not aid in the production of the minor third. Now, since Tartini understood the necessity of this doubling, we do not understand why he stopped at this sixth term.[48]

I will say nothing about the two following rules because they are of no practical use, but I notice in the seventh rule a fact borrowed from Rameau for the formation of dissonant chords because this rule is stated thus: ". . . it is not possible to have a dissonant chord that is not based on a consonant chord."[49] As can be seen, it is the generation of dissonances by the addition of thirds, and leaving aside the determinations of tonality. One can see what I have said about the drawbacks of this system in the examination of Rameau's theory.

In the eighth rule Tartini wishes ". . . that the dissonance be prepared by a consonant note on the same degree, and that it be resolved by descending a tone or a semitone."[50] It is apparent from this rule that he did not understand that there are natural dissonances that result from tonal relationships. There are others that arise from the artful device of prolongation, and these are the only ones that must be prepared.[51] This rule and the preceding suffice to destroy a whole harmonic system from its foundation.

[48]Tartini undoubtedly stopped at the sixth term because these are the terms contained in the resonance of sonorous bodies. Like Rameau, Tartini is confining his theory to the consonance of the major triad as it is expressed in the *senario*.

[49]". . . che non si dà, nè può darsi posizione alcuna dissonate, se non fondata sopra la posizione consonate." (Tartini, *Trattato*, 77.)

[50]". . . che la dissonanza sia apparecchiata da nota consonante unisona, e sia risoluta in nota consonante, che a ragguaglio della dissonanza discenda per tuono, o semituono." (Ibid., 84.)

[51]It is noteworthy that Fétis, with his obsession for the preparation and resolution of dissonance, did not comment about Tartini's resolution of the augmented twelfth *down* rather than up. (Ibid., 82.)

Tartini did understand, contrary to Fétis' assertion, that there are natural dissonances. In the *Trattato* he wrote (129), "On the dominant, which forms the harmonic [perfect] cadence with the tonic, the 7th is used without being prepared. In final cadences it is the almost universal practice to add the 7th to the penultimate note. There is no rule here, rather it is against the rule, since such a 7th is not prepared, but nature is stronger than art." (Trans. D. P. Walker.)

I have nothing to say about the ninth rule, which is found in the following chapter and which is of little interest because it concerns only the dissonances or notes that never create harmony. To touch upon such a subject, I would be obliged to say that there are no discordances other than the tones that lack justness, and that every interval, whatever it may be, is harmonic. But this subject, which contains a complete order of new harmonic considerations, would not be proper here and would involve me too much. One will find it dealt with theoretically in my *Philosophie de la musique* and practically in my *Traité complet de l'harmonie*.

The analysis that I have just given of Tartini's system seems to me to show the radical defects of its conception, its inadequacy as a practical method, and its inferiority with respect to the fundamental bass system. It has often been said that its obscurity hurt its success. I believe that the opposite is more exact, that because one did not understand it, one assumed profundity. If it had been more intelligible, its faults would have been perceived more easily.

I am obliged to go back a few years before the publication of Tartini's system for another theory that, not having been noticed when it appeared, was reproduced in various forms later. Levens, *maître de musique* of the Bordeaux cathedral, was the first who made it known in his book entitled *Abrégé des règles de l'Harmonie pour apprendre la Composition, avec un Nouveau Projet sur un Système de Musique sans Tempérament, ni cordes mobiles* (Bordeaux: Chapiers, 1743, 92 p. in quarto). In the first part of this work Levens proves that he was a good musician, and that he wrote more correctly than the majority of the authors of music treatises. This first part concerns the practice of harmony, such as it was known in France in his time, and according to Rameau's doctrine which the author does not always understand and sometimes contradicts. The second part of the book offers more interest with the plan for a new system of which Levens is the inventor, as he himself says, because first he substitutes the arithmetic progression for the harmonic progression that has been employed until his time for the generation of intervals.[52] He had noticed that the harmonic progression cannot generate a complete scale, the fourth note not being necessarily its product because, he said, none of the numbers of this progression could find another that would be in the proportion of 4:3, which is that of the fourth, with it. This consideration leads him to propose to turn to the arithmetic progression, jointly with the harmonic progression to the tenth term (the latter rising, the other falling). From this progression he divides two strings, of which the first gives him a series of ascending tones the intervals of which are those of the natural tones of the horn and trumpet.

Example of the ascending progression

C2	C3	G3	C4	E4	G4	B-flat4	C5	D5	E5
1	1/2	1/3	1/4	1/5	1/6	1/7	1/8	1/9	1/10

Proceeding in the reverse manner for the second string by means of the arithmetic progression, he finds a descending series that gives him the fourth degree and the lowered sixth degree.

Example of a descending progression

C5	C4	F4	C3	A-flat3	F3	D3	C3	B-flat2	A-flat2
1	2	3	4	5	6	7	8	9	10

In his system, Levens found three different whole tones, namely the "major tone" in the proportion of 7:8; the "perfect tone" in that of 8:9; finally the "minor tone," as 9:10. From the experiment that he did, he said, a very acceptable variety of different tones followed. To complete the chromatic scale, he only had to divide the major tone into two unequal tones in the proportions of 14:15 and 15:16; the

---

[52]An arithmetic progression is a series of numbers in which each term, after the first, is obtained by adding a fixed number called the "common difference" to each preceding term. In the series 1, 3, 5, 7 the common difference is 2, and, in the series 1/2, 2, 7/2, 5 the common difference is 3/2. A harmonic progression, on the other hand, is a series of fractions in which the numerator is common and the denominators create an arithmetic progression. For example, 1, 1/2, 1/3, 1/4, 1/5; or 60, 30, 20, 15, 12 (60, 60/2, 60/3, 60/4, 60/5).

perfect tone into two other semitones of which the proportions are 16:17 and 17:18; finally the minor tone into two minor semitones, as 18:19 and 19:20.[53]

The main defect of this system, a defect that makes it crumble at its foundation, is, on the one hand, that it does not correspond to the constitution of any tonality, and, on the other hand, that the intervals' proportions do not correspond in the various octaves and, consequently, false sensations hurt the ear. For example, at the two extremes of the scale one finds the distance from c to d represented by a "major tone" on one end, and by a "perfect tone" on the other end.[54] But these difficulties do not stop Levens and do not preclude him from building, with the harmonic progression, a minor seventh chord (*c, e, g, b-flat*) on the tonic, although the note that forms the seventh may not be in the key; a dominant seventh chord (*g, b, d, f*), forgetting that this last note does not exist in the first ten terms of the harmonic progression and that what he substitutes is not the true fourth degree of the key; the six-five chord (*f, a, c, d*), although the first two notes of this chord are also missing in the first ten terms of the harmonic progression; finally, with the harmonic progression, the dominant seventh chord, although the third of this dominant is formed with a note lower than the true leading tone.[55]

---

[53]To derive each of the new tones, Levens had to find the harmonic mean of each proportion, which is the average obtained by doubling (the new tones will occur an octave higher) the ratio of each proportion. The harmonic mean becomes the "mean proportional" in the expression a:b = b:c. In 2(7:8), the harmonic mean is 15; therefore the expression a:b = b:c is 14:15 = 15:16. In 2(8:9), the harmonic mean is 17, and the expression is 16:17 = 17:18. Thus Levens ended up with six different semitones that range in size from 119 cents (14:15) to 89 cents (19:20). Levens also obtained seven more semitones by quadrupling each of the two minor thirds (5:6 and 6:7). (Levens, 72.) These semitones vary in size from 84 cents (20:21) to 63 cents (27:28). (See J. Murray Barbour, *Tuning and Temperament: A Historical Survey* [East Lansing: Michigan State College Press, 1953], 147). By dividing each tone equally to form the chromatic tones that he needs, Barbour asserts that Levens' meantone temperament created "deviations that are as great as for some varieties of just intonation" (145).

[54]In this case, the "two extremes of the scale" are the upper portion of the ascending harmonic progression and the lower portion of the descending arithmetic progression.

[55]Levens used the harmonic progression to derive his five fundamental chords in major, which, in addition to the seventh chords Fétis has cited, included the "large

Nevertheless, it is the essential feature of this system that was taken up much later by Ballière, geometrician and member of the Academy of Science of Rouen, and later still by Jamard, Canon of Sainte-Geneviève. If we compare Levens' book to the one that Ballière published under the title *Théorie de la musique* (Paris: Didot, 1764), we recognize at first glance that the latter was a much less competent musician but a better educated mathematician. After having established in nearly the same way as his predecessor the necessity to extend the harmonic progression beyond six to complete the scale, he arrives at Rameau's objection against the natural tones of the horn and the trumpet: "The tones 1/7, 1/11, and 1/13, being not at all harmonics of 1 and 3, are always false[56] on these instruments" (*Génération harmonique*, 62). Rameau, like all those who have expressed the same opinion, had not seen that this ratio of the number seven was precisely the one that could give the fourth note of the key its attractive character with the leading tone, as Euler saw so well (see the above mentioned). Ballière did not see so far. He was content to make this weak reply to Rameau's statement:

> If by the word 'false' one means that they deviate from the principles that musicians have established, fine. But if one means to say that they deviate from the natural laws, the word 'always' prevents one from accepting this proposition. How can I believe, in fact, that a tone that nature 'always' presents is not that which it ought to

---

sixth": *c, e, g, a*. In minor Levens generated five seventh chords using the arithmetic progression: (1) a minor seventh chord on tonic (*c, e flat, g, b flat* [48:40:32:27]), (2) a "large sixth" on tonic (*c, e-flat, g, a* [12:10:8:7]), (3) the six-five chord (*f, a-flat, c, d* [36:30:24:21]), (4) a dominant seventh chord (*g, b, d, f* [32:25:21:18]), and (5) a "dominant seventh chord altered by a major semitone" (*a-flat, b, d, f* [30:25:21:18]). As a result, Levens ended up with two different dominant-seventh chords: one with the ratios 12:15:18:21 in major, and one with the ratios 32:25:21:18 in minor. (Levens, 79-81.) It is this latter dominant seventh (that formed by the arithmetic progression) to which Fétis is referring; the interval from *b-c* in the arithmetic progression is 71 cents, and it is 112 cents (15:16) in the harmonic progression. (See J. Murray Barbour, *Tuning and Temperament*, 145-46.)

[56]Rameau undoubtedly means that these notes are out-of-tune to just intonation, because he omits the tone 1/9.

present? One is more justified to believe that the principles of musicians lack exactitude.[57]

In place of "principles of musicians," he ought to have said the "principles of geometricians," because musicians have felt precisely by instinct the necessity for the number seven, not for the seventh degree but for the fourth, and Euler saw quite well that for that reason he had to change the generating note from the tonic to the dominant.

Ballière, like Levens, understood the necessity for the descending progression that he calls *sous-doubles*; he does not create it in the same way. In order to arrive at the same result, while avoiding the monstrous faults of Levens' inverted progression, he uses a geometric construction that gives him the proportional lengths of strings for each note, and which, basically, is identical to the properties of the sections of the circle analyzed by Gibel in his *Introductio musicae theoreticae didacticae*. With the artificial introduction of intermediary tones to the products of the inverse progressions, Ballière forms the following two ascending and descending scales:

c,	d,	e,	f,	g,	a,	b-flat,	b-natural,	c
c,	b-natural,	b-flat,	a,	g,	f,	e,	d,	c

That settled, Ballière searches for the principle of chords in the combinations of numbers, and after having established that the sounds 1, 3, 5, which form the perfect chord, are the principle of harmony, he does not see any difficulty, "the impression of 1 being given," with this chord being followed by those of the same form: 7, 9, 11 (*b-flat, d, f*), or 9, 11, 13 (*d, f, a*). He does not concern himself for an instant with the dreadful succession of these tones, absolutely foreign to each other, because he is satisfied that there was a geometric progression in the formation of these chords.[58] And so that you do not believe that I am attributing a meaning to his words that they do not have, and that Ballière was considering these chords in isolation and not in succession, here it is as he expresses it:

---

[57]Charles-Louis-Denis Ballière de Laisement, *Théorie de la musique* (Paris: Didot, 1764), § 7, p. 5.

[58]The progression that creates these chords is arithmetic and not geometric.

The perfect chord 1, 3, 5, therefore, is the principle of harmony, and every piece of music commences with this expressed or implied chord. The impression of 1 being given, one can follow this chord with other notes of the progression such as

$$
\begin{array}{ccccccccc}
7 & 9 & 11 & 3 & 9 & 15 & 9 & 11 & 13 \\
\textit{b-flat,} & \textit{d,} & \textit{f;} & \textit{g,} & \textit{d,} & \textit{b;} & \textit{d,} & \textit{f,} & \textit{a;}
\end{array}
$$

and this is what we call chord succession.[59] [Fétis' italics.]

After this sample of Ballière's harmonic organization and the basis of his system, I do not believe I have to pursue an analysis when it is easy to perceive the results.[60] Jamard's *Recherches sur la Théorie de la musique* would not occupy me further, if I did not find in it a hint of logic that is lacking in Levens' and Ballière's books. Jamard, who possesses a veritable philosophical method, retreats from none of the results of the principle of the arithmetic progression, and carrying them to the end, he arrives at the destruction of the fundamental bass system that was the object of Levens' adoration. On this system, he says:

Mr. Levens pushed his division only as far as *e* 1/10; undoubtedly he was afraid of *f* 1/11. This is what I do not understand at all. One continually repeats that in music the ear is *the great judge*. Now, what could concern me more than to support this proposition, since I do not know a single experiment done on these tones that does not seem to follow my principles and that does not serve to confirm them? This tone *f* 1/11 certainly is not at all offensive on the hunting horn when it is not accompanied by other instruments that play *f* 3/32. Why, then, should it be more false than the *f* 3/32? If these two *f*s sound together, the ear is torn, I agree, but does it follow from that that one of the two is false? Unquestionably no. Because, since these two tones heard separately always have a good effect, it simply follows that they are not intended to be heard together at all. It is this, I believe, on

---

[59]Ibid., [par. 73], 36.

[60]Krehbiel ("Harmonic Theories of J.-P. Rameau") believed that Ballière's theory of harmony, which is demonstrably inconsistent in logic, is not only a diatribe against the musical practice of his era, but also against a theory of modulation, since the scale structure as Ballière stated it is nonmodulating: the principal note (C2) determined the scale structure of all tonalities (179-97).

which everyone agrees. Let us return to Mr. Levens, and agree that so skillful a musician, who was occupied with our ordinary practice, who regarded the rules of chords and the system of fundamental bass as the foundation of all harmony, or rather of all music, admit, I say, that he must have had a great deal of trouble rejecting f 3/32, the subdominant of the mode, from his system in order to admit f 3/33 in its place, since by rejecting f 3/32 he had to renounce absolutely the whole system of fundamental bass.[61]

We think that we are dreaming in reading such things, and we cannot refrain from deploring the blindness of this mania for a system of harmony which, since that of Rameau, possessed the mind of a multitude of scholars and men of letters, or musicians jealous of the glory of the author of fundamental bass. At first they intended only to explain what was the art such as it existed, but just as the philosophical school of this era was preoccupied with the sole thought of searching for the origin of ideas instead of first devoting themselves to making a strict analysis and rigorous classification of intellectual faculties, they stuck to searching for the origin of the scale in lieu of accepting the scale as a fact whose properties it was necessary to analyze in order eventually to deduce its systematic results. What was happening in this research, too delicate and too difficult for the capacity of those who had devoted themselves to it? It is that encountering some insurmountable difficulties from the point of view where they stood, they ended up refusing to explain, in order to establish something more or less different, which they did not fail to present as real music, if only by means of some experiment or calculation that could give an appearance of regularity to the system. The various viewpoints under which the construction of the scale according to the arithmetic progression occurred in Levens', Ballière's, and Jamard's books are some of the most striking examples of the facility that certain writers have to take appearance for reality, and of the degree of absurdity to which a false system, pushed to its ultimate consequences, could arrive. Un-

---

[61][Canon] Jamard, *Recherches sur la Théorie de la musique* [Paris: Jombert, 1769], 35-36[n].

doubtedly the tones 1/11 and 1/13 enter into the combinations of music today, but with neither the form nor the name that Jamard gives them. I do not need to explain the harmonic results of the latter's system; we see at first glance where they could lead. Moreover, I am not done with the principle of this system. We will see it treated again by a musician as erudite as a harmonist as a mathematician, and who strayed, nevertheless, onto a false path.

In the midst of the music and harmonic systems that followed each other and clashed since the publication of Rameau's, a methodical harmony book freed from every consideration of number and physical phenomena appeared. This book is the *Traité des accords et de leur succession, selon le système de la basse fondamentale* by Abbé Roussier.[62] It is divided into three parts. I have nothing at all to say about the first two parts, because they contain only a classification and an analysis of chords following Rameau's principles.[63] I will, at least, remark that although he had little skill in the art of writing and his early education as a musician had been neglected, Roussier shows much more sense of method than the system's inventor, and he was the first in France to turn to the very important consideration of harmonic succession.[64] But we are astonished by the third part, if we consider the time of its publication, because Abbé Roussier proposes introducing into music a certain number of chords unknown then. Here is what he says:

> Those who absolutely wish to confine themselves to their circle of knowledge will probably dislike *my daring to propose some chords that have never been heard of*; others may reject them as too harsh, too dissonant. As for the first, . . . by [expressly] declaring here that this

[62][Pierre-Joseph Roussier]. Paris: [Duchesne], 1764.

[63]For a succinct and concise discussion of the first two parts of this treatise, see Mitchell, ("A History of Theories"), pp. 87-90; for a comprehensive study, see Richard Dale Osborne, "The Theoretical Writings of Abbé Pierre-Joseph Roussier" (Ph.D. diss., The Ohio State University, 1966).

[64]Günter Birkner claims that it was Rameau's *Traité de l'harmonie* that provided Roussier with an introduction to the theoretical facts of music. Moreover, the *Traité de l'harmonie*, which Roussier discovered at age twenty-five, was the agent that stimulated Roussier's future endeavors into the new-found science. ("Roussier, Pierre-Joseph" *MGG* 11, cols. 1018-19.)

third part is not intended for them, they have nothing more to say to me. As for the others, I ask them to be willing to examine the matter attentively before making a decision.[65] [Fétis' italics.]

Truly there is cause to marvel at seeing that, guided by analogy and the musical feeling that was in him, Roussier foresaw the possibility of making good use of certain harmonies that only Mozart's genius and a small number of his contemporaries and successors had known how to bring into play. It is thus that the "augmented sixth," or as was said then, *superflue*, is controlled by the law of inversion for the chord of the diminished third and just fifth, and that of the minor sixth and minor third with a major fourth (tritone). Thus it is, moreover, that by moving from the chord of the "diminished third and just fifth" to that of the dominant seventh, he conceived the possibility of altering the third as in the perfect chord. If he had been content to alter some of the chords' natural intervals, either original or modified by prolongation or substitution, he would have rendered the greatest service to the advancement of the art and science, and we would be forming the highest opinion of his instinct, his taste, and his experience. But it is not at all so, because the barbarity of his ear caused him to imagine some intolerable harmonies in which the feeling of any tonality is destroyed: for example, a chord that he calls the "diminished eleventh" (*g-sharp, d-sharp, f, a, c*), a chord of the "augmented fifth with a minor fourth and seventh" (*g, d-sharp, f, a, c*), a chord of the "augmented seventh with minor sixth and ninth" (*e, d-sharp, f, a, c*), etc.[66] Moreover, scarcely able to discern true dissonances, he makes very poor applications of a good rule that he had found by reasoning, and which he expresses thus: "All major dissonance must rise one degree; all minor dissonance must descend one degree" (p. 42). The first part of this rule would be incontestable if Roussier had applied it to the dissonances formed by the leading tone or ascending alterations. But Rameau's

[65][Ibid.], 158n. 59.

[66]Each of these "new" chords was created by "supposing" a root below the German o3 chord (a German augmented sixth with the sixth inverted), which Roussier contended (158) was less harsh than the French augmented sixth chord (*f, a, b, d-sharp*), because the latter had four dissonances (*a-b, f-d-sharp, f-b, a-d-sharp*), while the former (*d-sharp, f, a, c*) had only three dissonances (*d-sharp-f, d-sharp-a, d-sharp-c*).

"double employment" led him so far astray that he finds no application for his rule except for the six-five chord on the fourth degree (*f*, *a*, *c*, *d*) because he takes the sixth as a dissonance, while analysis reveals that when two notes clash at the second, it is the lower note that is the dissonance.[67]

In spite of the extensive faults that I have pointed out, the *Traité des accords* and the complement of this work that Roussier published under the title *Harmonie pratique, ou exemples pour le traité des accords* (Paris: [Bailleux], 1775) could have rendered eminent service to harmonic theory in France by calling attention to the consideration of the succession of chords, which Rameau's system had forgotten, if Roussier himself had not lost sight of his practical works by a return to a theory of numbers applied to music, of which he gave the first indication in the notes of his *Observations sur différens points d'harmonie*,[68] then in his *Lettre à l'auteur de Journal des Beaux-arts et des Sciences, touchant la division du Zodiaque et l'institution de la semaine Planétaire, relativement à une progression géométrique, d'où dépendent les proportions musicales*[69] and which is found developed in his *Mémoire sur la musique des anciens*[70] and

---

[67]According to Roussier, the consonant intervals are those formed by disjunct degrees of the scale. There are, therefore, four consonant intervals: the third, the fourth, the fifth, and the sixth. The dissonant intervals, formed by conjunct degrees of the scale, are the second and the seventh, with the seventh being conjunct to the octave (*Traité des accords*, 6). While the sixth as such is consonant, within the context of the supertonic six-five, the sixth is dissonant because it forms a conjunct degree with the fifth. If one accepts the concept of interval roots and the value-order of interval roots set down by Hindemith in Series 2 as a valid basis for root determination, Roussier's analysis is substantiated because the best interval in the chord is the perfect fifth. Thus, *d* is "dissonant." As for his rule about the resolution of dissonance, Roussier stated explicitly on page 42, that the major dissonance is the sixth of the subdominant, and the minor dissonance is the seventh of either the dominant or the leading-tone seventh. All of the other dissonances are "accidental."

[68](Paris: [d'Houry], 1765), 217-25. [On pages 11-23 in *Observations*, Roussier explains the twelve differences between the added sixth chord (*f*, *a*, *c*, *d*) and the large sixth chord (*f*, *a*, *c*, *d*).]

[69]Paris, 1771. [This letter was published in the *Journal des Beaux-Arts & des Sciences* in November and December 1770.]

[70]*Mémoire sur la musique des anciens, où l'on expose le principe des proportions authentiques, dites de Pythagore, et de divers systêmes de musique chez les grecs, les chinois et les égyptiens, avec un parallèle entre le systême des égyptiens et celui des modernes* (Paris: [LaCombe], 1770).

in his *Notes [et observations] sur le mémoire de P. Amiot concernant la musique des chinois.*[71] A passage from Timaeus of Locris, reported by Plato, and the dreams of Censorin had turned Roussier's head. Thence he drew the idea of a geometric progression of twelve terms, which he calls a "triple progression" because the proportion of the just fifth 3:1, tripled from fifth to fifth, gives him the following descending progression: 1:3:9:27:81:243:729, etc.,[72] which, extended to the twelfth fifth or the thirteenth term, gives the figures 531:441, an expression, according to him, of the comma between *c-flat* and *b*. His point of departure is this last note, because in the order of the planets corresponding to the hours of day and to the days of the week, Saturn is first. Now, what we have seen in all of the other systems has happened to Roussier's system—in wishing to explain music, he undid it. Finding this game of numbers in opposition with the result of so called harmonic proportions, he denied the reality of the latter and threw in many suppositions that the most cursory examination does not support. For example, an antique bronze cited by Montfaucon in *Antiquité expliquée*, where one can see the series of seven main divinities, beginning with Saturn and ending at Venus, gives him the scale that he considers fundamental: *b, c, d, e, f, g, a*. It is from that that he starts to make his progression of twelve fifths: *b, e, a, d, g, c*, etc. Furthermore, by long chains of reasoning, he arrives at the opinion that the tones of the musical scale of the Greeks were interpreted as descending, an opinion now held by Pepusch[73] and reproduced these days by Mr. de Drie-

---

[71]Paris: [Nyon l'aine], 1780.

72
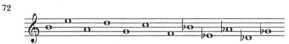

[73]John Christopher Pepusch, "Of the various Genera and Species of Music among the Ancients, with some Observations concerning their Scale," in *Philosophical Transactions of the Royal Society of London* 44 (Oct.-Dec. 1746): 266-74. Pepusch is arguing to consider a descending scale as well as an ascending scale, and that "the first Sound in each was the *Proslambanomenos* (269).

[74]Friedrich von Drieberg, *Die praktische Musik der Griechen* (Berlin: Trautwein, 1821).

[75]Fétis chastised von Drieberg and Pepusch on two counts: (1) the *hypate* is the *first* and *lowest* note of the scale; (2) Greek scales (to which he ascribed the names of the church modes) consist of an *ascending* series of sounds. (Fétis, "Résumé philosophique de l'histoire de la musique" in *BUM* 1 [Paris: Fournier, 1835], cv-cvi n.)

berg,[74] as I have said in my *Résumé philosophique de l'histoire de la musique*.[75] Finally, he insists in many places on the necessity of redoing all modern music; as if the arts could be created by such processes, and as if the forms of the scales were not determined by laws set much higher than in the arbitrary properties of numbers; as if in this very system the numbers were not reduced to a hypothetical value! After all, the reality of the facts represented by numbers are be believed when these numbers are the expression of the dimensions of sonorous bodies or of the frequency of vibrations from which the measure of the intervals of sounds result. But where can one find the laws of this triple progression which one wishes to make the criterion of art and science, if it is not in the alleged analogies with a planetary system and an ancient calendar? Have we to establish a real science or a useless hermetic theory? Are we musicians, or ought we to form a kind of gnostic sect, a new breed of illuminati? What would make one believe that Abbé Roussier leaned towards this latter conversion of the seekers of harmonic theories is that in many places in his *Mémoire sur la musique des anciens* and his *Lettres sur les rapports du zodiaque et du la semaine planétaire avec la gamme* he speaks highly of the wisdom of the Egyptian priests who revealed the secrets of their musical doctrine only to those whom they initiate into the mysteries of their theo-philosophy. But we have dwelt long enough on the aberrations of intellectual pursuit inserted into the creation of a harmonic system. Let us return to theories more positive and more consistent with the object of art.

But first, before turning our attention to the works undertaken outside of France to accelerate the progress of harmony with respect to both art and science, let us say a word about the last two systems that closed the sphere of speculation on this subject at the end of the eighteenth century. One, published by Mercadier de Belestat[76] under the title *Nouveau système de musique théorique et pratique*, the other by the Chevalier de Lirou.

Engrossed with the idea of a reconciliation between the exigencies of mathematical theory and musical feeling, Mercadier begins by establishing the necessity of the absolute justness of octaves. This is why, taking two strings at the unison, he leaves the first in its

---

[76]Jean-Baptiste Mercadier was commonly surnamed "de Belestat" because he was born in the borough of Belestat. (Fétis, *BUM* 6:90.)

entirety so as to make it a constant point of comparison, and cuts the second string into two equal parts, from which the octave in the proportion 1/2 results. He also stresses a great deal the nearly absolute analogy of this octave with the principal tone, and thus borrows from Rameau the idea of the identity of octaves. For the other intervals, he consults the ear and finds his own sense of accord with experience and theory in the justness of the fifth resulting from the proportion 2/3. The inversion of this proportion gives him the interval of the just fourth in 3/4. For the other intervals, he said, mathematical exactitude is no longer rigorously necessary for the ear. Thus the major third employed in music will not always be represented exactly by the proportion 4/5, nor that of the minor third by 5/6. But this matters little, because the ratios of the tones' accordance are frequently determined in practice by considerations independent of that of absolute justness. The farther away we get from the simplicity of the primary ratios, the less rigorous accuracy is necessary, according to Mercadier's doctrine.

This result attained, the author of this theory forms the perfect chord of the tones produced by the ratios 1/2, 4/5, and 2/3, and seeks the other consonant chords that can be formed in the same way with tones produced by less simple proportions.[77] Next taking the tone 2/3 from the division of the first string as the generator, he proceeds in the same manner and, seeking the fifth in 2/3 of the total length of the string tuned to the unison of the sound produced by this proportion and the third in 4/5 of this same string, he obtains the two new tones necessary for the formation of the scale. Now let us assume that the sound 1 is *c*; the sound 1/2 will be its octave, the sound 2/3 will be *g*, and the sound 4/5 will be *e*. Next taking the tone

[77]Having demonstrated that there are but two perfect consonant chords (major and minor), Mercadier used the proportions for the major, exclaiming, "*Experience teaches us actually that it likes the perfect chord a great deal more in this disposition 1 5/4 3/2, than in the other 1 6/5 3/2.*" (Jean-Baptiste Mercadier, *Nouveau Système de musique théorique et pratique* [Paris: Valade, 1776], 20-21.) Hindemith opposed this irrational procedure of measuring intervals, claiming, "Construction by means of a series of fifths and thirds does not represent a primeval method of erecting a scale. One is simply taking the scale already present in practical music and trying to explain the intervals of the series . . . ." (Paul Hindemith, *The Craft of Musical Composition*, trans. Arthur Mendel, Bk. 1 [4th ed.; New York: Associated Music Publishers, 1945], 33.)

g as the new generator on a new string, 2/3 of this string will be *d*, and the tone 4/5 will be *b*. To tell the truth, these tones will not have a mathematical precision, but they will satisfy the ear, and, according to Mercadier's theory, it is the exact result at which he wished to arrive. Therefore the tones obtained thus far are *c*, *d*, *e*, *g*, *b*, *c*. Let us go on, and taking for the third generator the tone 2/3 of the second generator, i.e., *d*, tuning a string at the unison of this new tone, and then taking the tone 2/3 of it, i.e., *a* (the fifth of this *d*), nothing more will remain except to find the last tone to have a complete scale. But here a difficulty arises, because the tone 4/3 of the third generator is not the *f* that we need, but an *f-sharp* that does not appear in this scale. We remove this difficulty by taking, with the compass on the first generating string, one fourth equal to that which is found between the tone 2/3 and that of 1/2. Next, by bringing all the tones into their natural, successive order by means of the identify of octaves, we will have all of the scale: *c*, *d*, *e*, *f*, *g*, *a*, *b* such as the ear indicates, with a natural temperament that will avoid the comma from the succession of a dozen fifths.[78] To be brief in this exposé, I have omitted all the calculations with which Mercadier backed up his system.

Thus after having formed his scale, an object of complete satisfaction for him, Mercadier had no difficulty borrowing from Rameau his generation of chords by the addition of thirds, his inversion of these chords, and even his fundamental bass, after having made a harsh enough critique of the learned musician's system in his preliminary discourse.[79] There is more; because on

[78]Barbour declares that Mercadier was propounding an irregular temperament in which some of the fifths are pure (the 3:2 fifth of just tuning or 702 cents), while the others are tempered by either 1/6 comma (698 cents) or 1/12 comma; the latter comma is the temperament of the equal-tempered fifth (700 cents). In summing up the labyrinth of calculations into which Mercadier leads the reader, Barbour says, "He directed that the fifths from C to E should be flat by 1/6 syntonic comma [80:81], and those from E to G-sharp flat by 1/12 comma. Then G-sharp is taken as A-flat, the next three fifths are to be just, and the fifth F-C then turns out to be about 1/12 comma flat" (168). (J. Murray Barbour, *Tuning and Temperament*, 167-69.)

[79]Mercadier also adopts Rameau's theory of chords by supposition (Pt. 6, chap. 3, pp. 204-10) and his *double emploi* (chap. 9, p. 235).

examining it closely, his melodic generation is drawn, like that of Rameau, from the fundamental movement of fifths. Mercadier had not noticed that he put into opposition the two principles that he wished to make the foundation of his system. Obliged to turn to the feeling of the ear in order to oppose the laws of arithmetic that indeed cannot engender a scale, he ought to have noticed that sound structured from numbers became useless, I would say almost ridiculous. The good tuners of keyboard instruments do not make so much fuss; they also satisfy the ear, but they do not pretend to make a system. What is more, on the relation of harmony considered in its theory as in its practice, Mercadier lagged behind Roussier, although he may be a few years later. His system did not have any success.

As well as Mercadier de Belestat, the Chevalier de Lirou, author of *Explication du système de l'harmonie pour abréger l' étude de la composition, et accorder la pratique avec la théorie,*[80] attempts to extract the scale from the harmonic construction of several perfect chords, but he proceeded differently, as we shall see presently. Jamard had proved that the logical consequences of Levens' and Ballière's systems would lead to the abandonment of fundamental bass, but this consideration is all theoretic in his book. The Chevalier de Lirou was the first French writer who, in a harmony book, broke away completely from this system of fundamental bass, which had become the guide for all harmonic theorists among us, and which resisted the attacks of its adversaries for a long time. A rather precise observation of the phenomena of the chords' successions led de Lirou to search for the laws of these successions in the affinities of tonality, which actually are the unquestionable basis for all music. Unfortunately, the writer's ideas lacked clarity with respect to this criterion of the science and art. In lieu of the quest for the principle of the tonal affinity of sounds by the order of succession, he took the harmonic resonance of sonorous bodies, supposedly uniform, as his point of departure. He says *c* produces *e, g; g* generates *b, d;* moreover, *c* can be considered the fifth of *f,*

---

[80]Jean-François-Espic de Lirou, *Explication du système de l'harmonie,* . . . (London, 1785).

whence f, a, c.[81] Thus c being placed as an intermediary, the following tones are found in the harmonic resonance of f, c, and g: e, f, g, a, b, c, d, e, which include all of the intervals of our major scale and correspond to the two tetrachords of Greek music: e, f, g, a and b, c, d, e. And because he had succeeded in finding the notes that constitute the scale with a mechanical and arbitrary process, he believed he had tonality and persuaded himself that he only needed to change the disposition of these notes by beginning on c instead of e. He did not know that all the difficulty is exactly in determining the first note of the scale. Having reached this result, de Lirou arranged the notes in a circle that represents the two ascending and descending progressions: c, e, g, b, d, f, a; and c, a, f, d, b, g, e, which he considered as the basis for all chordal constructions, harmonic successions, the modes, and modulation.[82] Like most of the French harmonic theorists of his time, de Lirou had only an imperfect command of the art of composition, so that several chord successions that he presents as admissible are not. But he is, I think, the first who specified sufficiently good rules, although incomplete, for the movement of keys and modes in modulation.

After de Lirou's book, which appeared in 1785 and was scarcely noticed, the eighteenth century closed in France with respect to science with the *Traité d'harmonie et de modulation*, which was published in 1797 by Langlé, the librarian of the Conservatory. A certain reputation as an expert harmonist had been achieved by this artist through the Naples school. In this book, numerical theories of

[81]Since de Lirou contends that ". . . the fifth is the basic interval, the interval *par excellence*" (18), and that music emanates from "a common center," tonic, in effect, represents duality: it is the generator of a triad as well as the fifth of a triad. This concept is not unique to de Lirou, but is reminiscent of Rameau's triple progression (1:3:9) where the tonic is represented by the number 3, the subdominant by the number 1, and the dominant by the number 9. (Rameau, *Nouvelles Réflexions sur le principe sonore* [Paris, 1790], 196n.) This concept recurs again in Moritz Hauptmann when he talks about "having" a dominant and "being" a dominant. (Shirlaw, *Theory of Harmony*, 352-62.)

[82]The arrangement of the pitch material in this disposition permits, according to de Lirou, each note of the scale to be either a tonic, a third, or a fifth of a perfect chord. (de Lirou, 26.)

intervals or acoustic phenomena no longer are seen as the basis for the system of harmonic generation. Langlé's declared pretension was to search for the true foundation of the science in artistic practice. From the first words of the foreword that he put at the beginning of his treatise, we are tempted to believe that he had grasped the true principles of this science, because he protests against previously published books in which chords are considered in an isolated way, regardless of the laws of succession that control them. But immediately following, we see him advance this singular proposition: *there is only one chord, that of the third, of which combinations produce all the others.*[83] And as proof of this principle, he offers this series of thirds as the example: *f, a, c, e, g, b, d, f*; then he extracts from this series the perfect chord on the fourth degree (*f, a, c*), the perfect minor chord (*a, c, e*), the tonic chord (*c, e, g*), the relative minor chord of the dominant (*e, g, b*), the dominant chord (*g, b, d*), the major seventh chords (*f, a, c, e* and *c, e, g, b*), the minor seventh chord with the minor third (*a, c, e, g*), and the dominant seventh chord (*g, b, d, f*). Now, with this classification, Langlé confuses everything by making, through his generation of thirds, chord classes of the seventh, for example, of every type, as if these relations existed by themselves in music and leaving aside every consideration of the formation of chords by alteration, prolongation, and substitution. For this reason, he finds himself in obvious contradiction with the beginning of his book. This fault which, although not analyzed by its readers, cast much obscurity on his system just the same, and was detrimental to the book's success. Moreover, shocking imperfections in the chord successions that he gives as examples caused his book to be rejected in the examination that was made of the various harmonic systems in 1800 by the assembly of the Conservatory, and from that time his system fell into oblivion.

After the examination that I have devoted to the efforts made in the eighteenth century in France for the formation of a rational

---

[83]Langlé has been misquoted by Fétis. Here is what Langlé said: "I recognize in harmony only one unique interval, generator of all chords; this interval is the third. By its multiplication, it produces a unique chord that contains all of them." (Honoré François-Marie Langlé, *Traité d'harmonie et de modulation* (Paris: Cochet, 1797), 1.)

system of the science of harmony, I need to consider the influence that the idea of a similar creation exercised in Germany and Italy.

As I have said, the idea of a theory of chord generation had not occurred to any German harmonist prior to the publication of Rameau's *Traité de l'harmonie* and the *Nouveau système*, and Mattheson, who published the second edition of his *Große Generalbass-Schule* in 1731, not only had not adopted the idea that brought so much honor to Rameau, in spite of the errors into which let himself be led, but in lieu of a reasoned discussion, he stooped to write these coarse insults in his *Critica musica*:

> In the works of the organist of Clermont, one generally finds 1,000 hundred-weight of toilsome research and feeble observations; 500 of vain pretensions at originality; about 3 pounds of new or borrowed knowledge; 2 ounces of common sense; and scarcely a grain of good taste.[84]

The *Treulicher Unterricht im General-Baß* of David Kellner, published in 1742 and frequently reprinted, had not pulled science from the empirical viewpoint where Heinichen and Mattheson had left it.[85] Therefore the middle of the eighteenth century had arrived before the German harmonic theorists became interested in a theory of the art that they taught by practice. But from this time on, we will see that all Germany was agitated for the creation of a similar theory.

Sorge, organist at Lobenstein, was the first who, without adopting anything from Rameau's theory, seemed to be won over to the idea of the necessity for a scientific foundation for the proceed-

---

[84]Since Fétis gives neither the volume number nor the page on which he found this quotation in the alleged work, he probably was relying on his memory and meant to refer to the *Kleine General-Bass-Schule* where Mattheson castigates Rameau with these very words in a footnote on pages 220-21; the *Kleine General-Bass-Schule* appeared later (1735) than either the *Critica musica* (1722-25) or the *Große General-bass-Schule* (1731).

[85]Since no edition of Kellner's treatise appeared in 1742, this publication date is a misprint for either the first edition (Hamburg: Kiszner, 1732), or the third edition (Hamburg: Christian Herold, 1743). The eighth and last edition appeared in 1796 (*MGG*, s.v. "Kellner, David"). Arnold (*Art of Accompaniment*, 1:269-70) and Joel Lester (*Compositional Theory in the Eighteenth Century* [Cambridge, Mass. and London: Harvard University Press, 1992], 125-26) have a very brief discussion of this treatise.

ings of art.[86] He states his principles in a book that is titled *Vorgemach der musicalischen Composition, oder: Ausführliche, ordentliche und vorheutige Praxin hinlängliche Anweisung zum General-Baß* . . . (Lobenstein: The Author, 1745[-47]).[87]

Although Sorge does not make himself clear on this subject, there is reason to believe that the reading of Euler's *Tentamen novae theoriae* made an impression on him, and that it is from this book that he drew the idea of a system founded on the numerical ratios of sounds. But instead of adhering to the consideration of the degrees of suavity of chords because of the simplicity of numerical ratios, he adopted the opinions of musicians regarding the consonant and dissonant qualities of chords. Like them, he divided the chords into consonant and dissonant harmony, and he considered as consonant any chord that was composed of only three tones from the intervals of the third, fourth, fifth, or sixth of varying nature. But because several of these chords were not the product of pure harmonic progression, he resorted to the arithmetic progression in which he found the appropriate expressions for these same chords. In the ratio 4:5:6 he found the perfect major chord, and he remarks (chap. 6, p. 14[-15]) that some experiences of various kinds prove that this chord exists in the resonance of several sonorous bodies. The natural tones of the trumpet give him the perfect minor chord that he calls *trias minus perfecta* (chap. 7, p.16) and that he represents with the numbers 10:12:15 from the arithmetic progression. The same instrument gives him the chord *e, g, b-flat*, which he calls *trias deficiens* and which is commonly called the "perfect diminished chord" in the modern school. A propos of this *b-flat*, he introduces the number seven into the calculation without any difficulty, and represents the chord following the proportions 5:6:7 (chap. 8, p. 18). For the perfect chord

[86]James M. Martin, II ("The *Compendium Harmonicum* [1760] of Georg Andreas Sorge [1703-1778]: A Translation and Critical Commentary" [Ph.D. diss., Catholic University of America, 1981]) has noted that in his *Vorgemach der musikalischen Sorge* "published his discovery of the phenomenon of combination tones (summation tones and difference tones) and appeared to recognize that this phenomenon ensued from the overtone series. His appears to have been the first account in print, antedating Tartini's by nine years" (18).

[87]*Antichambre de la composition musicale, ou instruction détaillée, régulière et suffisante pour la pratique actuelle de la basse continue.*

with the augmented fifth, he is obliged to raise the terms of the arithmetic proportion to 48:60:75 (chap. 9, p. 20). Finally, the perfect chord with the diminished third, as *a-sharp, c, e,* leads Sorge up to the numbers 180:225:256.

In the second part of his work, he deals with the chords of the sixth, and the six-four, derived from the preceding perfect chords that he calls "fundamental" (*Haupt-Accords*). But in this distinction of fundamental and derived chords, he does not mention Rameau, to whom it belongs, and does not call to his readers' attention what is important in the consideration of inversion.

The third part of Sorge's book is devoted to dissonant chords. Just as the tones of the trumpet gave the perfect diminished chord (*e, g, b-flat*), they provide that of the minor seventh, *c, e, g, b-flat* or its transposition, *g, b, d, f,* represented by the numbers 4:5:6:7. Sorge also forms some dissonant chords of the same kind by adding the minor seventh to the perfect minor chord, following the arithmetic progression 10:12:15:18; to the perfect diminished chord, following the numbers 45:54:64:80; to the perfect augmented chord, in the proportions 48:60:75:85; finally to the perfect chord with the diminished third in the proportions 180:225:256:320.[88]

All these chords and their derivatives are ranked by Sorge among those where the dissonance is natural, i.e., attacked without preparation; as for all other dissonances, they appear to enter into the category of transitional notes or of prolongation, following the ancient theory formulated by Johann Crüger in these words:[89] "Dissonantiae, concentum Musicum magnoperè exornantes, ingrediuntur harmoniam duobus modis: vel enim celeritate, obliterantur, vel Syncopationibus."[90] Observe this carefully, because here we have arrived at one of the most important facts of the history of harmony: it is the second

---

[88]Sorge, who calls the *b, d-sharp, f, a* chord a "trias manca mit der kleiner Septime," gives the figures 45:56-1/4:64:80 for the diminished third chord (345); Fétis has apparently multiplied these figures by 4 to avoid the fraction.

[89]Sorge cites this quotation from Crüger on page 337 of *Vorgemach der musicalischen Composition.*

[90]*Synopsis musica,* chap. 12, p. 127. [Dissonances, greatly elaborating a musical resolution, attain harmony in two ways: they are obliterated either quickly or by syncopation.]

period of genuine discoveries in this science, and the glory of this discovery belongs to the humble organist of Lobenstein, neglected by all music historians until today. For the first time he has established that a dissonant chord exists by itself, apart from any modification of another harmony, and he states that this chord is completely different from the other dissonant harmonies.[91] It is true that he is mistaken in granting the same character to the minor seventh chord added, according to him, to the perfect minor chord, although this chord is formed and used only as a product of prolongation and of another kind of modification of which I will speak later. But if the aspect of regularity in the formation of chords led Sorge astray, he grasped, nevertheless, the fundamental character of the dominant seventh chord and of modern tonality. In this he deserves to take a place in the history of harmonic science immediately after Rameau, who first perceived the foundations of this science and established them in the theory of chord inversion. I did not own the books of this erudite musician, and I had not read them when I wrote, in the article "Kirnberger" in my *Biographie universelle des musiciens*, that his theory of the prolongation of notes in the succession of chords was the only substantial thing done for the advancement of the science of harmony since Rameau's classification of fundamental and derived chords until Catel. A fortunate accident having put these very rare books into my hands, I saw there, with as much astonishment as delight, the fact that I have just pointed out—a fact that ought to become one of great importance subsequently.

Rameau's works, having reached Germany, made a profound impression on Marpurg. A trip that he made to Paris in 1746, moreover, had made him see the enthusiasm that the theory contained in these books excited among musicians. Back in Berlin, he devoted himself to studying this theory, and it was from this, with modifications, that he drafted his *Handbuch bey dem Generalbasse und der Composition . . .* , published in 1755.[92] There he reproduced the

[91]Shirlaw pointed out Fétis's factual error. Rameau, not Sorge, was the first to recognize that the dominant seventh chord could be taken without preparation. (Shirlaw, *Theory of Harmony*, 307.)

[92] David A. Sheldon contends that the use of the term "thoroughbass" in the title of Marpurg's treatise is "simply anachronistic" because "Marpurg's main concern

principle of the generation of chords by the addition of thirds;[93] the inevitable consequence of this principle is to isolate all chords and remove their actual formation from the laws of tonality and succession. As for his particular ideas, they consist of a multitude of special cases in which he slipped many errors among some facts. In a classification of *dominant seventh, leading tone seventh,* and *dominant ninth* chords, he considers them *quasi-consonant,* although in reality they have a character exactly opposite to consonance, since they are more gravitational than any other harmony, and imperatively demand resolution.[94]

Fifteen years after the publication of his first work, Sorge issued an abstract freed from all consideration of numbers with the title *Compendium harmonicum.* There he attacked Rameau's theory in its double employment; the *eleventh* chord, which he proved to be only a suspension of the third of the perfect chord; lastly in the construction of a dominant seventh chord, which he maintained is an immediate product of nature and a necessary result of the arithmetic

---

is composition." (*Marpurg's Thoroughbass and Composition Handbook: A Narrative Translation and Critical Study* [Stuyvesant, NY: Pendragon Press, 1989], x.)

[93]While Rameau suggested building chords by the superposition of thirds, Marpurg established it as the fundamental principle of chord construction. (Krehbiel, "Harmonic Principles of J.-P. Rameau," 166.)

[94]In the *Traité complet de la théorie et de la pratique de l'harmonie,* Fétis included the following paragraph about Marpurg:

> Without entering into greater expositions, it is easy to understand the spirit of this system. Its advantage over Rameau's system consists of keeping the place that harmonies ought to occupy on the degrees of the scale, in lieu of searching for their formation on arbitrary notes. Marpurg removes the considerations of numerical proportions and acoustical phenomena from his theory. He replaces them with that of tonality, retaining from his predecessor's system only the mechanical formation of dissonant chords by the addition of thirds. This is why he himself qualifies his theory as 'eclectic' in his preface. But, with this procedure, he, like Rameau, confuses the natural dissonant chords with those that can arise only from the circumstances of succession, and he turns them into so many isolated facts that it is impossible to perceive their application ahead of time. This mechanical formation of dissonances is absolutely arbitrary and has no connection with the processes of art. (Bk 4, § 301, p. 211.)

progression 4:5:6:7. Marpurg also received a large part of the criticism in the *Compendium harmonicum* for having, said Sorge (in his preface), added new errors to those of his model.[95]

Marpurg's reaction was not expected; less than six months after the publication of *Compendium harmonicum*, Marpurg published an analysis of this book[96] in which he attacked his adversary on the substitution of the arithmetric progression for the geometric progression, and on some inaccuracies in the examples given by Sorge concerning harmonic successions.[97] But he did not touch at all on the fundamental things and really did not make any solid objection against the facts established by the latter, although he must have devastated him with this epigraph: "Vous l'avez voulu, George Dandin . . . ."[98] Nevertheless, the power of known names and the confidence that they inspire is such that Marpurg evidently conquered in this conflict, passed as the victor, and editions of his *Handbuch bey dem Generalbasse* multiplied, while the misunderstood

[95]In his preface, Sorge's fundamental criticism of Marpurg is the latter's adoption of Rameau's concept of an undertone series—an idea from which Rameau had since retreated—as a basis for the chords of supposition. Sorge, who asserts that Marpurg compounded Rameau's error by extending it to thirteenth chords, closes his preface with "Either the truth must prevail, or the order of Nature must be reversed." (Martin, "The *Compendium Harmonicum*," 152.)

[96][Friedrich Wilhelm Marpurg], *Herrn Georg Andreas Sorges Anleitung zum Generalbass und zur Composition mit Anmerkungen* (Berlin: [Gottlieb August Lange], 1760).

[97]Jonathan W. Bernard, who discussed the main tenets of the conflict in "The Marpurg-Sorge Controversy" (*MTS*, 11 [Fall 1989]: 164-86), contends that this controversy reveals ". . . the general nature of the conflict between the fundamental-bass and figured-bass schools of thought in mid-eighteenth-century Germany as well as a record of the specific arguments that two important theorists brought to bear in support of their opposing positions" (164). Marpurg was the promulgator of the fundamental-bass school and Sorge the figured-bass school.

[98]The phrase, "You have what you asked for," has been taken from Molière's comedy *George Dandin*, which was produced on 15 July 1668 at Versailles. George Dandin, a rich peasant who, to rise on the social scale, enters an arranged marriage with the daughter of a poor nobleman, makes this comment on his own misfortunes in act 1, sc. 9. The satire in *George Dandin* "is directed . . . not against a social system, but against individuals who have their own stupidity to blame." (Joan Crowe, "Reflections on *George Dandin*" in *Molière: Stage and Study. Essays in honour of W. G. Moore*, ed. W. D. Howarth and Merlin Thomas [Oxford: Clarendon Press, 1973], 9.)

book of the poor organist from Lobenstein fell into utter disrepute and did not sell at all.[99]

A contemporary of Sorge and Marpurg, Daube, a musician in the service of the Duke of Würtemberg, was worried, as they all were, about the necessity for a systematic theory of harmony. But, cutting himself off from every consideration of numbers and acoustical phenomena, he conceived the usefulness of this theory only by making it conform to practice. Actually, what he published with the title *General-Baß in drey Accorden, gegründet in den Regeln der alt-und neunen Autoren, . . . (L'harmonie en trois accords, d'après les règles des auteurs anciens et modernes, . . .)* is less a theory than a classification of chords because of their function in tonality.[100] Although this work only appeared in 1756, he had finished it, nevertheless, two years earlier as the preface, dated 28 December 1754 in Stuttgart, proves. Consequently, Daube wrote it before knowing Marpurg's *Handbuch bey dem Generalbasse*. Sorge's book, published nine years previously, does not seem to have been employed. Either he was too unacquainted with the science of calculations to read it with profit, or he simply wished, as he indicates in several places, to replace Heinichen's and Mattheson's empirical and obsolete works with a systematic treatise.

With the title *General-Baß in drey Accorden*, Daube proposes three fundamental chords, existing by themselves, as the results of tonality and under a law of the intimate connection of their constituent intervals. These three chords are the perfect chord, the dominant seventh chord, and the six-five chord on the fourth degree. It is a long way from Rameau's unique perfect chord and the construction of the other chords by the addition of thirds and the suppression of intervals. However it is evident that Daube borrowed his chord on the fourth degree from the double employment of the French

---

[99]James M. Martin contends that Fétis was the first scholar and ". . . the only major nineteenth century theorist to have recognized the importance of Sorge's theories, and thus to have supported Sorge's theoretical position in the dispute with Marpurg." ("The *Compendium Harmonicum*," 83.)

[100] For a comprehensive discussion of this treatise, see Barbara K. Wallace, "J. F. Daube's *General-Bass in drey Accorden* (1756): A Translation and Commentary" (Ph.D. diss., North Texas State University, 1983).

harmonist,[101] as he owes to Sorge, of whom he does not speak, the idea of the original existence of the dominant seventh chord. Finally, Rameau also gives him the theory of the inversion of the fundamental chords. Daube does not explain the motive that makes him accept the six-five chord as fundamental, rather than that of the seventh on the second degree.[102] But from what he says in the second chapter concerning the dissonance of the second which generates the seventh, and not the seventh giving rise to the second, there is reason to believe that this is the motive that causes him to consider the six-five chord as fundamental, because the interval of the second exists between the fifth and the sixth.

The three chords that have just been mentioned appear to the system's author to constitute all harmony, because he says (chap. 3, p. 20) they and their derivatives suffice to accompany all the degrees of the ascending and descending scale. And to demonstrate it, he gives this tonal formula with harmonies drawn from these very chords, but some of these harmonies are as poor with respect to tonal feeling as with that of the succession of intervals. For example, Daube places the six-four-three chord on the ascending sixth degree, followed by the minor fifth and sixth chord on the seventh, whence it follows that the dissonance of the chord on the sixth degree has no possible resolution. This fault, and the six-four chord on the dominant, which deprives this degree of its chord of repose, makes the harmonic formula of this system's author inadmissible. Marpurg sharply criticized this scale and many other things, under the mask

---

[101]After Marpurg harshly criticized Daube's work in the second and third volumes of his *Historisch-kritische Beyträge zur Aufnahme der Musik*, 5 vols. (Berlin: Lange, 1754-60), Daube replied on 30 November 1756 that he had read only Rameau's *Démonstration du principe de l'harmonie* about five years earlier "for only a few hours; I could not have been able to obtain it before the summer of 1754, at which time my book had already been handed over to the publisher" (3:69-70). Barbara K. Wallace ("J. F. Daube's *General-Bass*," 14-15) argues that Daube could have gotten the idea of the added-sixth chord on the fourth degree from Gasparini.

[102]Daube, in giving the figured bass for the inversions, lists the six-four-three as the *first* inversion and the fundamental seventh chord as the *third* inversion. (Johann Friedrich Daube, *Generalbaß in drey Accorden gegründet* [Leipzig: J. B. Andrä, 1756], 17.)

of anonymity, in the second volume of his *Historisch-kritische Beyträge zur Aufnahme der Musik* (464-74).

Daube considers all the other chords either as complete prolongations of the primary chords or derived from cadential activity, or as alternations of the natural intervals of these chords—a system in which Sorge preceded him.

Let us not be astonished by Daube's error as regards the six-five chord on the fourth degree, because this harmony, derived from certain modifications of which we will speak later, has been the stumbling block of all harmonic theorists until today. By considering it as primary, the whole concept of a complete rational system is made impossible. Actually Daube added nothing to the basic foundations of those systems laid down by Rameau and Sorge. Nevertheless, some good modulatory formulas are found in his book, which enjoyed a certain vogue in Germany.

After Daube, a remarkable book appeared that, nevertheless, escaped Germany's attention, or which at least was not appraised at its just worth. I wish to speak of what Schröter, organist at Nordhausen, published in 1772 under the title *Deutliche Anweisung zum Generalbaß* (*Instruction claire sur la basse continue*).[103] An educated man, not only in music but also in letters and sciences, Schröter had strengthened his ideas on a theory of harmony, the object of so many fruitless efforts, in meditation and in the calm of a small village. He had read everything that had been published on this science, had carefully analyzed the work of his predecessors, and had resumed his observations and his analysis in a history of harmony; unfortunately the manuscript perished in 1761 in a pillage of Nordhausen by the French army. Too elderly to begin a similar work again, Schröter limited himself to giving a résumé in the excellent preface of his *Deutliche Anweisung zum Generalbaß*.[104] Nevertheless, I ought to add that this interesting man had an erroneous moment by taking

---

[103]Christoph Gottlieb Schröter, *Deutliche Anweisung zum Generalbaß, in beständiger Veränderung des uns angebohrnen harmonischen Dreyklanges mit zulänglichen Exempeln* (Halberstadt: J. H. Groß, 1772).

[104]Sections of the résumé and the treatise have been translated by Arnold (*Art of Accompaniment*), 1:295-308.

part in the discussion of Sorge and Marpurg, and declaring himself in favor of the latter with some observations Marpurg inserted in his *Kritische Briefe*.[105] But later Schröter severed himself from Marpurg in the most important points of the theory.

In the eighth chapter of this book (p. 38), Schröter establishes that only the perfect chord exists by itself, and that all the others are the products either of the inversion of this chord, or of the substitution of the seventh for the octave for the formation of the dominant seventh chord, or of prolongation for the construction of the seventh on the second degree and the harmony that derives from it; or, finally, of the anticipation.

Here then is a great step in the true theory, in that the harmony of the minor seventh and those chords that are derived from it are considered in their real point of view, i.e., under that of a prolongation that retards the natural intervals of a consonant chord. In this phenomenon, Schröter considers only the effect of a retardation; this is why he gives it the name *Verzögerung* (*retardatio*). If one had asked him what this *retardement* is, he would have been at a loss to find a satisfactory response, because it is evident that when the retardation ceases, for example, in the chord d, f, a, c, one will have d, f, a, b for the resolution, which is not a consonant harmony. Now there is some other circumstance that, in the chord d, f, a, c, unites with the retardation of c, but Schröter's analysis did not dig so deeply—it stopped at the discovery of the fact of *retardement*. One cannot deny that this discovery is of great importance, in that it furnishes the first element for a classification of dissonant chords that do not exist originally as the results of tonality. This was the first blow raised against the false theory that had ranked the seventh chord with the minor third in the same class of harmony as that of the seventh with the major third.

Concerning the latter, Schröter took a step backward by considering the dominant seventh as the product of the substitution of the seventh for the octave of the perfect chord, because this dominant seventh chord, characteristic of modern tonality, exists by itself in

---

[105]F. W. Marpurg, ed., *Kritische Briefe über die Tonkunst* (2 vols.; Berlin: F. W. Birnstiel, 1760-63), 1:137.

this tonality of which it is the generator. This is what Euler and Sorge had seen so well.

In chapters nine to seventeen, Schröter develops the results of the theory set forth in the eighth; the eighteenth chapter is devoted to alterations, and the nineteenth to the *retardements* of all natural and altered harmonies. In the latter the author gives proof of great sagacity. Some of his insights are more advanced than the state of the art of his time, and by instinct he foreshadows some of the harmonic aggregations that Mozart, Beethoven, Weber, and Rossini subsequently introduced into practice.

In my article on Kirnberger (*Biographie universelle des musiciens*, 5:341), I said that we have conceded too much to this theoretician for the perfection of the theory of harmony. I myself conceded too much in this work, because I knew neither Sorge's books nor that of Schröter, and because music historians who spoke of it had not understood its merit. All the writers who have cited Kirnberger's book *Die wahren Grundsätze zum Gebrauch der Harmonie* (*Les vrais Principes concernant l'usage de l'harmonie*)[106] say that he reduced the fundamental harmony to the perfect and seventh chords. Even he, in the prefaces of his various works, and especially in that of his *Grundsätze des Generalbasses* [Berlin: J. J. Hummel, 1781],[107] which are the practical development of the preceding work, even he, I say, congratulates himself on having arrived at this simplicity. But just as he considers the three-note chord under its three tonal forms, namely, the perfect chord with the major third, the same chord with the minor third, and, finally, the minor third and minor fifth chord

---

[106]Berlin and Königsberg: G. J. Decker & G. L. Hartung, 1773. This treatise has been translated by David Beach and Jurgen Thym, "The True Principles of the Practice of Harmony," *JMT* 23 (Fall 1979): 163-224. Although "The True Principles of the Practice of Harmony" actually was written by Johann Abraham Peter Schulz (1747-1800) who had studied with Kirnberger from 1765 to 1768, it is, according to Beach, an accurate presentation of Kirnberger's harmonic theories (164).

[107]David Beach states that this work, which was written to provide the beginning student with instruction in figured bass and four-part harmony, was to be an introduction to *Die Kunst des reinen Satzes in der Musik*. (Johann Philipp Kirnberger, *The Art of Strict Musical Composition*, trans. David Beach and Jurgen Thym [New Haven and London: Yale University Press, 1982], xii n. 5.)

(on the seventh degree), so he considers the seventh chord as original, whether it has the major third, as in *g, b, d, f,* or whether this third is minor, as in *a, c, e, g,* or, finally, whether the third and fifth are minor, as in *b, d, f, a,* or even whether the third and seventh are major, as in *c, e, g, b.* These forms, Kirnberger says, differ only in the quality of the intervals. But the quality of the intervals is precisely what establishes the difference in the natural or artificial existence of the chords with respect to tonality. If the difficulty were not that, there would be nothing at all in it.

As for the seventh chord on the second degree, Kirnberger derives it from the retardation of the sixth in the sixth chord on the same degree, which is derived from the minor third and minor fifth chord. Thus formed, his chord is composed, therefore, of *d, f, c,* retarding *d, f, b*; sometimes the fifth is introduced, he says, to fill in the harmony. But by virtue of what law and by what technique is this foreign note introduced into the chord? This is what he has not seen, and what he does not even attempt to explain, restricting himself to pointing out a fact of experience. This difficulty is the most important in the whole rational theory of harmony, and it has been the stumbling block of all harmonic theorists.[108]

After Kirnberger, several musicians in Germany who enjoyed honorable reputations wrote harmony and *basso continuo* treatises during the last part of the eighteenth century. But among them only one appears to me to have wanted to create a system that does not appear to have been conceived from a single attempt, if we judge from the first writings intended for propagation, compared to his last works in which he set forth his system. The author of this system was Abbé Vogler, who, having founded a school of music in 1776 in Mannheim, published in the same year a sort of manifesto of the principles that he taught there in a book entitled *Tonwissenschaft und Tonsetzkunst* (*La science de la musique et de la composition*), followed by a sort of commentary on these principles, published under the title of *Kuhrpfälzische Tonschule* (*École de musique du Palatinat* [Mannheim,

---

[108]For a detailed and comparative analysis of the theories of Marpurg and Kirnberger, see Joyce Mekeel, "The Harmonic Theories of Kirnberger and Marpurg," *JMT* 4 (Nov. 1960): 163-93, and Joel Lester (*Compositional Theory*), 231-57.

1778]), and a journal of the school's progress with the new method entitled *Betrachtungen der Mannheimer Tonschule* (*Examens de l'école de musique de Mannheim*). The necessity for all these explanations does not give a favorable view of the lucidity of the system. The doctrine's obscurity and the incoherence of its elements actually were the faults for which the critics of his era reproached him. Weisbecke, professor of law at Erlang, attacked this theory in writings published in 1783 and 1784; Knecht, a pupil of Vogler's first school, was obliged to go to the defense of his master, and the *Musikalische Zeitung* of Speyer became the journal of a polemic on this subject. Later, Vogler reproduced his system in Copenhagen, writing in Danish, and undertook a new demonstration of his principles in a school founded for this purpose. Finally, in 1800, he published in Prague, where he taught a course on his theory, *Handbuch zur Harmonielehre und für den Generalbaß, nach den grundsätze der Mannheimer Tonschule* (*Manuel de la science de l'harmonie et de la basse continue, d'après les principes de l'école de Mannheim*). There, in a long preface, he complains with bitterness about the attacks against his work and his person, and about the accusations of charlatanism that have been hurled in his face. Whatever opinion one has of Vogler's doctrine and writings, one is deeply affected to see a man who has had the glory of training, in his last school in Darmstadt, two of the most prominent German musicians of the present time, Carl Maria von Weber and Meyerbeer, obliged to debate the legitimacy of his claims for the respect of artists. After this digression, which seemed necessary for those who do not know Vogler's works, I am returning to the analysis of his system.[109]

This system is taken, as far as its theoretical part, from Levens' book, and, as for its practical applications, from Vallotti's principles, of which I will speak presently. Taking a string that he divides harmonically on the one hand, and in an arithmetic progression on the other, he obtains the harmonic and diatonic intervals in the lower and middle notes, in accordance with the acoustical construction of

[109]In *Viennese Harmonic Theory from Albrechtsberger to Schenker and Schoenberg* (Ann Arbor: UMI Research Press, 1982), Robert W. Wason gives a précis of the theories in Vogler's *Handbuch* on pages 12-16. For a comprehensive study of Vogler's theories, see Floyd K. Grave and Margaret G. Grave, *In Praise of Harmony: The Teachings of Abbé Georg Joseph Vogler* (Lincoln: University of Nebraska Press, 1987).

the trumpet and horn, and the chromatic intervals in the highest notes. Like Levens, he establishes three whole-tones of which the proportions are different, namely, a major tone of *b-flat* to *c*, in the proportion of 7:8; a middle tone, *c* to *d*, as 8:9; a minor tone as 9:10 (*Tonwissenschaft*, 122-23).[110] The arithmetic progression, extended to the thirty-second term, gives Vogler a chromatic scale, a major scale with the notes *c, d, e, f, g, a, b*; an enharmonic scale of *c-sharp* and *d-flat, d-sharp* and *e-flat, e-sharp* and *f-natural*, etc.; finally a minor scale.

From the division of his string by the arithmetic progression, Vogler also obtains the perfect major chord (*c, e, g*), the perfect minor chord (*g, b-flat, d*), the chord of the minor third and minor fifth (*e, g, b-flat*), the minor seventh chord with a major third (*c, e, g, b-flat*), the major-ninth chord (*c, e, g, b-flat, d*), the minor seventh chord with a minor fifth (*e, g, b-flat, d*); finally all the harmonies, without excepting those whose intervals are generally designated by the name "chromatic." Therefore according to the author of this system, it no longer is a question of putting each of these harmonies on the degree where it is most correctly placed. Undoubtedly this would be a radical difficulty with respect to tonality if Vogler accepted the formulas of tonality that might expressly define the place of each because of certain functions of successions. But he does not doubt that the arithmetic progression gives not only a scale, but a chromatic scale, and, faithful to his principle, he establishes that all of the possible chords, fundamental or derived, can be formed on each of the notes of this scale. Although he may be obliged to conform to usage and establish the keys of *c, d, e-flat, f*, etc., he maintains that in these keys every tone that does not seem to belong there, every harmony that is foreign to it, may be put in place without resulting in actual modulations, unless cadential action sets up the new key. In the formation of this monstrous system, so completely contrary to every feeling of the most delicate, the most

---

[110]Vogler observed that the differences among each type of whole tone is equal to a comma, the very discrepancy in just intonation that led to the emergence of mean-tone temperament. Vogler also noted the existence of two kinds of half-steps: the "major" half-step (15:16) occurs diatonically between *e-f* and *b-c*, while the "minor" half-step (24:25) occurs chromatically, as *c* to *c-sharp*. ([Georg Joseph] Vogler, *Tonwissenschaft und Tonsetzkunst* [Mannheim, 1776], 12-13.) Fétis's page references are most curious—the treatise has only 86 pages!

sensitive part of the art, it is true that he forgets a greater difficulty, namely, that the tendencies determined by the inequalities of the intervals' justness, under the terms of the arithmetic progression, do not permit the harmonies to be transferred to notes other than those fixed by these tendencies, without affecting the ear by the discomfort that false intervals produce, because the ratios are no longer the same. For example, the number 7, which gives the gravitational dissonance of the fourth degree with the dominant, sets up a ratio that can only exist between these two notes, according to their functions which consist of foreshadowing the return of tonic or the preparation for a necessary modulation. Further, let us say that such a theory is the negation of every true theory, because it reduces the art and science to a collection of disconnected facts. The laws of harmonic succession are destroyed in such a maze of heterogeneous chords, and all of Knecht's efforts to establish these laws, without destroying his master's system, in the book conforming to this theory, which he published with the title *Elementarwerk der Harmonie und des Generalbaß*, etc.[111] (*Traité élémentaire de l'harmonie et de la basse continue*, etc.), have been fruitless.

Such was the last harmonic system that closed the eighteenth century in Germany, and that was not a success, in spite of the public teaching that its author did in several large cities. As for the treatises of harmony and *basso continuo* of Albrechtsberger,[112] Türk,[113] Portmann,[114] Kessel,[115] and several others, I do not believe I have to give an analysis, because they contain more or less new views only in

[111][Justin Heinrich Knecht] Augsburg and Stuttgart, 1792, 1794, 1798; 2nd ed., Munich: Falter & Son, 1814, with one vol. of plates.

[112][Johann Georg Albrechtsberger], *Kurzgefaßte Methode den Generalbass zu erlernen* (*Méthode abrégée pour apprendre la basse continue*) (Vienna [& Mainz: Artaria], 1792).

[113][Daniel Gottlob Türk], *Kurze Anweisung zum Generalbaßspielen* (*Instruction sur l'accompagnement de la basse continue*), (Halle & Leipzig 1791); 2nd ed. (Halle & Leipzig 1800). [The second edition, which is expanded into two volumes encompassing nearly 800 pages, drops "Kurze" from the title.]

[114][Johann Gottlieb Portmann], *Leichtes Lehrbuch der Harmonie, Composition und des Generalbasses, zum Gebrauch für Liebhaber der Musik, angehende und fortschreitende Musici und Composition* (*Méthode facile d'harmonie, de composition et de basse continue . . .*) (Darmstadt: [J. J. Will], 1789).

[115][Johann Christian Bertram Kessel], *Unterricht im Generalbasse zum Gebrauche für Lehrer und Lernende* (*Instruction sur l'usage de l'harmonie pour les professeurs et les élèves*) (Leipzig: [Hertel], 1791).

detail, and only in what concerns more or less easy methods of teaching.[116] It is in this way that I have proceeded with certain books of the same type published in France in the second half of the eighteenth century, e.g., Béthizy[117] and Bemetzrieder,[118] who belong to the same category.[119]

Before dealing with Catel's reform of the harmonic system, which opened the nineteenth century in France, it remains for me to cast a glance on what was done in Italy and England in the last part of the eighteenth century.

Tartini's theory was unsuccessful in Italy, because it contained only vague speculations that did not have any direct application in practice. It was not the same with respect to a theory, both systematic

---

[116]Arnold (*Art of Accompaniment*, 1:318-22) has a summary of Türk's treatise. David A. Shelton (*Marpurg's Thoroughbass*, 249-60) discussed how Türk's attempt to synthesize Kirnberger's and Marpurg's ideas for the beginning student of thoroughbass resulted in an eclectic approach to harmony.

[117][Jean-Laurent de Béthizy], *Exposition de la théorie et de la pratique de la musique, Suivant les nouvelles découvertes* (Paris: [M. Lambert], 1754; [2d ed., Paris: Deschamps, 1764]).

[118][Anton Bemetzrieder], *Nouvel essai sur l'harmonie, Suite du Traité de Musique* (Paris: [The Author and Onfroy], 1779).

[119]Krehbiel ("The Harmonic Principles of J.-P. Rameau") has a précis of Béthizy's harmonic principles on pp. 198-200. For a substantive study, see A. Louise Hall Earhart, "The Harmonic Theories of Jean-Laurent de Béthizy and Their Relationship to Those of Rameau and d'Alembert" (Ph.D. diss., The Ohio State University, 1985).

The treatise Fétis has cited for Bemetzrieder (*Nouvel essai sur l'harmonie*) was not concerned at all with *basso continuo*. Bemetzrieder's *basso continuo* treatise was *Traité de musique, Concernant les Tons, les Harmonies, les Accords et le Discours musical* (Paris: Onfroy, 1776) with its accompanying *Exemples Du Traité de Musique* . . . . In the preface to the *Traité de musique*, Bemetzrieder stated that "in order to learn this amiable science properly and steadily, one must study this book in front of a clavecin or in front of a fortepiano; go step by step, and make each proposition tangible on the instrument." And for those who did not know how to read music or to play the clavecin, Bemetzrieder suggested that they obtain his "Leçons de clavecin which can be found at Bluet, Libraire sur le Pont St. Michel" (iii-iv). In "A propos des *Leçons de clavecin* (1771): Diderot et Bemetzrieder" (*Revue de musicologie* 66 [1980]: 125-78), Jean Gribenski suggests that Bemetzrieder's patron, the Encyclopedist Denis Diderot (1713-84), either assisted Bemetzrieder or wrote the *Leçons de clavecin* for Bemetzrieder.

and practical, conceived by P. Vallotti, a grand-cordelier monk of the monastery at Padua, who formed a school developed by the students of this savant musician, and whose doctrine was very different from that of other schools in some essential points. Contemplated in the cloister's quiet and during a long life, Vallotti's theory came to its point of maturity when the author decided to publish it. But he had then reached the age of eighty-two, and he died unexpectedly before he was able to bring it to light. Only the first part was published under this title: *Della scienza teorica, e pratica della moderna musica* (Padua: [Stamperia del Seminario (Giovanni Manfrè)], 1779); it is purely speculative.[120] The other three parts, unpublished to this day, were expected to deal with the practical elements of music, counterpoint, the rules of harmony and accompaniment.[121]

Today we would not know, except by tradition, the applications Vallotti made of his speculative theory to the practice of the art and to the harmonic system, if his student and successor, Sabbatini, had not made them known in his treatises on harmony[122] and fugue.[123] The first of these works alone must occupy us here.

Sabbatini's method was purely empirical. You should not search for a general view of systematic construction; the facts are ascertained by their existence, without searching for their origin. Thus Sabbatini finds the perfect major chord on tonic, the perfect minor chord on the sixth degree, and a progression of these chords by a series of bass movements descending a fifth and rising a fourth leads him to the minor third and minor fifth chord, which is formed on the seventh

[120]Given the numerous algebraic calculations in Vallotti's treatise to derive intervals and chords, it is quite astonishing that Fétis said nothing about them.

[121]Books 2, 3, and 4 were finally published in 1950 as *Trattato della moderna musica* (Padua: Il messaggero di S. Antonio [Tipografia della provincia Patavina]). This publication, which was edited by Bernardino Rizzi and Giancarlo Zanon, is called an "unscholarly edition" by Sven Hansell in *NGrove* 19:506.

[122]Luigi Antonio Sabbatini, *La vera idea delle musicali numeriche segnature diretta al giovane studiosò dell' armonìca* (Venice: [Valle], 1799).

[123]*Trattato sopra le fughe musicali . . . Sabbatini . . . corredato da copioso saggi del e le opere del Padre F. A. Vallotti* (Venice: [Valle], 1802).

degree of the scale. As far as this last chord is concerned, he has shown more sagacity than all of his predecessors, because the former considered it as a natural chord in the place that it occupies, while Sabbatini, or rather Vallotti, saw quite well that this chord, which responds to no tonal condition of the major or minor modes, is effected only by analogy in a progression of perfect, nonmodulatory chords.[124] It is remarkable that more modern, recent harmonic theorists have proven less advanced on this point. As for harmony derived from the fundamental, Vallotti and Sabbatini follow Rameau's doctrine.

Considering the chromatic scale as a true scale, these authors do not show the augmented fifth, the diminished third, or the other modified intervals of consonant chords as alterations of the natural intervals of the perfect major, minor or diminished chords, but as an arbitrary employment of intervals that are all assumed in this chromatic scale.[125]

Moving ahead to the dissonant chords, Sabbatini constructs them by the addition of intervals to the perfect major, minor, and diminished chords.[126] Thus, the addition of a major third above the perfect major chord on tonic gives him a major seventh chord (c, e, g, b), which he considers as the first in order. Likewise, the addition of a minor third above the perfect minor chord on the sixth degree

[124]Sabbatini classified the third, the sixth, the perfect fourth, and the perfect fifth as consonant intervals; the sixth and perfect fourth were "secondary consonances." The leading-tone triad, containing the dissonant interval of a diminished fifth, was classified as *consonant harmony by analogy* (*armonìe consonanti per rappresentanza*). (Sabbatini, *La vera idea*, 12).

[125] At no point did Sabbatini discuss "the chromatic scale as a true scale," nor is the use of the augmented triad and diminished-third triad arbitrary. The augmented-fifth triad and the diminished-third triad (as well as their inversions) are, like the diminished-fifth triad, *consonant harmony by analogy*, and they are derived by chromatic alteration from a specific chord in minor. The augmented-fifth triad occurred on the mediant and resolved to the tonic in a dominant-like manner. The diminished-third triad occurred on the raised subdominant and preceded the dominant. (Ibid., 16-19.)

[126]Sabbatini was obviously well-versed with Tartini's *Trattato*, because Sabbatini's precept for the formation of dissonant chords from consonant chords (". . . che non si dà nè può darsi posizione dissonante, se non fondata sopra la posizione consonante" [20]) is almost verbatim what Tartini stated on page 77 of his treatise. (See n. 49 *supra*.)

creates a minor seventh chord (a, c, e, g). From these two fundamental chords, he draws, by inversion, the six-five, six-four-three, and second chords.[127] Finally, a major third added above the minor third and minor fifth chord creates the leading-tone seventh (b, d, f, a). Next, Sabbatini says (*La vera idea delle music musicali numeriche segnature*, art. 5, p. 32) that there is another minor seventh chord that is formed on the fifth of the principal tone of the key; it is composed of the major third, just fifth, and minor seventh, as g, b, d, f. That one, he says, differs from the other seventh chords in that it does not need to be prepared, whereas the dissonance of the former must always be heard beforehand as a consonance.

We see that the absence of a good classification of the original chords throws the author of this system into a great confusion of ideas here; the logical order that we have seen from the authors of the most erroneous systems no longer occurs here. Because, what is this seventh chord which exists outside of the system of practical generation adopted by the author, which has different conditions for its use, and which resembles them only by the necessity of resolving the dissonance by descending?[128] And how is it, that having found from practice that this dissonant chord does not need preparation, Vallotti and Sabbatini did not conclude that it was the constituent chord of tonality, as well as the perfect major and minor chords? Finally, how is it that the necessity to prepare the dissonances of the other seventh chords did not make them see that these chords had an origin other than the addition of thirds to the perfect chords? Many other imperfections arise from this system, but I hasten to arrive at the

---

[127]The complete figuring, six-four-two, is more commonly abbreviated four-two or two. Marpurg, in his discussion of the "chord of the second," described it thus: ". . . the lower end of it, and accordingly the bass, contains the dissonance, since the parent chord is standing on its head here." (Marpurg, *Handbuch bey dem Generalbasse* [2d ed.; Berlin, 1762], § 44, p. 66.)

[128]For the special privilege accorded the major minor seventh chord, Sabbatini took refuge in the seventh partial of the overtone series which, while not consonant, was also not a "true dissonance." To support his theory, he cited both Tartini (*Trattato*, 126ff.) and Vallotti (*Della Scienza teorica*, 115). (Sabbatini, *La vera idea*, 32-34.)

peculiarities that caused this system to be rejected by the purist schools of Italy, with regard to practice.

The addition of a minor third above the perfect diminished chord of the minor mode leads Vallotti and Sabbatini to the diminished seventh chord. The same addition to the same chord with a chromatic or diminished third, produces the diminished seventh chord with the diminished third (*d-sharp, f, a, c*).[129] Finally, the addition of a minor third above the perfect augmented chord gives rise to the major seventh chord with an augmented fifth (*c, e, g-sharp b*).[130] All of the harmonies derived from these chords are formed by their inversion.

Up to that point, if the theory is unsatisfactory, the practical examples of harmony in Sabbatini's book conform to what is done in the modern school. But here is a new part, an unexpected part where the ear is offended by the strange association of sounds whose movements cannot give the sensation of resolved dissonances, inasmuch as the notes on which the resolution are made are already heard in the chord. Thus, in the perfect chord *c, e, g, c* in which he even doubles intervals, Sabbatini says that when the ninth is added, so that the chord he gives is composed of *c, e, g, c, d, e, g, c*,[131] the first derived harmony is a seven-six chord (*e, g, c, d*), the second is a six-five-four chord (*g, c, d, e*), and the complete inversion is a seven-four-two chord (*d, e, g, c*).

Thus it is in this manner that Sabbatini, following Vallotti, adds a dissonance of the eleventh to the perfect major or minor chord in which the intervals are doubled. The chord thus composed occurs in this form: *c, e, g, c, e, f, g*. Its first derivative is the nine-eight-six-three chord (*e, g, c, e, f*), the second is the seven-six-four chord (*g, c, e, f*), and the third inversion is the seven-five-two chord (*f, g, c, e*).[132]

[129]This seventh chord with the diminished third occurs on the raised fourth degree in minor and resolves immediately to the dominant. (Ibid., 69-71.)

[130]Unlike the augmented triad, this mediant seventh chord in minor resolved to a dominant seventh chord. (Ibid., 72-74.)

[131]While Sabbatini does have this "doubled" ninth chord, it does not occur in a musical context, but in a figure that gives the figured bass and illustrates the dissonant interval (9) as it occurs between 8 and 10; neither this chord nor any other chord in a "figure" is resolved. (Ibid., 78.)

[132]All of the ninth and eleventh chords in Sabbatini's musical examples are dominant harmonies. (Ibid., 80-81, 86-87.)

And yet who would believe that there harmonies, so harsh,[133] so devoid of the means of good resolution, were conceived by a savant musician—educated in purer principles—only for wanting a system, and because he did not understand the technique of suspension that delays the natural intervals of the chords! If he had grasped the theory of this technique, he would have seen by this alone that when a note is delayed in a chord, it cannot be heard at the same time as the suspension. Consequently, instead of composing the ninth chord of *c, e, g, c, d*, he ought to form it of *c, e, g, d*, delaying *c, e, g, c*.[134] Thus, he would have avoided all the harmonic horrors that he presents as derivatives of his primary harmony. Likewise, the principle of suspension would have proven to him that his so-called eleventh is only a fourth, that this fourth delays the third, and, consequently, that the third and fourth cannot be heard simultaneously. Thus, instead of a chord composed of *c, e, f, g, c*, which does not occur in any well-written piece of music, he should have had *c, f, g, c*, delaying *c, e, g, c*; its derived harmonies would have the same regularity.

I do not need to extend the examination of this bizarre theory any further in order to make clear that, when Vallotti's students began to propagate it, those provoked against it were distinguished Italian composers. The theory was special in that it alone had the pretension of reforming the art of writing; all of the other systems had restricted themselves to giving more or less false explanations of the facts, more or less close to the truth, or creating simple, speculative hypotheses.

We cannot consider the *Regole musicali per i principianti de cembalo, nel sonar coi numeri e per i principianti di contrappunto* (Naples: Mazzola,

---

[133]This is a germane observation by Fétis, because eleventh chords tend to lose their identity when the *root* occurs above the eleventh in an upper voice. The resultant clash between the major third and "eleventh" is undoubtedly what Fétis meant by "harsh."

[134]Fétis' criticism here is wholly unwarranted, because (1) all of the musical examples use only four voices; (2) the ninth is a suspended dissonance and not a true harmonic member, and (3) in none of Sabbatini's musical examples is the note of resolution present with the suspension. In the example that Sabbatini gave on page 80, he had the ninth chord composed of *c, e, g, d*, which does, indeed, delay *c, e, g, c*. Furthermore, the fundamental bass for each example was clearly marked "9 8."

1775) of [Fedele] Fenaroli as the exposé of a harmonic theory. It is only a practical outline of the tradition, pure but outmoded, of Durante's school; it did not represent the current state of the art.

In the eighteenth century, England did not have any harmonic theorists whose works are worthy of any notice. Five well-known musicians, as a matter of fact, published some harmonic treatises there, but four of these artists were German, and the fifth was Italian. The first, Gottfried [Godfry] Keller, settled in London about 1702. Like all of Rameau's predecessors, it was not Keller's intent to create a harmonic system in his *Méthode complète pour apprendre à accompagner la basse continue* but to formulate some rules for accompaniment,[135] as the title of the book indicates.[136] There is more analysis in Pepusch's work, which has *A Treatise on Harmony*[137] for a title, but this musician, also German by birth, does not seem to have known the *Traité d'harmonie* of the French theorist, and in lieu of presenting a system of generation and classification of chords, applied himself to considering harmony in the art of composition. The first systematic book published in England dealing with harmony is that of John Frederick Lampe, German by birth, who published a method of *basso continuo* based on Rameau's principles of fundamental bass[138] in 1737.[139] A few years later the celebrated violinist Geminiani published his *Guide harmonique*[140]

---

[135]Arnold (*Art of Accompaniment*, 1:247-50) discussed some of Keller's rules. What Arnold failed to mention is that both the layout and the quality of printing in the 1731 edition (the Appendix in William Holder's *A Treatise of the Natural Grounds, and Principles of Harmony* [London: W. Pearson, 1731]) was inferior to the undated edition.

[136]*A Compleat Method For Attaining to Play a Thorough Bass Upon Either Organ, Harpsichord or Theorbo-Lute* . . . (London: [Printed for John Cullen, 1707]).

[137][Johann Christoph (John Christopher) Pepusch], *A Treatise on Harmony: containing The Chief Rules for Composing in Two, Three, and Four Parts.* . . . [2d ed.] (London: W. Pearson, 1731).

[138]Lampe calls the fundamental bass the "natural bass" because it "keeps its place as *Ground-Note* of the Cord" and gives the chord its name (18).

[139]*A Plain and Compendious Method of Teaching Thorough Bass, After the most Rational Manner* . . . . (London: [Wilcox], 1737).

[140][Francesco Saverio Geminiani], *Guida Armonica, o Dizionariò Armonico being A Sure Guide to Harmony and Modulation* . . . , [Op. 10] (London: [Johnson], 1742).

(production worse than mediocre), which cannot be considered a systematic treatise of harmony, because it is only a kind of dictionary of chordal succession and modulations.[141]

Kollman, the last of the writers mentioned above, had come from Germany about 1782 to settle in London. Fourteen years later he published a book called *Essai sur l'harmonie musicale, suivant la nature de cette science et les principes des autres les plus célèbres*[142] These principles are those of Kirnberger, whom Kollman frequently limited himself to translating. But in endeavoring to supplement some gaps in Kirnberger, he borrowed some ideas from Marpurg, not understanding the contradictions that are found between the doctrines of these two theorists. Later he noticed the anomaly of the two systems that he had tried to reconcile in this work, believed he had found a more rational and homogeneous theory in Ballière's book, and published it in his *Nouvelle Théorie de l'harmonie musicale*.[143] The analysis that I have done of the principles of Ballière exempts me from examining Kollman's book.[144]

---

[141]The third part of Serre's *Observations sur les principes de l'harmonie, occasionnées par quelques écrits modernes sur le sujet*, . . . (175-206) is a critique of Geminiani's treatise. Although Geminiani intended to produce a work that would "be of the Greatest Use to the Students of Harmony, by enlarging their Ideas, and giving them just and Compleat Notions of Harmony and Modulation" (Preface, n.p.), the author restricted the treatise to the minor mode and, as both Fétis and Serre observed, merely created a poorly organized dictionary in which each figured bass (between two and five notes in length) was followed by an annotation that directed the student to other pages to select a continuing progression. This process continued until the progression ended with a cadence. Geminiani responded to his critics by issuing a *Supplement to the Guida Armonica, With examples Shewing its Use in Composition* (London: For the Author by K. Johnson, n.d.) to "explane [sic] my Design more fully, and satisfy the Lovers of the Art, by Instructing them in the Method of making the intended Use of My Work" (Preface, n.p.). The latter work used six different figured basses from the *Guida* to instruct the learner how to write in different styles using from two to four voices.

[142][Augustus Frederic Christopher Kollman], *An Essay on Musical Harmony, According to the Nature of that Science and the Principles of the Greatest Musical Authors* (London: [J. Dale], 1796).

[143]*A New Theory of Musical Harmony, According to a Complete and Natural System of That Science* (London: [W. Bulmer], 1806).

[144]Erwin R. Jacobi discussed Kollman's writings on pages 136-42 of his article "Harmonic Theory in England after the Time of Rameau" in *JMT* 1 (Nov. 1957): 126-46.

CHAPTER III
THE NINETEENTH CENTURY—THE DEVELOPMENT OF THE ART
A Complete and Definitive Formation of the Theory of Harmony

After the discovery of the natural harmony of the dominant, which created modern tonality and the first means of actual modulation, composers, placed under the influence of this tonality, devoted themselves to developing the immediate consequences; and more than fifty years elapsed before they felt the need for new means of effects. It was only toward the end of the seventeenth century that musicians began to introduce ascending or descending alterations of the natural intervals in the consonant chords. The first of these alterations consisted of raising the sixth of a sixth chord on the sixth degree of the minor mode by a semitone, which created an attraction analogous to that of the leading tone. For example, the sixth chord on the sixth degree of the key of *a* minor (*f*, *a*, *d*) becomes an augmented sixth chord (*f*, *a*, *d-sharp*). This *d-sharp*, placed in the relationship of a tritone with *a*, determines a necessity for an ascending resolution. But this same interval of a tritone or major fourth can be thought of as a minor fifth, if the *d-sharp* is transformed into *e-flat*. The intonation in voices and instruments of variable pitch differs only a tiny amount, which determines a descending attraction. Now let us suppose the augmented-sixth chord *f*, *a*, *d-sharp* can be spontaneously changed into the seventh chord *f*, *a*, *eb*; an unexpected modulation will result from it since, following the law of tonality, the seventh chord *f*, *a*, *eb*, being the dominant, immediately determines the key of *b-flat*. Likewise the dominant-seventh chord can be changed into that of the augmented sixth and, consequently, define a modulation from the key of *b-flat* to that of *a* minor.

From this power of unexpected change of key, the feeling of surprise results, a feeling that did not exist in music prior to the use of alteration in the natural intervals of chords. In my *Philosophie de la musique*, I called the category of harmonic facts resulting for this alteration the *ordre transitonique* of music. I discovered the principle of the variable proportions of intervals because of their resolution

tendencies, a principle that introduces new numbers into the calculation of these intervals; and, finally, a principle, unknown to all
theorists until today, whose unrecognized existence has been the
cause of so much bad reasoning and so many vain disputes.

For a long time the alteration of the intervals of consonant chords
was the expression of the composers' audacity. In the first part of the
eighteenth century, some isolated occurrences of alterations of dissonant chords were, as matter of fact, noticed individually every now
and then, but as the results of chance, and in a way sort of unknown
to the musicians who used them. Mozart was the first who, observing
the expressive accent that resides in alterations, increased usage with
a rare sagacity, and systematically inserted them into dissonant chords.
From that time, not only could he introduce a greater number of
dramatic accents in his songs, but he could also multiply and vary the
means of unexpected modulations; because we understand that a great
many new attractions were bound to be born in these combinations
that group the different kinds of dissonances together. Some of the
dissonances are ascending in their capacity as incidental leading tones,
and others descend as ordinary dissonances. For example, suppose
that an ascending alteration is introduced in the third of the minor
sixth and fifth (commonly called the diminished fifth) chord of the key
of C. We will have a chord composed of *b, d-sharp, f, g*, which will be
arranged in a more satisfying manner for the ear by making it *b, f, g,
d-sharp*. Because *d-sharp* is the expressive accent, it ought to be found
in the melody, namely, in the upper voice. Now, what will be the result
of this chord? A gravitational minor fifth between *b* and *f*, a dissonance
of the second between *f* and *g*, which will oblige *f* to descend; a
diminished third or augmented sixth between *d-sharp* and *f* which,
giving *d-sharp* the instantaneous character of a leading tone, will oblige
d-sharp to ascend; lastly, an augmented fifth or diminished fourth
between *g* and *d-sharp*.

Suppose that to all of these attractions, some combinations of
substituted notes (about which I will speak in the examination of the
definitive theory), and the retardation of one of the natural notes of
the chords happen to be joined together; the attractions will multiply, and the means of modulations will be increased in the same
proportion. Beethoven, Cherubini, Weber, and Rossini, having

followed in Mozart's footsteps, have extended the domain of the *ordre transitonique* by introducing there, with the means that I have just indicated, a multitude of new ways.[1] The last expression of this course is the one where the simple and multiple alterations are joined with all the combinations of varied tendencies that can be added there; we arrive at the solution of this problem: *A note being given, find the combinations and harmonic formulas so that it can be resolved in all of the keys and in all of their different modes.* Therefore, having come to the *ordre omnitonique*, the art will have no more harmonic discoveries to make, at least following the construction of our scale.

When the Paris Conservatory of Music was organized in 1796, the most renowned professors for each branch of the art who taught, each according to his ideas and method, were brought together because there was not enough time to prepare a main doctrine for a uniform education. This is why Rodolphe gave harmony lessons following his empirical method, which is lacking in any kind of analysis;[2] why Rey taught his course according to the system of fundamental bass; why Langlé developed the results of the theory that has been expounded earlier, and why Berton, freed from every consideration of system, employed the practical method with his students. It was only some years later that this celebrated composer conceived his family tree of chords and the dictionary that is its outgrowth.[3]

Still they soon became aware of the drawbacks of this diversity of method and system in a school where unity of doctrine ought to be the foundation of instruction. A commission composed of Cherubini, Gossec, Martini, Le Sueur, Méhul, Catel, Lacépède, Prony, and the

---

[1]In his *Traité complet de l'harmonie*, Fétis explores the concept of common tone modulation, which he calls an "intuitive attraction" because ". . . musical sense compensates for this implied harmony at the moment of the tonal change" (Bk. 3, chap. 3 § 270, pp. 180–81).

[2][Jean (Johann) Joseph Rodolphe (Rudolph)], *Théorie d'accompagnement et de composition, à l'usage des élèves de l'école nationale de musique* (Paris: [Naderman], 1779).

[3][Henri-Montan Berton], *Traité d'harmonie basé sur l'arbre généalogique des accords* (Paris: [Mme Duhan], 1804); *Dictionnaire des accords*, 3 vols. (Paris: [Mme Duhan], 1804).

professors who have just been named,[4] was appointed early in 1801 with a view to discussing and laying down the foundations of a system of harmony. That of Rameau, especially, was the object of serious examination, because it still had many followers in France. Méhul, named chairman of the commission, expressed it in this way in the last meeting:

> In a conflict of differing opinions, supported by the partisans or antagonists of the fundamental bass system, the commission, *being unable to distinguish the whole truth*, suspended its judgement when the work submitted for our action terminated all the discussion, by offering a complete system, simple in its principles and clear in its developments.[5] [Fétis' italics.]

This system, which presented so many advantages, according to Méhul, was the one that Catel published shortly thereafter under the title *Traité d'harmonie adopté par le Conservatoire, pour servir à l'étude dans cet établissement.*[6] The influence that the Conservatory exercised already in this era soon confirmed beyond all question what the most famous French musicians declared to be better.[7] This was the *coup de grâce* given to Rameau's system, and the destruction of the latter was more complete and rapid because the remaining sectaries were excluded from public teaching at this time.

What then was this theory, so satisfying that it was adopted without opposition by the most skillful French musicians, and which immediately acquired a vogue that had been Rameau's reward only after thirty years of work, struggles, and multiple publications? Catel discloses it in a single phrase: "In harmony only one chord exists in

---

[4]Langlé was not a member of the commission, but André Frédéric Eler (1764–1821) and Nicholas Etienne Framery (1745–1810) were members of the commission.

[5]*Arrêtés relatifs à l'adoption de Traité d'harmonie* as quoted in Charles-Simon Catel, *Traité d'harmonie adopté par le Conservatoire, pour servir à l'étude dans cet établissement* (ii).

[6][Charles-Simon Catel] (Paris: [Mme. Le Roy], 1802).

[7]The influence of the Conservatory extended beyond the borders of France and Europe. Thirty years after the publication of Catel's treatise, an edition appeared in the United States: *A Treatise on Harmony, Written and Composed for the use of the Pupils at the Royal Conservatoire of Music in Paris; . . . From the English Copy with Additional Notes and Explanations by Lowell Mason* (Boston: James Loring, 1832).

which all of the others are contained" (*Traité d'harmonie*, 5). What is this chord, and how is it formed? Here is a résumé of what Catel says in that respect.

If we take a string that is tuned to the lowest *g* on the piano, and if we divide it in half, we find its octave [G2]. Its third part gives the octave of its fifth [D3]; its fifth, the double octave of its third [B3]; its seventh, the twenty-first interval, or the double octave of its seventh [F4]; finally its ninth, its twenty-third interval or double octave of its ninth [A4]. Thus, a chord composed of *g, b, d, f, a* arises from this division of the chord. This chord is the one to which in practice we give the name "dominant ninth." It contains the perfect major chord (*g, b, d*), the perfect minor chord (*d, f, a*), the perfect diminished chord (*b, d, f*), the dominant seventh chord (*g, b, d, f*), and the leading-tone seventh (*b, f, d, a*). By continuing the operation of the division of the string to the third octave, namely, starting from the sound 1/8 [G4], we find the sounds 1/10, 1/12, 1/14, and 1/17, which produce the dominant "minor" ninth (*g, b, d, f, a-flat*) and the "diminished-seventh" chord (*b, d, f, a-flat*). All of these chords are natural and fundamental.[8] By inversion of the intervals, we obtain natural chords like them, which, the same as the fundamental ones, are attacked without preparation, as arising from the formation of tonality.[9]

Notice that the geometrician de Prony, who had joined the commission, had no difficulty admitting the sound 1/7 as the true *f* of the scale, and the sound 1/9 as *a*, although these proportions are not those of geometricians for these notes, with the exception of Euler, whose memoir on the first of these numbers appears to have been unknown or unnoticed by the other mathematicians.[10] As for the

---

[8]"Fundamental" means *root* position.

[9]All harmony having its origin in the first nine partials of the monochord or sonorous body—perfect triads, dominant seventh or ninth, and the half-diminished seventh chord—constitutes "natural or simple harmony"; thus, the dissonance does not have to be prepared.

[10]Euler was one of the first mathematicians to employ logarithms for the calculation of intervals. Baron Gaspard Riche de Prony (1744–1839) lamented the lack of influence engendered by Euler's *Tentamen novae theoriae musicae*, which was either unknown or scarcely known in France. ("Du rapport fait à l'académie des sciences sur cet ouvrage," in Baron Blein's *Principes de mélodie et d'harmonie déduits de la théorie des vibrations* [Paris, 1838], x.) Following Euler, de Prony used logarithms to

consent of de Prony, it is verified with these words from the minutes of adoption printed at the beginning of the *Traité d'harmonie*: "Citizen Catel develops his system of harmony. After the fullest deliberation, the general assembly adopts it *unanimously*, . . ." [Fétis' italics.]

The natural chords being found, as we have seen, Catel establishes that all harmonic combinations other than the former are formed by notes foreign to the chords, what we call "passing notes," by prolongations that suspend or retard the natural intervals of the chords, or, finally, by alterations of these same intervals.[11] As for substitution, about which I will speak later, Catel did not see it at all, but he had a sort of intuition about it when he said, in reference to the analogy of using the "diminished fifth" chord (fifth and sixth minor) and of those of the leading-tone seventh and diminished seventh:

> The similarity[12] that exists between these chords proves their identity, and clearly demonstrates that they have the same origin (14).

> Everything that has been said about the leading-tone seventh, as far as its relation to the dominant seventh, applies to the diminished seventh (16).

It is a fruitful idea to search for the origin of harmonies and their analogy in the destination that they have, in accordance with the order of tonal succession. If Catel had delved further into this consideration, he would have left nothing for his successors, because he would have found the complete system of which he has shown only some parts.

---

determine intervals, and in *Instruction élémentaire sur les moyens de calculer les intervalles musicaux* (Paris: Didot, 1822), he pointed out the advantage obtained by utilizing logarithms based on two for determining intervals. Moreover, de Prony also calculated a table of logarithms on the twelfth root of two, a table that is used for equal-tempered tuning (*Larousse de la musique* [1957], 1:555).

[11]These harmonic combinations, which are built on the natural chords, Catel calls "composed harmony" (6).

[12]The two chords, the dominant seventh and the half-diminished seventh, have three common tones, and both of the chords resolve to the tonic.

With respect to prolongation, although he did not formulate the theory in a general sense, and although he paid too much attention to some special cases, he knew the technique well in what concerns consonant chords and some of the dissonant chords. But the obstacle against which some of the preceding theories had run aground still recurs in Catel's and leads to a similar ruin. This obstacle is, as we quite expect, the minor seventh chord on the second degree and the harmonies that are derived from it. We have to recall that in the major dominant ninth chord, produced by the division of the string, he found the perfect minor chord d, f, a. Therefore this chord exists, for him, on the second degree of the scale, although this is not the one that exists there in the determination of modern tonality. According to him, in the succession of this perfect chord to that of the tonic, if this tonic is extended, it produces the seventh chord with which he is concerned. But more difficulties arise here: (1) the perfect minor chord on the second degree does not belong at all to the tonality, although the prolongation that produces the seventh chord is tonal. (2) Catel can only show this alleged origin of the seventh chord by writing in five parts,[13] in order to have it complete, which is an exception contrary to the principles of unity on which a wholly veritable theory ought to rest. (3) Lastly, the principle of the artificial construction of chords by prolongation demands that the prolongation coming to a close, the delayed chord occurs immediately. Now every prolongation that produces a dissonance must inevitably resolve by descending a degree. The application of this fundamental rule cannot find its place here, because if c, the seventh of d, f, a, c descended to b, we would have a new dissonant six-five chord, d, f, a, b, which does not belong to this key, and which would be that of the fourth degree of the relative minor key. Catel understood this difficulty well, but not knowing how to get out of it, and not having been able to prove the true origin of the chord, he had recourse in this arbitrary rule whose falseness is evident, and which he expresses thus: "The prolongation can be made, as well, on an already complete chord, in which the prolonged

---

[13]Catel uses five parts for the root position, first, and second inversion seventh chords.

note will not have any resolution. But it should resolve, of course, in the following chord by descending a degree" [21]. If Catel's views had been more general, and if he had known the technique of substitution and the combinations of collective modifications of natural chords, he would have avoided the stumbling block against which a part of his system has shattered.

If we search for what is innovative in Catel's theory and what was borrowed from his predecessors, or at least what was said only after them, we will see that Sorge was the first to consider (in 1745) consonant harmony and the dominant seventh harmony as forming the class of natural chords, but that the latter has been mistaken in classifying the minor seventh on the second degree in the same class, while Catel saw quite clearly that he was creating an artificial harmony, although he did not discover the nature of the device. Sorge also saw well that some of Rameau's and Marpurg's chords, notably those of the eleventh, were only the products of the prolongation that formed artificial chords. But Schröter (in 1772) was the first who saw that the seventh chord on the second degree is one of the chords of this class, although he could not say how the prolongation was effected. Finally, Schröter was the first who clearly analyzed the facts of the alteration of the intervals of the natural chords and the new aspects that they give to these chords. If Catel had no knowledge of these authors' books, all he did at least was to "reinvent" what they had already published. But what appertains to him in particular is the view of the analogy of the major and minor dominant ninth chords, the leading-tone seventh, and the diminished seventh with the dominant seventh chord. Also, it is the order that he put into the various parts of the system, and, lastly, the analysis of the facts of practice where he demonstrated the skillfulness of a great musician.[14] Consequently, we are not astonished at the great success that his theory achieved in France during the first fifteen years of the nineteenth century. Notice, on the other hand, how many motives seemed to be compelled to stand in opposition to

---

[14]The modern term "plagal cadence" appeared for the first time in Catel's treatise (34).

a backward step that Reicha and some other harmonists tried to have done to the science for twenty-five years.

The great reputation that Reicha enjoyed in France and even in Germany during these twenty-five years obliges me to enter into more details than I would like about his system, which is, in a way, only the reproduction of old theories outmoded by the discoveries of Sorge, Schröter, Kirnberger and, above all, by Catel's method.

Reicha, setting aside the consideration of the succession of chords that had made such great strides in the science since Sorge, and, consequently, the phenomena of harmonic construction resulting from prolongation, returns to the system of isolated chords, of which he forms an arbitrary classification following certain considerations that are peculiar to him. His theoretic foundation is composed of thirteen consonant and dissonant chords, among which a certain number are primary, and the others are products of alteration.[15] From the first few pages Reicha offers in the exposition of his principles,[16] we perceive an undisputed confusion in rudimentary ideas that throws the system into a labyrinth of a multitude of particular facts, a quite singular fault for a man who had taken courses in philosophy, jurisprudence, and mathematics in Germany.

The two primary chords of Reicha's classification are the perfect major chord and the minor. The third is a perfect diminished chord (third and fifth minor), which he makes a dissonant chord. In this respect, with the classification of isolated chords, he differs from the other authors of harmonic systems who

---

[15]The thirteen chords are grouped into three classifications: (1) triads, (2) seventh chords, and (3) ninth chords. Those chords that are the products of alteration include $\begin{smallmatrix} +6 \\ 5 \\ 3 \end{smallmatrix}$ $\begin{smallmatrix} +6 \\ 4 \\ 3 \end{smallmatrix}$ $\begin{smallmatrix} 7 \\ +5 \end{smallmatrix}$ $\begin{smallmatrix} +5 \\ 3 \end{smallmatrix}$.

Only the major and minor chords were classified as consonant chords by Reicha ("the others are more or less dissonant"), the "fundamental" chords included the major, minor, and diminished triads; four types of seventh chords (the fully-diminished seventh is excluded), and the dominant ninth chords. (Reicha, *Cours de Composition*, 9.)

[16][Anton Joseph Reicha], *Cours de composition musicale, ou Traité complet et raisonné d'harmonique pratique* (Paris: Gambaro, n.d.)

recognized as dissonances only the sounds that clash by seconds, or in their inversions and doublings, of the seventh and ninth. What induces Reicha to classify this chord among the dissonant ones is that, as a result of the very construction of the diminished (minor) fifth interval, there is a kind of attraction between the two sounds that compose this interval.[17] But he ought to have seen that this attraction is not so overbearing that it vanishes in a succeeding modulation to this chord, which does not take place with respect to true dissonance, unless it takes the characteristic of the leading tone enharmonically. The fourth chord of the classification is that of the augmented fifth. But here the confusion of the author's ideas about the system already appears, because in the chapter where he deals with this chord, he admits that this is only a perfect major chord with an altered fifth.[18]

The fifth chord is that of the dominant seventh, which he calls the "first kind." Then comes the sixth chord, which is this chord of the minor seventh with a minor third, the object of so many errors by all the harmonists. Reicha gives it the name of the seventh of the "second kind," and restricts himself to saying that this chord ". . . is employed primarily on the second degree of the major scale" (36), with no more concern about its original formation than that of the other chords.[19]

The seventh with the minor fifth, called the "third kind" by Reicha, and the major seventh or the fourth kind, the major ninth and

---

[17]Since Reicha defined consonance as ". . . the intervals that produce an agreeable and sweet sensation for us, the effect of which leaves nothing to be desired," the diminished fifth has to be classified as a dissonance (Ibid., 7).

[18]Fétis has distorted Reicha's statement. Reicha wrote that the alteration of the fifth made the chord dissonant. Thus, the alteration and resultant dissonance automatically preclude the inclusion of the augmented triad in the classification of consonant chords. Reicha called the augmented triad the "first altered chord," and he stipulated that (1) the augmented triad can occur only in the major mode on the tonic or dominant if the key has been well established; and (2) that the augmented triad usually resolves to the perfect major chord a perfect fifth below. (He cites one exception—V^+ to V^6/vi.) In four of Reicha's five examples, the augmented triad arises from a chromatic passing tone. (Ibid., 44.)

[19]Reicha included a footnote to this sentence which said, "One also finds it on the third and sixth degree of the same scale." (Ibid., 36.)

the minor ninth are regarded equally as primary chords of the same rank by him.[20] Although chords 11, 12, and 13 are only alterations of chords derived from the augmented sixth (with a fifth and with a fourth) and the dominant seventh chord (with an augmented fifth), he places them, nevertheless, in his fundamental classification.[21]

Such is the system that was very popular among some artists in Paris, because the professor who had invented it lived down its shortcomings in the explanations and practical applications that he gave to his students. But that is, all the same, the least rational theory that it might be possible to conceive, and the most deplorable return to the flagrant empiricism of the early methods at the beginning of the eighteenth century. This system annuled the good that Catel's method had done in France and reopened the door for a multitude a false theories that have been produced in this country and elsewhere for some years. All the more dangerous because this system was supported by a name justly esteemed in other parts of the art, it again called into question what was decided by the authority of intellect and experience; and it formed partisans who declared it a genius' conception, while actually it could have led to the destruction of the science if it had not found in its path a theory both scientific and experimental, of which I will speak shortly, and which averted the harm that Reicha's false system could have produced.

[20]The seventh chords of the second, third, and fourth kind need preparation. The first kind (dominant seventh) may be taken without preparation because this seventh chord determines the tonic and is ". . . the most pleasant of the dissonant chords *after the diminished chord*." (Ibid., 34.) With all of the seventh chords, Reicha specifies the mode and the scale degree on which it can occur. The half-diminished seventh is restricted to the second degree in minor (37), and the major-major seventh occurs "ordinarily on the sixth degree of a minor scale, or on the fourth degree of a major scale" (38).

Reicha explains that each type of ninth chord occurs on the dominant, but "almost always without its principal note," and, to avoid any confusion between the seventh chord of the third type (half-diminished) and the incomplete ninth, Reicha gives a comparative chart of the two chords. As for the incomplete Mmm9 chord, Reicha states (43) that "it is called a diminished seventh chord."

[21]It is quite astounding that Fétis had nothing to say about Reicha's assertion that this altered dominant seventh chord can occur "on the tonic or on the dominant of a major key" in root position, and in first and third inversions. (Ibid., 45.)

Catel's and Reicha's systems first attracted my attention amid those that France has known in the first twenty years of the nineteenth century, because these are the ones that were most successful. I still must speak about some attempts made about the same time, in order to challenge the adoption of other systems that, although announced with more ambitious pretensions, have not had the same repercussion.

The first of these systems, in the order of dates, is the one that its author, de Momigny, set forth in a book called *Cours complet d'harmonie et de composition d'après une théorie neuve et générale de la musique, basée sur les principes incontestables puisés dans la nature, d'accord avec tous les bons ouvrages pratiques anciens et modernes, et mis par leur clarté à la portée de tout le monde* (3 vols.; Paris: The author, 1806).[22] Since then, and until 1834, de Momigny reproduced or explained his system in polemic writings where he treated his adversaries haughtily,[23] and in various works[24] that have not been popularly received.

---

[22]Momigny, as printer and publisher, released his *Cours complet* in installments during 1803–05. He reissued the treatise in 1806 and 1808 with no substantive changes. See Ian Bent, "*Momigny's Type de la Musique and a Treatise in the Making,*" in *Music, Theory and the Exploration of the Past*, eds. Christopher Hatch and David W. Bernstein (Chicago: University of Chicago Press, 1993), 309–40.

[23]When Alexandre-Jean Morel (1776–1825), a mathematics professor and amateur musician who believed that the principle for perceiving tonality resided in the structure of the ear, published his *Observations sur la seule vraie théorie de la musique, de M. de Momigny* (Paris: Bachelier, 1822), de Momigny replied that he was being presented with "another affront as the author of the only true theory of music" because he had failed to mention Morel in his work and did not base his "theory of music on the structure of the ear and the various contractions of the nerves." Momigny contended that despite "cowardly and vile intrigues," his theory would triumph over the "odious detractors." (J.-J. de Momigny, *Réponse. Aux observations de M. Morel, ou à ses attaques contre la seule vraie Théorie de la Musique, ouvrage de M. de Momigny* [Paris: Hocquet, n.d.], 1–2.)

[24]Jérôme-Joseph de Momigny, *La seule vraie théorie de la musique, utile à ceux qui excellent dans cet art, comme à ceux qui en sont aux premiers élémens*, . . . (Paris: [The Author], 1821).

    Encyclopédie méthodique. Musique publiée par MM. Framery, Ginguené et de Momigny. (2 vols.; Paris, 1791–1818).

    Cours général de musique, de piano, d'harmonie et de composition depuis A jusqu' à Z, pour les élèves, quelle que soit leur infériorité, et pour tous les musiciens du monde, quelle que soit leur supériorité réelle; . . . (Paris: The Author, 1834).

Starting from the point of view of Levens, Ballière, Jamard, and Sorge for the pursuit of the bases of scale construction, de Momigny, following the arithmetic progression, finds them in the divisions of a sonorous string, which gives the resultant scale: *c, d, e, f, g, a, b-flat*.[25] But, since this scale does not conform to that of the music of modern Europeans, and since *b-natural* is found only in the fifteenth division of the string, de Momigny, in lieu of adopting an eight-note scale with *b-natural* and *b-flat*,[26] like Levens and his imitators, dreams up the idea of not considering the string as a tonic, but as a dominant; hence his scale is *g, a, b, c, d, e, f*. He enumerates at length the advantages that result from the position of the tonic in the middle of the scale, ". . . as the sun at the center of our planetary system" [26]. For example, find the two semitones in the seven notes without resorting to the repetition of the first at the octave, divide the scale into two just fourths, and have the semitones in the same place in these fourths. One of de Momigny's most severe objections against the scale form commencing on tonic rests on the major fourth or *tritone*, which is created between the fourth and seventh note, not noticing that it is precisely this relationship that is basic to tonality, and that leads to the final conclusion of all melody and all harmony.

The divisions of the string, considered as a dominant, led de Momigny to the same harmonic results that Catel had obtained with the same means. But whatever his pretensions in this regard may be, he states them with a great deal less clarity. In this way, like Catel, he arrives at the formation of the perfect chords and of those of the dominant seventh and leading-tone seventh, which he considers the sole natural chords. As for the others, in lieu of explaining what devices create them, he declares them "chords that are not," and names them "discords in major" and "discords in minor," in such a way that the exact analysis of a harmony devised from many prolon-

---

[25]Momigny, following the arithmetic progression, begins on G1 and extends the progression to the fourteenth term, F5; the resultant scale is "the true scale," because (1) it is given by nature, (2) the two tetrachords of which it is composed (G4 to C5, and C5 to F5) are regular and symmetrical, and (3) tonic (C5) is in the center of the tetrachords. (Momigny, *Cours complet d'harmonie*, 26.)

[26]de Momigny rejects an eight-note scale with *b-flat* and *b-natural*, because ". . . this would demand that we admit a part of the chromatic genre into the diatonic genre" (Ibid., 27).

gations that are joined with alterations of different kinds would be impossible for anyone who had read only de Momigny's fastidious explanations. Moreover, nearly all of the examples that he gives of the use of chords are poorly written and prove that this author had only confused notions about harmonic use.

If de Momigny's pretensions at originality are duly examined, one must admit that he borrowed the arithmetic progression from Levens, Ballière, and Jamard; the transfer of his fundamental tone of the scale to the dominant from Sorge; the division of this string from Catel in order to arrive at the primary harmony; the combinations of thirds for the formation of the natural chords from Langlé, and the progressions of fourths and fifths for the formation of scales from Abbé Roussier. A few insights that are quite sound about the measure and rhythm,[27] and a pretentious phraseology arising from neologism are really all that belongs to the one who raised his voice so high for thirty years in favor of a system rejected by musicians.

At this point I do not believe that I have to examine the efforts made by Rey, an opera musician,[28] and his namesake[29] to re-establish the system of fundamental bass some years after the publication of Catel's book. Barren efforts could not revive a theory whose mission had ceased. I will observe the same silence towards a pretended *Théorie musicale* conceived by Emy-de-Lylette,[30] an ill-

---

[27]In his *Cours complet d'harmonie*, de Momigny states that "the measure is one of the greatest mysteries of music" (408). He suggests that when musicians have called the downbeat the first beat, they "are speaking according to their eyes and not from their *tact*, their judgement, or their ear" because ". . . they believe that a measure is confined between two barlines" (409–10). Working from the premise that musical units proceed from the upbeat to the downbeat, de Momigny propounds that simple duple meter should be counted as 1 | 2 1 | 2 1 | 2, etc.; simple triple meter should be either 1 2 | 3 1 2 | 3 etc. or 1 | 2 3 1 | 2 3 1 | 2 3, etc., because the segmentation of each *proposition musicale* occurs more naturally before the anacrusis.

[28][Jean-Baptiste Rey], *Exposition élmentaire de l'harmonie. Théorie générale des accords d'après la basse fondamentale*, . . . (Paris: [The Author and Naderman], 1807).

[29]*V. F. S. Rey, L'art de la musique théori-physico-practique générale et élémentaire, ou exposition des bases et des développements du système de la musique* (Paris: [Godefroy], 1806).

[30][Antoine-Ferdinand Emy-de-Lylette], *Théorie musicale, contenant la démonstration méthodique de la musique, à partir des premiers éléments de cet art jusques et compris la science de l'harmonie* (Paris, 1810).

digested extract of Lirou's ideas, and no less defective in its applications than in its systematic conception. There is more merit in the book that G. L. Chrétien published with the title *La musique étudiée comme science naturelle, certaine, et comme art.*[31] This book is also a sort of regeneration of Rameau's system, but considered from a new point of view.[32] According to Chrétien's ideas, all music resides in the phenomenon that expresses the perfect major chord in the resonance of certain sonorous bodies. All of the theories based on the divisions of the monochord and on the calculations of geometricians for the ratios of intervals are false, he says, *because the monochord and calculations can only have a force of inertia and not a generating force.* The monochord and calculations can serve to measure and to verify the justness of intervals, but they would not know how to generate either a scale or a harmony (42). Observe this thought whose correctness in incontestable, and which can be considered new, although it is only a positive expression of the vague theory of the Aristoxenians. Unfortunately, it does not lead Chrétien toward the consideration of the metaphysical origin of this scale and this harmony, the object of his quests. His enthusiasm for the phenomenon of harmonic resonance does not permit him to see that this phenomenon cannot be more than the division of a string, the principal generator of tonality. Moreover, the way this theoretician pursues an argument is not very demonstrative, because it is almost always restricted to affirmations. He says,

> I *affirm* that from this point of view [that of his theory], quantity of precepts and doctrines, which seemed unintelligible, acquire a lustre that was largely found overshadowed (9).

> They [the geometric theoreticians] have meant the truth; I love to believe it, but many have deceived themselves, I *affirm* (13).

> I *affirm* that this natural and inspiring way that he [Rameau] called the resonance of the sonorous body, and which I call the phenomenon of harmony, at all times was the unseen cause of music itself, and that

[31]Paris: [The Author and L.-G. Michaud], 1811. A volume of text and a *cahier* of plates with a mobile clavier.

[32]In the editor's note, Chrétien states that his work is "purely elementary . . . and the fruit of forty years of work" (n.p.).

it is the sole foundation on which musicians ought to turn their attention (40). [Fétis' italics.]

Let us examine what arises from all of Chrétien's affirmations.

There is only one chord, the perfect major chord, produced by the harmonic phenomenon. *The perfect minor chord is created by analogy with this unique chord by lowering, with the consent of the ear, the third a semitone.*

The perfect major chord, *dissonant* with the seventh, produces the dominant seventh chord.

The perfect minor chord, *dissonant* with the seventh, generates the seventh on the second degree.

The perfect major chord, *dissonant* with the sixth, produces the six-five chord on the fourth degree (fundamental according to Rameau's system).

The perfect minor chord, *dissonant* with the sixth, produces the six-five chord of the minor mode.

Every interval of a semitone holds the place of a tone and represents it. It is thus that the dominant seventh, derived from the dissonance added to the perfect major chord, its lower note being altered, gives rise to the "diminished seventh" chord, which represents it. It is thus that all the harmonies of the preceding six chords are formed, regardless of the aspect in which they appear.

It is regrettable that with his love for the harmony given by nature, Chrétien did not learn that there are sonorous bodies that utter, in the midst of all their tunings, the perfect minor chord; that there are others that give the constitutive interval of the dominant harmony, and even the altered harmonies. With this help he might have greatly simplified his theory.

However that may be, in the state where he left it, in nature there is only the perfect major chord. But the perfect major chord (*c, e, g*) gives only three notes of the scale, and Chrétien taught us that we have to find the diatonic scale in the resources that nature gives us. This difficulty did not stop him for long, because needing the perfect major chord of tonic, that of the fourth degree, and that of the dominant to form his consonant and dissonant harmonies, he simply takes three sonorous bodies of which one gives him *c, e, g*, another *f, a, c*, and a third *g, b, d; voilà, c, d, e, f, g, a, b, c*.[33] After so simple a thing, he has only to *affirm* that a minor third is included in the resonance of a perfect major chord, since in *f, a, c* the third *a, c* is found. It is necessary only to add the fifth *e*, originating from the perfect chord *c, e, g* to have the perfect minor chord, and, consequently, to find the types of major and minor modes in these combinations. Such are the results at which one can arrive with a strong faith in any one fact, proven or only perceived.

Choron is one of the French musicians who, with the greatest perseverance, turned his attention to the theory of harmony. Yet I cannot attribute any particular theory to him because his opinions have been in incessant fluctuation from the publication of his *Principes d'accompagnement des écoles d'Italie*[34] to his *Manuel de musique*,[35] namely in the space of thirty years. Canceling in his *Principes de composition des écoles d'Italie*[36] what he had done in his preceding work, establishing there an eclectic doctrine that seems to be his last word, then adopting Albrechtsberger's method, in which, nevertheless, he harshly criticized the details in the notes of his translation. Next, becoming enthusiastic for a new theory that he thought he had discovered, abandoning it before the impression of his work was complete and stopping its publication. Finally, returning to Marpurg's false theory towards the end of this life, and making it the basis for his *Manuel de musique*, although he also made a stinging critique of the details of this doctrine in multiple and extended notes.[37] Such was Choron's career in the theory of harmony. Doubt tormented his mind with respect to the

[33]Chrétien does not "simply take three sonorous bodies." Like de Lirou and Rameau, he generates them from a fifth, ". . . the *basic interval* of perfect chords" (76). Thus, the fundamental note of the perfect major chord *c, e, g* is the generator of the perfect chord *g, b, d*, and the fifth of the perfect chord *f, a, c* (76–79). With this manipulation of sounds, Rameau, de Lirou and Chrétien destroy *c* as tonic: when a perfect fifth (*f*) is added below the tonic (*c*), the *f* becomes the generator of the series of fifths.

[34]Paris: [Imbault], 1804.

[34][Alexandre-Étienne Choron], *Nouveau manuel complet de musique vocale et instrumentale, ou encyclopédie*, 6 vols. (Paris, 1836–38), and 2 vols. of examples.

[36]Paris: [le Duc], 1808.

[37]In his various books, Choron published some of the earliest French translations of treatises by Albrechtsberger, Marpurg, and Martini.

existence of a complete and rational harmonic system, and his works are, in a way, canceled in the history of this science.[38]

With respect to Germany, since the commencement of the sixteenth century, a multitude of methods and writings relative to the theory of harmony is found. But in the midst of the many volumes published on this subject, there is little that merits a place in the history of the progress and divergences of this science, so difficult to coordinate in all its parts, according to a clear principle. Among those that have found some partisans, I will cite only (1) *Les principes d'harmonie*[39] of Schicht, director of Thomasschule in Leipzig [1810-23], in which the dominant of the key is taken as the basis for the perfect major chord *g, b, d*; from the seventh chord *g, b, d, f*, he extracts the perfect diminished chord (*b, d, f*); from the ninth chord *g, b, d, f, a*, he extracts the leading-tone seventh (*b, d, f, a*) and the perfect minor chord (*d, f, a*); from the eleventh chord *g, b, d, f, a, c*, he extracts the minor seventh (*d, f, a, c*); finally, he extracts the major-seventh chord (*f, a, c, e*) from the thirteenth chord *g, b, d, f, a, c, e*. The fortuitous chromatic alteration of the intervals of these chords complete the empirical harmonic system conceived by Schicht.

(2) Still more strange to the conception of a veritable theory of harmony are the books of Preindl,[40] *Kapellmeister* of St. Stephen's Cathedral in Vienna, and of Göroldt,[41] director of music at Quendlinburg. These books, where the chords are all considered individually, can be ranked only in the class of practical manuals.

---

[38]For a précis of *Choron's Principes de composition*, see Byran Simm's article "Choron, Fétis, and the Theory of Tonality" (*JMT* 19/1 [1975]: 112–38). Simms contends that Fétis "derived many details, terms and concepts from Choron" (115). Fétis, on the other hand, stated that Choron left nothing "that had a positive value, either in the history or in the theory of the art and science." ("Mon testament musical," in *RGM* 20 (1853): 363.)

[39][Johann Gottfried Schicht], *Grundregeln der Harmonie und des Verwechslungssystems* (Leipzig: Breitkopf und Härtel, 1812).

[40][Joseph Preindl], *Wiener Tonschule, oder Elementarbuch zum Studium des Generalbasses, des Contrapunkts, der Harmonie-und Fugenlehre*, 2d ed. (Vienna: Haslinger, 1832).

[41][Johann Heinrich Göroldt], *Gründlicher Unterricht im Generalbasse und in der Composition oder, deutliche Erklärung von den Tönen, Tonarten, Intervallen, Accorden, Harmonien und Melodien*, 2 vols. (Quendlinburg & Leipzig: [Ernest], 1832).

(3) It is not the same with the *Traité élémentaire d'harmonie*[42] of Friedrich Schneider, today *Kappellmeister* in Dessau and a distinguished composer. Now, there is a theory, a false theory to tell the truth, whose origin is found in the books of Vogler, and which Gottfried Weber had developed previously in the work which will be spoken about presently. According to the fundamental principle of this doctrine, the perfect chord and the seventh chord are made on each of the notes of the scale where they occur. As for the nature of their intervals, they conform to the construction of the key and mode, having, because of the note where they are placed, either a major or minor third, either a just or diminished (minor) fifth, either a major or minor seventh. It is the same for the ninth chord, and it is only a question, in order to complete the nomenclature of the chords, of altering the various intervals.

I have just mentioned the name Gottfried Weber, whose system caused considerable stir in Germany for about fifteen years, and which has been nearly abandoned today. The work, which he published in 1817, has *Essai d'une théorie systématique de la composition*[43] for a title, and its success was such that it was necessary to make other editions in a few years.[44] We have just seen from what angle the chords are reckoned, but what distinguishes Weber's book from all of those of the same genre is the care that the author himself takes to damage confidence in this theory, and in every other one, declaring that he does not believe in the existence of a system with which all the facts of harmonic experience would agree, so that, according to him, the best work concerning harmony is that which contains the largest number of these facts in the analysis.[45] Thus he devoted himself to extending

---

[42][Johann Christian Friedrich Schneider], *Elementarbuch der Harmonie und Tonsetzkunst* (Leipzig: Peters, 1820; 2d ed., Leipzig: Peters, 1827).

[43]*Versuch einer geordneten Theorie der Tonsetzkunst*, 3 vols. (Mainz: Schott, 1817[–21]).

[44]A second edition, which appeared in 1824, was followed by a third edition in 1830–32.

[45]Weber, who believed that the musical art was not suited for a systematic establishment, labeled this theory *geordneten* to avoid ". . . the pompous title of system." Moreover, Weber contended that any "system" that had to resort to categories called "exceptions, liberties, licenses, ellipses, etc." to explain incongruent phenomena was very pretentious and rendered wholly vulnerable. (Weber, *Versuch*

as much as possible this analysis in this book.[45][6] This savant did not notice that his thesis took the science back to what it was in Heinichen's and Mattheson's time, and that by thus undermining his readers' faith in the possibility of a scientific principle, he was destroying the science itself. What would science be if it were only composed of isolated facts from which it would be impossible to establish methodical concatenation? Unquestionably it is Weber's pretention to deny the possibility of a rational theory that brought the premature renunciation of his own, and the swift reaction that took the Germans from admiration for this system to indifference.[47]

Now this long analysis of what has been done since the commencement of the sixteenth century for the creation of a science of harmony, and especially since Rameau had laid its foundation, should end. In summarizing the science of harmony, we find that all the systems have one of the following six methods for a principle: (1)

---

einer geordneten Theorie der Tonkunst 4 vols. [2d ed.; Mainz: Schott, 1824], 1:xiii–iv.) When Fétis reviewed the 3d edition of Weber's treatise in 1832 (RM 12:116–19) and again in 1839 (RGM 6:209–12, 219–21), he stated that since the treatise was not a "system," it should have been called a *Collection of Analytical Observations Concerning Various Parts of Music.* However, he continued, a treatise "that really contained everything that is relative to the art of writing in music would form more than twenty volumes." (*RM* 12:118.)

[46]In his preface to the English translation of Weber's theory, James F. Warner contends that "One valuable property peculiar to Weber is the *copious fulness* [sic] *and minute detail* with which he treats his topics. . . . The subjects which he takes up he *treats.* He makes us fully understand them. He leads us all around them, and shows us how they look on every side. If they are buried in rubbish, he clears them of that rubbish . . . ; if they are beset with difficulties, he is sure to notice the fact, and either remove those difficulties or tell us how to estimate them. The effect of all this is to give us clear, well-defined, and practical ideas—a species of knowledge that we can *use.*" (Gottfried Weber, *The Theory of Musical Composition* . . . Translated from the Third, Enlarged and Improved, German Edition, with Notes by James F. Warner of Boston, U.S. Edited, with Additions Drawn from the German Original by John Bishop of Cheltenham, 2 vols. [London: R. Cocks & Co., 1851], 1:vii.)

[47] In both his 1832 and 1839 reviews, Fétis maintained that Weber's second volume was quite good because it contained "many ingenious views from which the science could profit." (*RM* 12:117; *RGM* 6:212.) However, Weber's main contribution was a system of analytical symbols (Mitchell, "A History of Theories," 128). These symbols consisted of using Roman numerals to indicate the root of the chord and its relationship to a tonic. The size of the numerals indicated the quality of the

the harmonic resonance of sonorous bodies, or, more generally, acoustical phenomena of different types; (2) the arithmetic progression determined by the harmonic series of the horn or the trumpet; (3) the triple progression; (4) the division of the dominant monochord according to the arithmetic progression; (5) the arbitrary construction of chords by the addition and subtraction of thirds; (6) finally, the arbitrary placement of certain model chords on all of the degrees of the scale. Thus it is evident that all of these systems more or less derive from sources that are not intimately tied to the music itself, namely, to the art as it appears in its immediate consequences, and that in all the systems it has been necessary, to a certain point, to adjust this art to the strange principle that was given to it.

The only thing that we have not thought of directly is the quest for the principle of harmony in the music itself, namely, in *tonality*. But what is "tonality"? However foolish this question may appear to be, it is, nevertheless, certain that few musicians would be able to answer it satisfactorily. For me, I will say that tonality resides in the order in which the notes of the scale are placed, in their respective distances, and in their harmonic relations. The composition of chords, the circumstances that modify them, and the laws of their succession are the indispensable results of this tonality. Change the order of the sounds, or change their distances, and the majority of these harmonic relationships will be destroyed. For example, try to apply our harmony to the major scale of the Chinese, *f, g, a, b, c, d, e,* to the minor scale of ancient Irish music, *a, b, c, d, e, f-sharp,* or to the incomplete scale of the Scottish highlanders—the successions of this harmony would become unworkable in these tonalities. Indeed, what can we do with a com-

---

triad—upper case for major, lower case for minor, and, for diminished, a superscript o before the lower case numeral. The appendage of 7 after the numeral identified the major seventh and a superscript 7 was used for the minor seventh. Since no harmony could occur on the third degree in minor (2:54), there is no symbol for an augmented triad. In his preface, Weber contended these symbols were stolen by Friedrich Schneider (1820) and Gottlob Werner (*Versuch einer kurzen und deutlichen Darstellung der Harmonielehre* . . . [Leipzig: Hofmeister 1818]) between the publication of his second and third volumes (1818–21). (*Versuch einer geordneten Theorie der Tonkunst,* 2d ed., 1:xv–xvi.) For a discussion of Weber's role in harmonic analysis, see David Beach, "The Origins of Harmonic Analysis," *JMT* 18 (1974): 274–306.

bined harmony such as that of our music in a major scale in which the fourth degree is a semitone higher than in our scale of the same genre and is separated only by a semitone from the fifth note, so that the attraction that, in our harmonic scale, exists between the fourth note and the seventh and composes the dominant harmony, is here between the tonic and the fourth degree and, consequently, makes every final cadence impossible? What can we do with a harmony similar to that of our minor mode in a minor scale in which the sixth degree is a semitone higher than ours, and which does not have the seventh note? It is evident that these things are not made to go together. Irish songs that have been published in collections of national songs are in the major mode, or belong to modern times, which has allowed them to be harmonized as best they can. It is the same for Scottish airs and those of the Gaelic countries, which, moreover, are frequently accompanied at the octave or with a pedal, because their tonal character does not allow the cadential action of our harmony. The strange character that we notice in these songs does not arise from the whim of their composers, but from the scale that they have used.

What I call tonality, then, is the succession of melodic and harmonic facts that arise from the disposition of the distances of tones of our major and minor scales. If one of these distances were inverted, the tonality would assume another character, and entirely different facts would be manifest in the harmony. The immediate consequences of this tonality are (1) to give certain notes a character of rest that does not exist at all in the others, and to place on these notes the terminal points of cadences, i.e., the perfect chord, such as the tonic, the fourth, the fifth, and the sixth degrees. This deprives the third and the seventh degrees of this character of rest, and, consequently, excludes the perfect chord from them. (2) To impose a resolutory attraction to the fourth and seventh degree, which gives the dissonant harmony of the dominant its own character and obliges it to be resolved with a perfect or imperfect cadence, or to be followed by a modulation. There is no middle course for the dominant harmony—it must resolve either in the cadence or in modulation. (3) The rules that forbid the immediate succession of fifths and major thirds are also the result of tonality, because two successions of fifths, ascending or descending, and two major thirds have the disadvantage of putting into immediate contact two tones that have no analogy between them. All of this, I repeat, inevitably derives from the form of the major and minor scales and constitutes what are called *the laws of tonality*.

But, we ask, what is the principle of these scales, and what has dictated the order of their sounds, if it is not the acoustical phenomena and the laws of mathematics? I reply that this principle is purely metaphysical. We form this order and the melodic and harmonic phenomena that flow from it as a result of our conformation and education. This is a fact that exists for us by itself, and independently of any extraneous reason for us. Well then, one would not wish to concede that our instinct sufficed, joined with experience, in order to place the grounds of the enjoyment intended for our intelligence in a scale, and one will search in some unknown acoustical phenomena for the secret reason for this organization of tonality made for our use! Notice that these acoustical facts, initially poorly analyzed, do not have the significance that one thoughtlessly accords them, because, for example, the production of the harmony of the perfect major chord, which one notices in the resonance of certain sonorous bodies, is accompanied by many other weaker resonances. It is the same with regard to certain other bodies that produce other harmonies. Moreover, experience has proven that different modes of vibration accorded to the same bodies give rise to diverse phenomena. Mr. Troupenas has shown (*Revue musicale*, 12:125[-27]) that the tritone interval discovered by Baron Blein in the resonance of a square metal plate struck on one of its corners is only the result of the vibration of this plate in the direction of its diagonal, whereas the vibration in the direction of one of the sides of the plate gives rise to the other phenomena.[48] Let us suppose, in order to give the greatest possible extension to the alleged natural foundation of harmony that in the course of time some acoustical phenomena that give all the possible harmonies for our system are discovered; are we to conclude that these unknown phenomena are the origin of these harmonies found *a priori* by great musicians? Truly, this would be

---

[48]In "Correspondance" (*RM* 12 (1832): 125–27), Troupenas articulates three fundamental mathematical, musical, and acoustical faults of Baron Blein's *Principes de mélodie et d'harmonie déduits de la théorie des vibrations* (Paris: Bachelier, 1832), and in closing Troupenas queries if Blein can avoid the reproach of being a "barbarous musician and an absent-minded geometrician" (127).

an odd encroachment on the action of hidden causes implied by certain sophists upon our determinations, and this would be a rude blow dealt to our philosophic liberty. To be sure, when Monteverdi found the dominant harmony that changed the character of music and constituted our tonality in major and minor modes, always uniform whatever the key may be, the existence of the diagonal vibration of the plate was naught for him, and he was impelled only by his instinct and by certain observations of analogy. His audacious thought did not create the fact, but it discovered it, and the principle that guided him is absolutely metaphysical.

Shall I speak about the acoustical phenomenon of the harmonic series of the horn and the trumpet, which coincides with the arithmetic progression? It furnishes, it is true, the elements of a false scale that is not ours, and we have seen what Levens, Ballière, and Jamard were able to do with it.

Shall I speak about the division of the monochord, by introducing there, at the seventh term, the number acknowledged as necessary by Euler, as Catel and de Momigny have done? It contains the harmony of the natural chords, but by stopping at the latter, one has neither all the notes of the scale, nor the elements of a tonality. In order to obtain these, it would be necessary to extend this division to all the sounds, g, b, d, f, a, c, e, as Schicht has done. But then the natural and artificial chords will be confused, and the rational classification of these chords will no longer exist. Shall I speak of the purely harmonic progression? It provides the exact measure of the unchanging intervals of plainchant, where no interval endowed with attraction exists, but it cannot lead to the formation of a scale. Moreover, even if the acoustical phenomena and mathematics were giving us the elements of our tonality, they would not provide the order in which they must be ranked in order to compose in this tonality; we have seen that this is where the radical difficulty resides.

If it is recognized that these foundations of the system are deceptive, that they have misled all those who have taken them as a point of departure, and that they are powerless to support the edifice of tonality, it is evident that there remains no other principle for the construction of the scale and of tonality than the metaphysical principle; a principle, both subjective and objective, the necessary result of the sensitivity that perceives the relationship of sounds, and the intelligence that measures them and deduces the results. After so many centuries of studies carried out in absolutely opposite directions, one manages to recognize that the Pythagoreans were mistaken in attributing a basis for tonal construction to numbers that does not belong to them. The Aristoxenians were no less mistaken in attributing a faculty of comparison to the ear that it does not have. The ear perceives the sounds; the mind compares their relationships, measures them, and determines the melodic and harmonic conditions of a tonality.

This laid down, the science of harmony is all done, because this science is nothing else than the systematic exposé of art. Tonic appears through the absolute feeling of repose that is felt there, and the dissonant harmony of the dominant puts the finishing touch by giving it this character with its attractive resolution on the consonant harmony of this tonic.

The fourth degree of the scale, the fifth, and the sixth are also recognized as notes of repose through the power of the ending of subordinate cadences with which these notes are provided. Consonant harmony, that is the perfect chord, then also belongs to them. These harmonies conform to the key and the mode, and are major or minor because of the natural state of the notes.

The third and seventh degrees, which are separated only by a semitone from their upper notes and because of this have attractive tendencies, can be considered neither notes of repose nor, consequently, support the harmony of the perfect chord, which has a conclusive character. According to tonal order, they can, therefore, be accompanied only with derived harmonies. The second degree of the scale, able to be the conclusion of cadential activity only in a sequential pattern, has a character only of equivocal repose. Thus it happens that the harmony of the perfect chord does not belong to it in the ascending and descending harmonic series of the scale; this note is accompanied in the same formulas only by a derived harmony.

Of the natural, fundamental chords, there are only the perfect chord and that of the dominant seventh. According to Rameau's beautiful discovery, admitted into all harmonic systems, the other natural harmonies are derived from the former through the inversion of the intervals of the fundamental chords.

With the natural fundamental and derived harmony, all harmonic tonality is established, and the faculty of modulation exists. All the other harmonic groups that can affect the ear are only modifications of these natural chords. On the one hand, these modifications have variety of sensations for their aim; on the other hand, these modifications establish a greater number of relationships among the various keys and modes. The modifications of chords consist of *substitution* of one note for another; the *prolongation* of one note that delays an interval of the chord; the ascending or descending *alteration* of the natural notes of the chords; *substitution coupled with prolongation*; *alteration coupled with substitution*; *alteration coupled with prolongation*; *collective ascending and descending alterations*; the *anticipation* and *passing notes*.

Substitution occurs only in the dominant seventh chord and in its derivatives.[49] The substituted note is *always* the sixth degree, which takes the place of the dominant. Thus, when the seventh chord is written in five parts, namely, *g, b, d, f, g*, if an *a* is substituted in the upper voice for the *g*, i.e, the sixth degree for the dominant, one has the *dominant ninth* chord which, conforming to the mode, is major or minor.[50] If a similar substitution is made in the first inversion (*b, d, f, g*), one has, in the major mode, the leading-tone seventh (*b, d, f, a*) in the major mode, and the diminished seventh (*b, d, f, a-flat*) in the minor mode. It is the same with all of the other inversions. What reveals the analogy of these chords and the origin of their formation is the identify of their use and their tonal resolutions. Indeed, Catel saw this identity and ascertained the fact of substitution of a chord for its analogue, but he did not know the technique of the substituted note. The technique is very important, since it leads to the demonstration

[49]"Derivatives" are chord inversions. For details about substitution, see Fétis' *Traité d'harmonie*, Bk. 2, chap. 5, §§ 117–31, pp. 46–58.

[50]Fétis is vulnerable to the same objection he raised against Catel's origin of the supertonic seventh: he can show it only by writing a five-voice chord.

certain other chords that have been the stumbling block of all the theories.

In the succession of two chords, every note descending or ascending a step can be prolonged into the following chord, where it delays the normal construction.[51] If the prolongation produces a dissonance, it ought to resolve by descending, like every dissonance that is not a leading tone. If the prolongation is a consonance, it effects its movement by ascending. It is thus that a prolongation that delays the octave of the perfect chord produces a nine-five-three chord; that the one that delays the third produces a five-four chord; that the delay of the sixth of the first inversion of the perfect chord produces a seven-three chord; and that that of the sixth of the six-four chord produces the seven-four. It is, moreover, in this way that the delay of the third of the seventh chord gives a seven-five-four chord; that the suspension of the bass note in the first inversion of this chord produces a five-four-two chord; that the retardation of the sixth in the second inversion creates a seven-four-three chord; finally, that the delay of the major fourth in the last inversion of the seventh chord produces a six-five-two chord. Notice that in the seventh chord and in its inversions, it is always the tonic that delays the seventh note. Except for substitution, the delay does not change the destination of the natural chords, and the use of the latter remains exactly the same after the prolongation is resolved.

If the circumstances of substitution are coupled with those of prolongation,[52] one has a nine-seven-four chord for a combined

---

[51]For details, see Fétis, *Traité d'harmonie*, Bk. 2, chap. 6, §§ 132–52, pp. 59–76.
[52]Ibid., chap. 7, §§ 153–60, pp. 77–89.

1. Natural harmony   2. Substitution

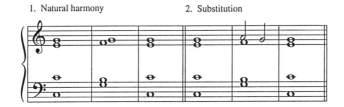

(cont. next page)

modification of the dominant seventh chord.[53] For that of the first inversion, a six-four-two chord; for that of the second inversion, a chord of the minor third, fifth, and minor seventh; finally, for that of the last inversion, a six-five-three chord. These combined modifications do not change the destination of natural chords; this destination remains the same as the resolution of the modifications. Thus such is the origin of these seventh chords of the second degree, of the fifth and sixth, etc., an origin that has been the stumbling block of all harmonic theories because their authors did not know the technique of substitution and the collective modifications of chords.

Every ascending or descending note of a whole tone in the succession of two chords can be altered a semitone. The ascending alterations can be made with the addition of a sharp or by the cancellation of a flat; every descending alteration can be effected by the addition of a flat or the cancellation of a sharp. Each note affected by an ascending alteration assumes the character of an incidental leading tone and inevitably is resolved by rising.

The alterations produce an immense quantity of modifications of natural chords and are combined with simple substitution, prolongation and substitution coupled with prolongation.[54]

The ascending and descending alterations can be prolonged into the succession of two chords.[55] When the prolongation is that of an ascending alteration, it ought to be resolved by ascending, al-

(Footnote 52, cont.)

3. Prolongation   4. Substitution coupled
                                  with prolongation.

[53]Fétis provides this illustration of the concept of substitution and prolongation on p. 77 of his *Traité d'harmonie*. (continued, next page)

[54]For details, see *Traité d'harmonie*, Bk. 2, chap. 8, §§ 161–83, pp. 89–10

[55]Ibid., chap. 9, §§ 184–98, pp. 104–12.

though dissonant, because the attractive character resulting from that of the incidental leading tone absorbs that of the dissonance.[56]

From these complex modifications of the natural chords, some multiple affinities result, which put all of the keys and their modes in touch, and they fulfill the last period of the development of harmony that I have called *ordre omnitonique* and provide the solution for this problem: *A note being given, find the combinations and harmonic formulas such that it can be resolved into all the keys and their various modes.* They also generate a large number of new chords not yet used by the composers, and whose form, destination, and usage I have determined *a priori*, by analysis.

The anticipation is a device by which one hears in a chord one of the notes of the chord that ought to follow it. This device is always melodic, because it is the melodious part that uses it.

Passing notes are those that, too rapid or of too little meaning in the shape of the melody or the accompaniment for each to have a particular harmony, are, nevertheless, necessary for the completion of these shapes. The ear accepts the use of these particular harmonic expletives provided their movement takes place by conjunct pitches when they are foreign to the chords.[57]

There are harmonic formulas called "progressions" or "sequences," because the bass makes a series of similar movements, such as to rise a second and descend a third, rise a fourth and descend a fifth, etc. In these progressions, the same chords that accompanied

---

[56]This example of the prolongation of altered notes is given on p. 105 of the *Traité d'harmonie*.

[57]In his *Traité d'harmonie*, Fétis explained that passing notes are those that "... are found on the weak parts of the beats of the measure." Those embellishing notes that occur on the strong beat or the strong part of the beat are appoggiaturas (Bk. 2, chap. 10, § 202, p. 114).

the pattern are placed on each completed movement of bass notes.[58] There are some of these progressions that modulate with each completed movement; there are others that do not modulate. In the latter, the mind suspends any idea of tonality and conclusion until the final cadence; the ear being occupied only with the analogy of movement, the scale degrees lose their tonal character. It follows that, in these non-modulating progressions, any one of the chords can be placed on any one of the notes. Thus in a progression that rises a second and descends a third, one will alternately put the perfect chord and the chord of the sixth on each of the notes; whence it will occur that the perfect chord, being placed on the seventh chord, will have a minor fifth. In this way, moreover, in a progression rising the fourth and descending the fifth (beginning with the seventh chord on the dominant), one will place the seventh chord on each of the degrees, and from this similarity of movements and of harmony it will come to pass that the chord that it concerns will be composed of the major third, just fifth, and major seventh on the fourth degree and on the tonic; of the minor third, just fifth, and minor seventh on the third degree and the sixth. Such is the origin of Vogler's, Weber's, and Schneider's theory, which placed the perfect chord and the seventh chord on each note of the scale, although actually such a use of these chords would destroy any sense of tonality if it were done anywhere else than in non-modulating progressions, where tonality is actually destroyed until the final cadence.

Having reached this point, the theory of harmony is at the last term of the art and science; it is complete and nothing can be added to it. It is this theory of which I have given the résumé in my *Méthod élémentaire d'harmonie et d'accompagnement*,[59] and of which my large *Traité d'harmonie*[60] contains the developments. Rameau, Sorge, Schröter, Kirnberger, and Catel found the first elements, and I have completed the theory by putting it on a solid base. The fact that it is, at the same time, the history of the progress of the art and the best analysis of the art of composition proves invincibly its excellence.

[58]A "sequence" is a *marches de basse*; each recurrence of the sequential pattern (*modèle*) is a progression.

[59]Paris: 1823; 2d ed., Paris: V. Lemoine, 1840.

[60]Now in press.

APPENDIX A

To the Director of the Revue et Gazette musicale

Sir:

Under the title "Note on a Point of the History of Harmony and Tonality," your issue of 29 November contains an article by Mr. Fétis in which I am sharply attacked. My celebrated compatriot defends his historic doctrines with a completely juvenile ardor; nothing more natural. What has the power to astonish me is that Mr. Fétis gives to understand that my opinions in this matter are dictated by considerations foreign to science. . . . Two times running, there is some mention of I do not know what occult aim that Mr. Fétis knows and that he does not wish to reveal. . . . I state here openly that the meaning of the allusions escapes me altogether. Therefore, I will not concern myself further, unless, however, Mr. Fétis decides to set aside his reservations and insinuations and explain himself clearly.

As for the scientific question, this is a different matter. Although I am loath to enter into an argument with a man whose age and important works inspire me with deep respect, it is my duty to uphold what I believe to be the truth.

Please, sir, do give a place in your gazette to this letter and the note that I have the honor of sending you. And do accept the assurance of my best feelings.

A Note in Reply to That of Fétis

In the intention of its author, this note was destined to refute the ideas that I expressed on the origin of our tonality in a conference of the Society of Composers held a few months ago, and of which the résumé appeared in the *Ménestrel* (issues of 8th, 15th and 22nd November 1868). Actually, my learned contradictor restricts himself to reproducing once more his favorite thesis: "The Invention of the Dominant Seventh Chord by Monteverdi." Although this is only one of the small aspects of the problem that I have dealt with, I accept the debate on the narrow ground that it has pleased Mr. Fétis to choose, and I am going to provide some new proofs in support of the arguments that I am putting forward.

These arguments, according to what Mr. Fétis says, are not new; I know nothing of that. Certainly, his are not new either, and I do not know that he has added an *iota* to them since 1835.

May I be so bold as to state precisely once more the point under discussion?

Is Monteverdi, *yes* or *no*, the oldest composer with whom the dominant seventh can be found in a form other than that of syncopation? Mr. Fétis says *yes*. Other more or less competent musicians say *no* . . . ,[1] and to Mr. Fétis' "affirmation," I offer the following facts:

First objection. The constant use, from the twelfth to the seventeenth century, of the second inversion of the chord in question (*d-f-[g]-b*), with suppression of the fourth (fundamental of the chord). This assimilation is not admitted by my contradictor, who sees in the aggregation *d-f-b* only a simple chord of the sixth *insignificant from the tonal viewpoint*. . . . What! insignificant from the tonal viewpoint, the chord that contains the *tritone*, the famous *diabolus in musica* of the middle ages! Is it not Fétis who writes in his *Traité d'harmonie* (§ 25, p. 9):

> It is remarkable that these *intervals [f-b, b-f] characterize modern tonality* through the energetic tendencies of their two constitutive notes: the leading tone calling the tonic after it, and the fourth degree generally followed by the third.

However that may be, Mr. Fétis finds my argument absolutely absurd, and, in an appeal a little theatrical for the occasion, he asks the musicians *of every country* to witness my ignorance! I suppose that he excludes from his appeal the majority of harmonic theorists who completely agree with me on this point. Among those whom I have at hand, I shall limit myself to citing two Germans: Reicha (*Cours de composition musicale*, 33) and Marx (*Die Lehre von der musikalischen Composition*, 1:141); two Frenchmen: Barbereau (*Traité de composition*, 1:41, 152) and Durutte (*Technie, ou Lois générales du système harmonique*,

---

[1]Illegible printing.

128); finally a Spaniard: Eslava (*Escuela de composicion, Tratado primero*, 43 [Madrid, 1861]). Unfortunately, I do not own any Italian, English, or Russian treatise of harmony, but it is not unreasonable to suppose that I would find still more evidence in favor of my opinion in them.

Second Objection. The existence of the complete dominant seventh chord among contrapuntists and notably Palestrina in his famous motet *Adoramus te Christe*. . . . Here is how Mr. Fétis twists this argument: "Like all of his predecessors, he (Mr. Gevaert) offers me some passages (?) of Palestrina on which I have explained myself twenty times, notably in my *Traité d'harmonie*." I have always read Mr. Fétis' writings eagerly; I know his *Traité d'harmonie* particularly well, but I have been unable to find anywhere a commentary on the passage in question.[2] I would be curious, I admit, to see this succession explained with only the technique of *syncope* or *ligature* in the meaning of the early contrapuntists.

Palestrina's example is the only one, moreover, that I have cited for the period of classical counterpoint. I could have added some others; I even could have cited a host of examples where this famous chord is complicated (according to Mr. Fétis' theory) by a "substitution" and a "prolongation." But it was not part of my plan to examine all the compositions of the middle ages in order to verify a fact really of secondary importance in my opinion.

I am arriving at my *third and last objection*, which I am reproducing verbatim to avoid all ambiguity.

> If one raised the objection that it concerns the use of the dominant seventh for *the condition directly and immediately preceding tonal repose*, we would respond that, even in this respect, Monteverdi cannot lay claim to priority. Actually, this example occurs in the majority of pieces in the *Nouve Musiche* (I have found it in more than twenty-five places), and notably in one of the oldest monodies of Caccini, the madrigal "Dovrò dunque morire," unquestionably composed before 1598.

---

[2]Although Fétis does cite some passages from Palestrina in his *Traité d'harmonie*, he makes no mention of this specific motet.

Mr. Fétis does not absolutely contest my date (I established it in my *Introduction historique*, which opens the first volume of *Gloires de l'Italie*), but he finds the argument worthless for the example in question, because, he says,

> the work from which the madrigal is taken appeared only in 1601, two years after the fifth book of Monteverdi's *Madrigals*. It is true that Caccini says, in his preface for the reader, that he had played these pieces several years earlier in Florence and Rome at the home of friends. But *that created no stir before the publication of the Nuove Musiche.*

One has reason to be astonished by an affirmation expressed in such absolute terms. What! works executed before an audience composed of gentlemen such as [Vincenzo] Galilei [*c*1528-91], [Girolamo] Mei [1519-94], [Ottavio] Rinuccini [1562-1621], [Jacopo] Peri [1561-1633], [Emilio de'] Cavalieri [*c*1550-1602]; would these works, repeated next before all of the city of Florence, the intellectual and artistic center of Italy, have remained unknown to Monteverdi? Does Caccini not expressly say that a long time before the publication of his volume, his madrigals and his airs were continually sung by the most famous Italian singers, and that all the composers had adopted his style? And the publication of *Nuove Musiche*, was it not precisely for the purpose of giving an exact version of these songs that had become altered in passing from hand to hand?

If Mr. Fétis were to doubt the influence exercised on Monteverdi by the Florentine monodists, then he should take the trouble to reread the celebrated letter of Pietro della Valle and some passages from Doni (among others chap. 9 of *Trattato della musica scenica*). He will see what the opinion of the contemporaries was in this respect. And not only did Caccini's compositions cause a sensation in Italy, they penetrated as far as northern Europe. The beautiful melody "Amarilli mia bella" had become popular in Holland in the days of the venerable poet Cats; so that one can be convinced of this, examine one of his chansons composed about 1630 (*Allen de Wercken van Jacob Cats* [Zwolle, 1862], 1:629). The same melody is shown in another Dutch songbook from the same era: Kruels, *Minne-Spieghel der deughden* (Amsterdam, 1640), 5 and 14.

If Caccini's novelties did not provoke the censure of theoreticians at their appearance, it is because of the milieu in which they appeared. The academicians of Florence cared very little for counterpoint, the destroyer of poetry (*laceramento della poesia*), according to them.[3] On the other hand, monody was a genre too much disdained by the *Artusi* for them to take the trouble to pick out the infractions of the established rules from there. . . .

Let there be no misunderstanding about the sense of my words. I do wish to raise altar against altar, to set Caccini against Monteverdi, to disparage the latter to exalt the former. I shall not imitate Mr. Fétis when he says of his hero, "that he was the sole genius from the sixteenth century to the first half of the seventeenth." If worst came to worst, it is a simple matter of personal taste. But yet Mr. Fétis ought to explain to us why he suddenly became so hard on Cavalieri, Frescobaldi, Giovanni Gabrieli, Gumpeltzhaimer, Hans Leo Hassler, Peri; why he withdraws from these illustrious contemporaries of Monteverdi the distinction of "genius," which he bestowed so generously on them in the second edition of his *Biographie universelle*?

How is Pure Gold Changed into Base Lead?

Farther on, we read that "it is to Monteverdi that we owe the first opera presented in the theaters of Venice." Mr. Fétis, however, cannot be unaware that this glory more legitimately belongs to Manelli, [Francesco] Sacrati, [(Pietro) Francesco] Cavalli and [Benedetto] Ferrari, whose operas preceded those of Monteverdi on the Venetian stages (see the catalogs of Ivanovitch and Groppo).

Now, that I have replied nearly line by line to Mr. Fétis' note, let him permit me to address a question to him. Why has he limited himself to an incidental point of my study and been silent about my general conclusions, which contradict much more severely his historic plan than my opinions on the dominant seventh? This silence surprises me all the more because I have carefully repeated these conclusions in the last part of my work.

[3]This remark about *laceramento della poesia* appeared in 1581 in Vincenzo Galilei's *Dialogo della musica antica e della moderna*.

Well then! Would Mr. Fétis find nothing to which to object in these propositions? But then, what happens to the question of Monteverdi? . . . A simple curiosity of a scholar, a small chronological problem.

If, on the contrary, as it is easy to suppose, Mr. Fétis does not abandon his convictions, let him rigorously defend what he calls the "tonality of plainchant," as well as the harmonic and melodic principles on which it is based; let him demonstrate to us that this tonality was not altered in its essential elements from the time of St. Gregory until the eve of the publication of these famous madrigals, and that the modifications that I observe, century by century, are a pure illusion; let him explain (always by the tenets of his system) the gradual fusion of the two major modes of antiquity, the appearance of the leading tone in the *dorius,* and the gradual extinction of the *phrygius,* and the existence of a unique major mode at the beginning of the sixteenth century.

Finally, at the end of sixteen century let him make us see clearly the destructive action of the dominant seventh on this tonality ten times secular, particularly let him not forget to explain to us how this chord, according to him, the "cause," the "direct agent" of the revolution, how, I say, this chord hardly foreseen, disappears almost completely for half a century, just at the moment when its presence is most necessary. When nothing more remains of everything that I have set forth; when my examples will be recognized apocryphals, my assertions unfounded, my conclusions incorrect; when it will indeed be proven that our tonality, this musical atmosphere that we breathe, this mould that was sufficient to contain the thought of a Bach or a Beethoven; when this essentially impersonal thing is the work of a single man, then Mr. Fétis can be justifiably proud at having revealed to the world an unique fact that has no analogies in the annals of the human mind. Then, but only then, it will be interesting to know if humanity ought to salute this new Prometheus named Monteverdi or Caccini.

Until then, let Mr. Fétis be reconciled to see his historic doctrines debated, his assertions inspected, and his hypotheses reduced to their just value.

Far be it from me to give Mr. Fétis a history lesson or to aspire for myself to the title of historian. I only aspire to the more humble role of popularizer. If sometimes I practised dealing with, in modest meetings, some subject having to do with past times of our art, my goal has been only to tell my colleagues all about the *positive* results of the science of our time, to focus their attention on too little-known works. Never have I drawn publicity to these attempts; still less have I sought to provoke polemics.

What I have always had my heart set on is to extricate myself from all bias, set forth only the facts as I have examined them myself; to admit my ignorance on the points that I had not studied sufficiently, to hold the opinions of others in esteem; and above all, never to assume a motive other than simple love of the truth in my contradictors.

F.-A. Gevaert

APPENDIX B

Example 1. de la Halle, Rondeau No. 15, "Tuat con je vivrai," mm. 9-11

Example 2. l'Escurel, "A vous, douce debonniare," mm. 1-2, 15-16, 6

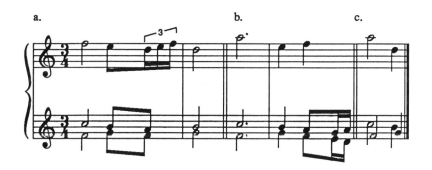

Example 3. Landini, "Non avà ma' pietà," mm. 2-4

Example 4. Dufay, Missa l'Homme Armé, "Kyrie" (trans. Kiesewetter)

BIBLIOGRAPHY
Books

Anonymous. *Refutation des Satyrischen Componistens, oder so genannten Phrynis, dem unpartheyischen Leser zu fernern Nachdencken vorgestellet von denen in aller welt berhmten Patz Tapinsmus,* ... n.p. 1678.

Allen, Warrren Dwight. *Philosophies of Music History.* 1939. Reprint. New York: Dover Publications, 1962.

Arnold, F[ranck] T[homas]. *The Art of Accompaniment from a Thorough-Bass.* 1931. Reprint. New York: Dover Publications, 1965.

Baini, Giuseppe. *Memorie storico-critiche della vita e delle opere di Giovanni Pierluigi da Palestrina,* ... 2 vols. Rome, 1828.

Ballière, Charles-Louis-Dennis. *Théorie de la musique.* Paris: Didot, 1764.

Barbour, J. Murray. *Tuning and Temperament: A Historical Survey.* 2d ed. East Lansing: Michigan State College Press, 1953.

Bemetzreider, Anton. *Nouvel essai sur l'harmonie, Suite de Traité de Musique.* Paris: The Author and Onfroy, 1779.

_____. *Traité de musique, Concernant les Tons, les Harmonies, les Accords et le Discours musical.* 2 vols. Paris: Onfroy, 1776.

Béthizy, Jean-Laurent de. *Exposition de la théorie et de la pratique de la musique, Suivant les nouvelles découvertes.* Paris: M. Lambert, 1754.

Blein, Baron. *Exposé de quelques principes nouveaux sur l'acoustique et la théorie des vibrations, et leur application a plusiers phénomènes de la physique.* Paris: The Author (J. Pinard), 1827.

_____. *Principes de mélodie et d'harmonie déduits de la théorie des vibrations.* Paris: Bachelier, 1832.

Bloom, Peter, ed. *Music in Paris in the Eighteen-Thirties.* Vol. 4 of *Musical Life in 19th-Century France.* Stuyvesant, NY: Pendragon Press, 1987.

Boyvin, Jacques. *Traité abrégé de l'accompagnement pour l'orgue et pour le clavessin.* Paris: Ballard, 1700.

Bridge, Sir [John] Frederick. *Twelve Good Musicians: From John Bull to Henry Purcell.* London: Kegan Paul, Trench, Trubner & Co., Ltd., [1920].

Brossard, Sébastien de. *Dictionaire de musique.* 2d ed. Paris: Ballard, 1705.

Buelow, George J. "Johann David Heinichen, *Der Generalbass in der Composition*: A Critical Study with Annotated Translation of Selected Chapters." Ph.D. diss., New York University, 1961.

_____. *Thorough-Bass Accompaniment according to Johann David Heinichen.* Berkley and Los Angeles: University of California Press, 1966.

Burney, Charles. *A General History of Music from the Earliest Ages to the Present Period (1789).* Ed. Frank Mercer. 2 vols. 1935. Reprint. New York: Dover Publications, 1957.

Cairns, David, trans. *A Life of Love and Music: The Memoirs of Hector Berlioz 1803-1865.* London: The Folio Society, 1987.

Campion, François. *Traité d'accompagement et de composition, selon la règle des octaves.* 1716. Reprint. Geneva: Minkoff, 1976.

Catel, Charles-Simon. *Traité d'harmonie adopté par le Conservatoire, pour servir à l'étude dans cet établissement.* Paris: Mme Le Roy, n.d.

Cavalieri, Emilio de'. *Rappresentatione di anima, et di corpo.* Rome: Nicolò Mutij, 1600.

de Chabanon. *Observations sur la musique, et principalment sur la métaphysique de l'art.* Paris: Michel-Paul Guy, 1779.

Chrétien, G-.L. *La musique étudiée comme science naturelle, certaine, et comme art, ou grammaire et dictionnaire musicale* Paris: The Author and L.-G. Michaud, 1811.

Couperin, François. "Règle pour l'accompagnement" in *Œuvres complète.* Vol. I. Paris: Éditions de l'Oiseau Lyre, 1933.

Coussemaker. *L'Art harmonique aux xiie et xiiie siècles.* Paris: A. Durand and V. Didrot, 1865.

_____. *Histoire de l'harmonie du moyen-âge.* Paris: V. Didron, 1852.

_____. *Les Harmonistes des xiie et xiiie siècles.* Lille, 1864.

_____. *Œuvres complètes du trouvère Adam de la Halle.* Paris, 1872.

_____. *Scriptorum de musica medii aevi.* 4 vols. Paris: Durand, 1864-76.

_____. *Traités inédits sur la musique du moyen age.* Lille, 1867.

Chrétien, G. L. *La musique étudiée comme science naturelle, certaine, et come art.* Paris: The Author and L.-G. Mihaud, 1811.

Crüger, Johann. *Synopsis musica continens 1. Methodum, concentum harmonicum purè & artificiosè constituendi:* .... Berlin: The Author and C. Rungi, 1634.

Dahlhaus, Carl. *Studies on the Origin of Harmonic Tonality.* Trans. Robert O. Gjerdingen. Princeton: Princeton University Press, 1990.

Dandrieu, Jean-François. *Principes de l'acompagnement [sic] du clavecin.* Paris: The Author, 1719.

Daube, Johann Friedrich. *Generalbaß in drey Accorden, gegründet in den Regeln der alt-und neunen Autoren,* ... Leipzig: A. B. Andrä, 1756.

Descartes, René. *Compendium musicae.* Utrecht: Trajecti ad Rhenum, 1650.

_____. *Compendium of Music*. Trans. Walter Robert with an Introduction and Notes by Charles Kent. Rome: American Institute of Musicology, 1961.

Desfossez, A., ed. *Document historique sur la priorité des Néerlandais sous le rapport de la science musicale à l'époque de la renaissance, . . .* LaHaye, 1855.

Doni, Giovanni Baptiste. *Lyra Barberina amphichordos accedunt eiusdem opera*. Ed. A. F. Gori and Giovanni Batista Passeri. 2 vols. Florence, 1763.

Drieberg, Friedrich von. *Die praktische Musik der Griechen*. Berlin: Trautwein, 1821.

Dufay, Guillaume. *Opera Omnia*. Ed. Heinrich Besseler. Vol. 3. Rome: American Institute of Musicology, 1951.

Dutrochet, René-Henri-Joachim. *Mémoire dur une nouvelle théorie de l'harmonie, Dans lequel on démontre l'existence de trois modes nouveaux, qui faisaient partie du systême musical des Grecs*. Paris: Allut, 1810.

Earhart, A. Louise Hall. "The Harmonic Theories of Jean-Laurent de Béthizy and Their Relationship to Those of Rameau and d'Alembert." Ph.D. diss., The Ohio State University, 1985.

Euler, Leonard. *Oeuvres complétes en français*. Éditées par l'association des capitaux intellectuels pour favoriser le développement des sciences physiques et mathématiques. 5 vols. Brussels, 1839.

_____. *Tentamen novae musicae musicae ex certissimis harmoniae principiis dilucidae expositae*. St. Petersburg, 1739.

_____. *"Tentamen novae theoriae musicae*. Transation and Commentary by Charles Samuel Smith." Ph.D. diss., Indiana University, 1960.

Fétis, François-Joseph. *Biographie universelle des musiciens et bibliographie générale de la musique*. 8 vols. Bruxelles: Meline, Cans et Compagnie, 1837; 2d ed., Paris: Didot Frères, Fils et Cie, 1860-65.

_____. *Esquisse de l'histoire de l'harmonie, considérée comme art et comme science systématique*. Paris: Bourgogue et Martinet, 1840.

_____. *Manuel des principes de musique, à l'usage des professeurs et d'élèves de toutes les écoles de musique. . . .* Paris: M. Schlesinger [1837].

_____. *Music Explained to the World*. Translated for the Boston Academy of Music. Boston: B. Perkins, 1842. Reprint, with New Introduction by Peter Bloom. New York: Da Capo Press, 1987.

_____. *La musique mise a la portée de tout le monde: Exposé succinct de tout ce qui est nécessaire pour juger de cet art*. 2d ed. Paris: E. Duverger, n.d.

_____. *Tratado completo de la teoría y práctica de la armonía*. Trans. Francisco de Asis Gil. Madrid: Salazar, [1850].

_____. *Trattato completo della teoria e della pratica dell' armonia*. [Trans. M. Mazzucato]. Milan: Ricordi, [1845].

_____. *Trattato completo della teoria e della pratica dell' armonia*. Trans. Emanuele Gambale. Milan: F. Lucca, n.d.

_____. *Traité du contrepoint et de la fugue*. Paris: Troupenas & Cie, 1825.

_____. *Traite complet de la théorie et de la pratique de l'harmonie contenant la doctrine de la science et de l'art*. 7th ed. Paris: G. Brandus and S. Dufour, 1861.

Forkel, J. N. *Allgemeine Geschichte der Musik*. 2 vols. Leipzig: Schwickert, 1801.

Gasparini, Francesco. *L'armonico practico al cimbalo. Regole, Osservazioni, ed Avvertimenti per ben suonare il Basso*, . . . Venice: Bortoli, 1708.

_____. *The Practical Harmonist at the Harpsichord*. Trans. Frank S. Stillings. Ed. David L. Burrows. New Haven: Yale University Press, 1968.

Geminiani, Francesco Saverio. *Guida Armonica o Dizionario Armonico being A Sure Guide to Harmony and Modulation*, . . . Op. 10. London: Printed for the Author by John Johnson, n.d.

_____. *A Supplement to the Guida Armonica, With Examples Shewing its Use in Composition*. London: Printed for the Author by John Johnson, n.d.

Gerbert, Martin, ed. *Scriptores ecclesiastici de musica sacra potissimum*. 3 vols. Typis San-Blaisianis, 1784.

Gevaert, François-Auguste. *Discours pronouncé a l'occasion du centième anniversaire de la naissance de F. J. Fétis*. Gand: C. Annoout-Braeckman, 1884.

_____. *Réponse à M. Fétis, sur l'origine de la tonalité moderne*. Paris: Kugelmann, 1868.

Girdlestone, Cuthbert. *Jean-Philippe Rameau: His Life and Work*. London: Cassell & Co., 1957.

Glareanus, Henricus. *Dodecachordon*. 1547. Reprint. New York: Broude Brothers, 1967.

Gori, A. F. and Giovanni Batista Passeri, ed. *Lyra Barberina amphichordos*. 2 vols. Florence, 1763.

Grave, Floyd K. and Margaret G. Grave. *In Praise of Harmony: The Teachings of Abbé George Joseph Vogler*. Lincoln: University of Nebraska Press, 1987.

Harriss, Ernest C. *Johann Mattheson's* Der vollkommene Capellmeister: *A Revised Translation with Critical Commentary*, Ann Arbor: UMI Research Press, 1981.

Hatch, Christopher, and David W. Bernstein, ed. *Music Theory and the Exploration of the Past.* Chicago: University of Chicago Press, 1993.

Hawkins, Sir John. *General History of the Science and Practice of Music.* 3 vols. London: Novello, Ewer & Co., 1875.

Heinichen, Johann David. *Neu erfundene und gründliche Anweisung, wie ein Music-liebender auff gewisse vortheilhafftige Arth könne zu vollkommener Erlernung des General-Basses, . . .* Hamburg: B. Schiller, 1711.

————. *Der General-Bass in der Composition, oder: Neue und gründliche Anweisung, wie ein Musik-Liebender mit besondern Vortheil, durch die Principia der Composition, . . .* Dresden: The Author, 1728.

Helmholtz, Herman. *On the Sensation of Tone.* Trans. Alexander J. Ellis. 2d ed. New York: Dover Publications, 1954.

Herlinger, Jan W. *The Lucidarium of Marchetto of Padua: A Critical Edition, Translation, and Commentary.* Chicago and London: University of Chicago Press, 1985.

Hindemith, Paul. *The Craft of Musical Composition.* Trans. Arthur Mendel. Book 1. 4th ed. New York: Associated Music Publishers, 1945.

Holder, William. *A Treatise of the Natural Grounds, and Principles of Harmony.* London: W. Pearson, 1731.

Horsley, Imogene. *Fugue: History and Practice.* New York: The Free Press, 1966.

Huys, Bernard; Godelieve Becquart-Robyns, Nicolas Meeùs, Paul Becquart, Paul Hooreman, Paul Raspé, Robert Wangermée. *François-Joseph Fétis et la vie musicale de son temps 1784-1871.* Brussels: Bibliothèque royale Albert Ier, 1972.

Jamard, Canon. *Sur la théorie de la musique.* Paris: Jombert & Mérigot pere & fils; Rouen: Machuel, 1769.

Johnson, Fredric. "Tartini's *Trattato di musica seconda la vera scienza dell' harmonica*: An Annotated Translation with Commentary." Ph.D. diss., Indiana University, 1985.

Keane, Sister Michaela Maria, S.N.J.N. *The Theoretical Writings of Jean-Philippe Rameau.* Washington, D.C.: The Catholic University of America Press, 1961.

Keller, Godfry. *A Compleat Method for Attaining to Play a Thorough Bass, Upon Either Organ, Harpsichord, or Theorbo-Lute. . . .* London: Printed for and Sold by John Cullen, 1707.

Kessel, Johann Christian Bertram. *Unterricht im Generalbasse zum Gebrauche für Lehrer und Lernende.* Leipzig: C. G. Hertel, 1791.

Kiesewetter, R. G. *Geschichte der europäisch-abendländischen oder unsrer heutigen Musik.* Leipzig: Breitkopf and Härtel, 1834.

Kirnberger, Johann. *The Art of Strict Musical Composition.* Trans. David Beach and Jurgen Thym. Introduction and Explanatory Notes by David Beach. New Haven and London: Yale University Press, 1982.

_____. *Die wahren Grundsätze zum Gebrauch der Harmonie, darinn deutlich gezeiget wird, ...* Berlin and Königsberg: G. J. Decker and G. L. Hartung, 1773.

Kollman, August Friedrich Christoph. *An Essay on Musical Harmony, According to the Nature of that science and the Principles of the greatest musical authors.* London: J. Dale, 1796.

Kosar, Anthony Jay. "François-Joseph Fétis' Theory of Chromaticism and Early Nineteenth-Century Music." Ph.D. diss., The Ohio State University, 1984.

Krehbiel, James Woodrow. "Harmonic Principles of Jean-Philippe Rameau and his Contemporaries." Ph.D. diss., Indiana University, 1964.

Krenek, Ernst. *Music Here and Now.* Trans. Barthold Fles. New York: W. W. Norton & Co., 1938.

Lampe, John Frederick. *A Plain and Compendious Method of Teaching Thorough Bass, After the most Rational Manner....* London: For J. Wilcox, 1737.

Langlé, Honoré François-Marie. *Traité d'harmonie et de modulation.* Paris: Cochet, 1797.

Leibnitz, Gottfried Wilhelm. *The Monadology and Other Philosophical Writings.* Ed. Robert Latta. 1898. Reprint. London: Lowe & Brydone, Printers, Ltd., 1951.

Lester, Joel. *Between Modes and Keys: German Theory 1592-1802.* Stuyvesant, NY: Pendragon Press, 1989.

_____. *Compositional Theory in the Eighteenth Century.* Cambridge, Mass. and London: Harvard University Press, 1992.

Levens. *Abregé des regles de l'harmonie, pour aprendre la composition avec Un nouveau projet sur un systême de musique sans tempérament, ni cordes mobiles.* Bordeaux: Jean Chappuis, 1743.

Lirou, Chevalier Jean-François Espic de. *Explication de système de l'harmonie pour abréger l'étude de la composition, et accorder la pratique avec la théorie.* London, 1785.

Loewenberg, Alfred. *Annals of Opera 1597-1940.* 3d ed. Revised and corrected. Totowa, N.J.: Rowan and Littlefield, 1978.

Lowinsky, Edward E. *Tonality and Atonality in Sixteenth-Century Music.* Berkeley and Los Angeles: University of California Press, 1961.

_____. *Secret Chromaticism in the Netherlands Motet*. Translated from the German by Carl Buchman. New York: Columbia University Press, 1946.

Macarry, Pierre. *Questions sur la diversité d'opinions et de doctrines des auteurs didactiques en musique*. Paris: Janet et Cotelle, 1827.

Mailly, Edouard. *Les Origines du Conservatoire Royal de Musique de Bruxelles*. Brussels: Hayez, 1879.

Maret, Hugues. *Elogue historique de Mr Rameau*. Dijon: Causse, 1766.

Marpurg, F. W. *Handbuch bey dem Generalbass und der Composition mit zwey-drey-vier-fünf-sechs-sieben-acht und mehreren Stimmen*. Berlin, 1755-58.

_____. *Historisch-kritische Beyträge zur Aufnahme der Musik*. 5 vols. Berlin: Lange, 1754-60.

_____, ed. *Kritische Briefe über die Tonkunst*. 2 vols. Berlin: F. W. Birnstiel, 1760-63.

Martin, James M., II. "The *Compendium Harmonicum* (1760) of Georg Andreas Sorge (1703-1778): A Translation and Critical Commentary." Ph. D. diss., Catholic University of America, 1981.

Masson, Charles. *Nouveau traité des regles pour la composition de la musique*. 2nd ed. 1699. Reprint. New York: Da Capo Press, 1967.

Mattheson, Johann. *Kleine General-Bass-Schule*. Hamburg: J. C. Kiszner, 1735.

Mercadier, Jean-Baptiste. *Nouveau systême de musique thèorique et pratique*. Paris: Valade, 1776.

Mickelsen, William C., trans. *Hugo Riemann's Theory of Harmony and History of Music Theory, Book III, by Hugo Riemann*. Lincoln and London: University of Nebraska Press, 1977.

Mitchell, John William. "A History of Theories of Functional Harmonic Progression." Ph.D. diss., Indiana University, 1963.

Momigny, Jérôme-Joseph de. *Cours complet d'harmonie et de composition d'après une théorie neuve et générale de la musique, ...* 3 vols. Paris: The Author, 1806.

_____. *Exposé succinct du seul système musical qui soit vraiment fondé et complet*. Paris: The Author, n.d.

_____. *Réponse. Aux observations de M. Morel, ou à ses attaques contᵛe le seule vraie Théorie de la Musique, ouvrage de M. de Momigny*. Paris: Hocquet, n.d.

Monteverdi, Claudio. *Tutte le opere*. Ed. G. Francesco Malipiero. Vol. 3. Vienna: Universal, 1926-42.

Morel, Alexandre-Jean. *Observations sur la seule vraie théorie de la musique, de M. de Momigny.* Paris: Bachelier, 1822.

Nichols, Robert S. "François-Joseph Fétis and the Theory of *Tonalité.*" Ph.D. diss., University of Michigan, 1971.

Niedt, Friedrich Erhard. *The Musical Guide: Parts I (1700/10), 2 (1721), and 3 (1717).* Trans. Pamela L. Poulin and Irmgard C. Taylor. Introduction and Explanatory Notes by Pamela L. Poulin. Oxford: Clarendon Press, 1989.

_____. *Musikalische Handleitung, oder Gründlicher Unterricht. Vermittelst welchen ein Leibhaber der edlen Music in kurzer Zeit sich so weit perfectioniren kan,* . . . Hamburg: Nicolaus Spieringk, 1700.

_____. *Musikalische Handleitung, oder Gründlicher Unterricht. Vermittelst welchen ein Leibhaber der edlen Music in kurzer Zeit sich so weit perfectioniren kan,* . . . Hamburg: B. Schiller, 1710.

_____. *Musikalische Handleitung, zur Variation des General-Basses,* . . . . Hamburg: B. Schiller, 1706.

_____. *Musikalische Handleitung* . . . . Op. posth. Hamburg: B. Schillers Erben, 1717.

Olleson, Edward, ed. *Modern Musical Scholarship.* London: Oriel Press Ltd., 1980.

Osborne, Richard Dale. "The Theoretical Works of Abbé Pierre-Joseph Roussier." Ph.D. diss., Ohio State University, 1966.

Parrish, Carl. *The Notation of Medieval Music.* New York: W. W. Norton & Co., 1957.

Pease, Edward Joseph. "An Edition of the Pixérécourt Manuscript: Paris, Bibliothèque Nationale, Fonds Fr. 15123." 2 vols. Ph.D. diss., Indiana University, 1959.

Pepusch, Johann Christoph (John Christopher). *A Treatise on Harmony: containing The Chief Rules for Composing in Two, Three, and Four Parts.* . . . 2d ed. London: W. Pearson, 1731.

Portmann, Johann Gottlieb. *Leichtes Lehrbuch der Harmonie, Composition und des Generalbasses, zum Gebrauch für Liebhaber der Musik, angehende und fortschreitende Musici und Componisten.* Darmstadt: J. J. Will, 1789.

Printz, Wolfgang. *Declaration oder Weitere erklärung der Refutation des Satyrischen componistens.* n.p. Cosmopolis, 1679.

_____. *Prynis oder Satyrischer Componist.* Quedlinburg: Okcl, 1676-77.

_____. *Pyrnis Mitilenaeus, oder Satyrischer Componist,* . . . Dresden and Leipzig: J. C. Mieth and J. C. Zimmermann, 1696.

Rameau, Jean-Philippe. *Complete Theoretical Writings.* Ed. Erwin R. Jacobi. 6 vols. American Institute of Musicology, 1967-72.

_____. *Démonstration du principe de l'harmonie, servant de base à tout l'art musical théorique et pratique.* Paris: Durand, 1750.

_____. *Génération harmonique, ou Traité de musique théorique et pratique.* Paris: Prault, 1737.

_____. *Nouveau système de musique théorique, où l'on découvre le principe de toutes les règles nécessaires à la pratique, pour servir d'introduction au traité d'harmonie.* Paris: Ballard, 1726.

_____. *Traité de l'harmonie reduite à ses principes naturels, divisé en quatre livres.* Paris: Ballard, 1722.

A Treatise on Harmony. Translated with an Introduction and Notes by Philip Gossett. New York: Dover Publications, 1971.

_____. *A Treatise on Harmony in which the Principles of Accompaniment are fully explained.* Trans. Griffin Jones. London: Longman & Broderip, n.d.

_____. *A Treatise of Music, containing the Principles of Composition.* London: For J. French, n.d.

_____. *A Treatise of Music, containing the Principles of Composition.* London: Robert Brown, 1752.

Reaney, Gilbert. *Répertoire International des Sources Musicales: Manuscripts of Polyphonic Music (c1320-1400).* Munich-Duisburg: G. Henle Verlag, 1969.

_____, ed. *Répertoire International des Sources Musicales: Manuscripts of Polyphonic Music 11th-Early 14th C.* Munich-Duisburg: G. Henle Verlag, 1966.

Reese, Gustav. *Music in the Middle Ages.* New York: W. W. Norton & Co., 1940.

_____. *Music in the Renaissance.* Rev. ed. New York: W. W. Norton & Co., 1959.

Reicha, Antoine (-Joseph). *Cours de composition musicale ou traité complet et raisonné d'harmonie pratique.* Paris: Gambaro, n.d.

Riemann, Hugo. *History of Music Theory, Books I and II.* Trans. Raymond Haggh. Lincoln: University of Nebraska Press, 1962.

Rivera, Benito. *German Music Theory in the Early 17th Century: The Treatises of Johannes Lippius.* Ann Arbor: UMI Research Press, 1980.

Roussier, Abbé Pierre-Joseph. *Lettre de M. l'Abbé Roussier, à l'Auteur de Journal des Beaux-Arts & des Sciences touchant la division zu Zodiaque, ...* Paris, 1771.

_____. *Traité des Accords et de leur succession, selon le système de la basse fondamentale.* Paris: Duchesne, 1764.

_____. *Observations sur différens points d'harmonie.* Geneva and Paris: Bailleux, 1755 [sic].

Sabbatini, Galeazzo. *Regola facile e breve per sonare sopra il Basso continuo nell'Organo, Manacordo, ò altro Simile Stromento.* Venice, 1628.

Sabbatini, Luigi Antonio. *La vera idea delle musicali numeriche segnature diretta al giovane studiosò dell' armonica.* Venice: Valle, 1799.

Saint-Lambert. *A New Treatise on Accompaniment With the Harpsichord, the Organ, and With Other Instruments.* Trans. and ed. John S. Powell. Bloomington and Indianapolis: Indiana University Press, 1991.

_____. *Nouveau traité de l'accompagnement de clavecin, de l'orgue et de quelques autres instruments.* Paris: Ballard, 1707.

Schneider, Friedrich. *Elementarbuch der Harmonie und Tonsetzkunst . . . .* Leipzig: C. F. Peters, 1820.

Schoenberg, Arnold. *Problems of Harmony.* Ed. Merle Armitage. 2d ed. New York: G. Schirmer, Inc. 1937.

Schrade, Leo, ed. *Polyphonic Music of the Fourteenth Century.* Vol. 4. Monaco: Éditions de l'Oiseau-Lyre, 1956-58.

Schröder, Christoph Gottlieb. *Deutliche Anweisung zum Generalbaß, in beständiger Veränderung des uns angebohren harmonischen Dreyklanges mit zulänglichen Exempeln.* Halberstadt: J. H. Groß, 1772.

Searle, Humphrey. *The Music of Liszt.* 2d rev. ed. New York: Dover Publications, 1966.

Seay, Albert, ed. *Johannis Tinctoris Opera Theoretical.* American Institute of Musicology, 1975.

Serre, Jean-Adam. *Essais sur les principes de l'harmonie, ou l'on traité de la Théorie de l'Harmonie en général, . . .* Paris: Prault fils, 1753.

_____. *Observations sur les principes de l'harmonie, occasionnés Par quelques Ecrits modernes sur ce sujet, . . .* Geneva: H. A. Gosse and J. Gosse, 1763.

Sessions, Roger. *Harmonic Practice.* New York: Harcourt, Brace & Co., 1951.

Sheldon, David A. *Marpurg's Thoroughbass and Composition Handbook: A Narrative Translation and Critical Study.* Harmonologia Series no. 2. Stuyvesant NY: Pendragon Press, 1989.

Shirlaw, Matthew. *The Theory of Harmony: An Inquiry into the Natural Principles of Harmony, with an Examination of the Chief Systems from Rameau to the Present Day.* DeKalb, Ill.: Dr. Birchard Coar, 1955.

Sorge, Georg Andreas. *Vorgemach der musicalischen Composition; oder, Ausführliche, ordentliche und vorheutige Praxim hinlängliche Anweisung zum General-Baß. . . .* Lobenstein: The Author, 1745-47.

Stillingfleet, Benjamin. *Principles and Power of Harmony*. London: J. and H. Hughs, 1771.

Stravinsky, Igor. *Poetics of Music in the Form of Six Lessons*. Trans. Arthur Knodel and Ingolf Dahl. 1947. Reprint. New York: Vintage-Knopf, 1956.

Strunk, Oliver. *Source Readings in Music History*. New York: W. W. Norton & Co., 1950.

————. *Essays on Music in the Western World*. New York: W. W. Norton & Co., 1974.

Tartini, Giuseppe. *Traktat über die Musik gemäss der wahren Wissenschaft von der Harmonie*. Übersetz und erläutert von Alfred Rubeli. Düsseldorf: Im Verlag der Gesellschaft zur Förderung der systematischen Musikwissenschaft e. V., 1966.

————. *Trattato di musica secondo la vera scienza dell' armonica*. Padua: Stamperia del Seminario (Giovanni Manfrè), 1754.

Thomson, William Ennis. "A Clarification of the Tonality Concept." Ph.D. diss., Indiana Uinversity, 1952.

Tinctoris, Johannes. *The Art of Counterpoint*. Translated and edited by Albert Seay. American Institute of Musicology, 1961.

————. *Proportions in Music*. Trans. Albert Seay. Colorado Springs: Colorado College Music Press, 1979.

Türk, Daniel Gottlob. *Kurze Anweisung zum Generalbaßspielen*. Halle and Leipzig: The Author, 1791.

————. *Anweisung zum Generalbaßspielen*. 2d ed. 2 vols. Halle and Leipzig: The Author, 1800.

Vallotti, Francesco Antonio. *Della scienza teorica, e pratica della moderna musica*. Padua: Stamperia del Seminario (Giovanni Manfrè), 1779.

Vogler, Abbé [Georg Joseph]. *Tonwissenschaft und Tonsetzkunst*. Mannheim: Kuhrfürstlich Hofdruckerei, 1776.

Wallace, Barbara K. "J. F. Daube's *General-Bass in drey Accorden* (1756): A Translation and Commentary." Ph.D. diss., North Texas State University, 1983.

Wangermée, Robert. *F.-J. Fétis, musicologue et compositeur. Contribution à l'étude du goût musical au XIXe siècle*. Académie royale de Belgique, Classe des Beaux-Arts, Mémoires, 2d Series, vol. 6, no. 4. Brussels: Palais des académies, 1951.

Wason, Robert W. *Viennese Harmonic Theory from Albrechtsberger to Schenker and Schoenberg*. Ann Arbor: UMI Research Press, 1982.

Weber, Gottfried. *The Theory of Musical Composition* . . . . Translated from the Third, Enlarged and Improved, German Edition, with Notes by James F. Warner of Boston, U.S. Edited, with Additions Drawn from the German Original by John Bishop of Cheltenham. 2 vols. London: R. Cocks and Co., 1851.

―――――――. *Versuch einer geordneten Theorie der Tonkunst zum Selbstunterricht.* 4 vols. 2d ed. Mainz: B. Schott, 1824.

Werckmeister, Andreas. *Die nothwendigsten Anmerckungen und Regeln wie der Bassus continuus, oder General-Baß wol könne tractiret werden* . . . . Aschersleben: G. E. Strunze, n.d.

Werner, Johann Gottlob. *Versuch einer kurzen und deutlichen Darstellung der Harmonielehre oder kleine Generalbaßschule für Anfänger und zum Selbstunterricht.* Leipzig: Hofmeister, 1818.

Wilkins, Nigel, trans. and ed. *The Lyric Works of Adam de la Halle (Chansons, Jeux-Partis, Rondeaux, Motets).* American Institute of Musicology, 1967.

―――――――. *The Works of Jehan de Lescurel.* American Institute of Musicology, 1966.

Williams, Peter. *Figured Bass Accompaniment.* 2 vols. Edinburgh: Edinburgh University Press, 1970.

Young, Irwin, trans. and ed. *The Practica Musicae of Franchinus Gaffurius.* Madison: University of Wisconsin Press, 1969.

Zarlino, Gioseffo. *The Art of Counterpoint, Part III of Le Institutioni harmoniche, 1558.* Trans. Guy A. Marco and Claude V. Palisca. New Haven: Yale University Press, 1968.

Articles

Beach, David. "The Origins of Harmonic Analysis." *Journal of Music Theory* 18 (1974): 274-306.

Beach, David W. and Jurgen Thym. *"The True Principles for the Practice of Harmony* by Johann Philipp Kirnberger: A Translation." *Journal of Music Theory 23 (1979): 163-226.*

Bent, Ian. "Momigny's *Type de la Musique* and a Treatise in the Making." In *Music Theory and the Exploration of the Past,* eds. Christopher Hatch and David W. Bernstein, 309–40. Chicago: University of Chicago Press, 1993.

Bent, Margaret. *"Resfacta* and *Cantare Super Librum." Journal of the American Musicological Society* 36 (1983): 371–91.

Bent, Margaret; Lewis Lockwood, and Robert Donington. "Musica Ficta." In *The New Grove Dictionary of Music and Musicians.* Edited by Stanley Sadie. Vol. 12, 802-11. London: MacMillan, 1980.

Bernard, Jonathan W. "The Marpurg-Sorge Controversy." *Music Theory Spectrum* 11 (1989): 164-86.

Besseler, Heinrich. "Franco von Köln." In *Die Musik in Geschichte und Gegenwart*. Edited by Friedrich Blume. Vol. 4, cols. 688-98. Kassel: Bärenreiter und Gegenwart, 1955.

————. "Johannes des Muris." In *Die Musik in Geschichte und Gegenwart*. Edited by Friedrich Blume. Vol. 7, cols. 105-15. Kassel: Bärenreiter-Verlag, 1958.

Birkner, Günter. "Roussier, Pierre-Joseph." In *Die Musik in Geschichte und Gegenwart*. Edited by Friedrich Blume. Vol. 7, cols. 1018-19. Kassel: Bärenreiter-Verlag, 1958.

Bloom, Peter. "A Review of Fétis's *Revue musicale*." In *Music in Paris in the Eighteen-Thirties*, edited by Peter Bloom, 55-79. Stuyvesant, NY: Pendragon Press, 1987.

Buelow, George J. "Printz, Wolfgang Caspar." In *The New Grove Dictionary of Music and Musicians*. Edited by Stanley Sadie. Vol. 15, 274-75. London: MacMillan, 1980.

Burnham, Scott. "Method and Motivation in Hugo Riemann's History of Harmonic Theory." *Music Theory Spectrum* 14 (1992): 1-14.

Castel, Père Louis-Bertrand. "Extrait de la Traité de l'harmonie." *Journal de Trévoux* 20 (1722): 1713-43, 1876-1910.

Ceulemans, Anne-Emmanuelle. "Fétis et les rapports entre l'harmonie et la mélodie." *Revue Belge de Musicologie* 44 (1990): 123-31.

Chailley, Jacques. "Rameau et la théorie musicale." *La Revue Musicale* numéro spécial 260 (1965): 65-95.

Christensen, Thomas. "Eighteenth-Century Science and the *Corps Sonore*: The Scientific Background to Rameau's Principle of Harmony." *Journal of Music Theory* 31 (1987): 23-43.

————. "The *Règle de l'Octave* in Thorough-Bass Theory and Practice," *Acta Musicologica* 64 (1992): 91-117.

Crowe, Joan. "Reflections on George Dandin." In *Molière: Stage and Study*. Edited by W. D. Howarth and Merlin Thomas, 3-12. Oxford: Clarendon Press, 1973.

Duckles, Vincent. "A French Critic's View on the State of Music in London (1829)." In *Modern Musical Scholarship*, edited by Edward Olleson, 223-37. London: Oriel Press Ltd., 1980.

Euler, Leonard. "Conjecture sur la raison de quelques dissonances généralement reçues dans la musique." *Mémoires de l'Academie Berlin* 20 (1764): 165-73.

————. "Du veritable caractère de la musique moderne." *Mémoires de l'Academie Berlin* 20 (1764): 174-99.

Ferand, Ernst T. "What is *Res Facta*" *Jopurnal of the American Musicological Society*, 10 (1957): 141–50.

Fétis, François-Joseph. "Cours de Philosophie musicale et d'Histoire de la Musique." *Revue musicale* 12 (1832): 131-33, 139-41, 155-58, 161-64, 169-71, 177-79, 184-87, 196-98.

_____. "Découverte de plusieurs Manuscripts intéressants pour l'histoire de la musique." *Revue musicale* 1 (1827): 3-11, 106-13.

_____. "Fétis, François-Joseph." In *Biographie universelle des musiciens et bibliographie générale de la musique*. 2d ed. Vol. 3, 226-39. Paris: Didot Frères et C243ie, 1878.

_____. "Gasparini, Francesco." In *Biographie universelle des musiciens et bibliographie générale de la musique*. 2d ed. Vol. 3, 414-15. Paris: Didot Frères et C243ie, 1878.

_____. "Grand Concert." *Revue et Gazette musicale de Paris* 3 (1828): 422-24.

_____. "Histoire de la musique." *Revue musicale* 12 (1832): 265-270.

_____. "Littérature musicale." *Revue musicale* 12 (1832): 116-19.

_____. "Littérature de la musique." *Revue et Gazette musicale de Paris* 6 (1839): 209-12, 219-21.

_____. "Mercadier, Jean-Baptiste." In *Biographie universelle des musiciens et Bibliographie Générale de la Musique*. 2d ed. Vol.6, 90. Paris: Didot Frères et Cie, 1884.

_____. "Mon testament musical." *Revue et Gazette musicale de Paris* 20 (1853): 281-84, 297-300, 313-16, 321-24, 347-50, 363-66.

_____. "Note." *Revue musicale* 6 (1830): 32-34.

_____. "Nouvelles de Paris." *Revue musicale* 5 (1829): 129-36.

_____. "Nouvelles dicussions [sic] sur l'Introduction d'un quator de Mozart." *Revue musicale* 8 (1830): 321-28.

_____. "Perne, François-Louis." In *Biographie universelle des musiciens et bibliographie générale de la musique*. 2d ed. Vol.6, 490-95. Paris: Didot Frères et C243ie, 1884.

_____. "Résumé philosophique de l'histoire de la musique." In *Biographie universelle des musiciens et bibliographie générale de la musique*. 1st ed. Vol. 1, xxxvii-ccliv. Paris: Fournier, 1835.

_____. "Romieu, . . ." In *Biographie universelle des musiciens et bibliographie générale de la musique*. 2d ed. Vol.7, 304-05. Paris: Didot Frères et C243ie, 1883.

_____. "Roquefort-Lamericourt (Jean-Baptiste-Bonaventure)." In *Biographie universelle des musiciens et bibliographie générale de la musique*. 2d ed. Vol. 7, 307–8. Paris: Didot Frères et C243ie, 1883.

_____. "Sur un passage singulier d'un quatuor de Mozart." *Revue musicale* 5 (1829): 601–6.

_____. "Sur l'état actuel de la musique à Londres." *Revue musicale* 5 (1829): 313-19, 361-9, 385-92, 409-17, 457-64, 481-88, 529-36, 560-67.

Gallo, F. Albert. "Marchetto da Padova." In *The New Grove Dictionary of Music and Musicians*. Edited by Stanley Sadie. Vol. 11, 661-63. London: MacMillan, 1980.

Gribenski, Jean. "A propos des 'Leçons de clavecin' (1771): Diderot et Bemetzrieder." *Revue et musicologie* 66 (1980): 125-78.

Gushee, Lawrence. "Jehan des Murs." In *The New Grove Dictionary of Music and Musicians*. Edited by Stanley Sadie. Vol. 9, 587-90. London: MacMillan, 1980.

Hamm, Charles. "Dufay [du Fay], Guillaume." In *The New Grove Dictionary of Music and Musicians*. Edited by Stanley Sadie. Vol. 5, 674-86. London: MacMillan, 1980.

Hansell, Sven. "Vallotti, Francesco Antonio." In *The New Grove Dictionary of Music and Musicians*. Edited by Stanley Sadie. Vol. 19, 505-07. London: MacMillan, 1980.

Hasse, Hans. "Kellner, David." In *Die Musik in Geschichte und Gegenwart*. Edited by Friedrich Blume. Vol. 7, cols. 818-19. Kassel: Bärenreiter-Verlag, 1958.

Herlinger, Jan. "Fractional Divisions of the Whole Tone." *Music Theory Spectrum* 3 (1981): 74-83.

Herlinger, Jan W. "Marchetto's Division of the Whole Tone." *Journal of the American Musicological Society* 34 (1981): 90-105.

Hindemith, Paul. "Methods of Music Theory." *Musical Quarterly*, 30 (1944): 20-28.

Hughes, Andrew. "Franco of Cologne." In *The New Grove Dictionary of Music and Musicians*. Edited by Stanley Sadie. Vol. 6, 794-97. London: MacMillan, 1980.

Jacobi, Erwin. "Harmonic Theory in England after the time of Rameau." *Journal of Music Theory* 1 (1957): 126–46.

Lester, Joel. "Root-Position and Inverted Triads in Theory Around 1600." *Journal of the American Musicological Society* 27 (1974): 110-19.

Lesure, François. "L'Affaire Fétis." *Revue belge de musicologie* 28-30 (1974-76): 214-21.

Lewin, David. "Concerning the Inspired Revelation of F.-J. Fétis." *Theoria* 2 (1987): 1-12.

McClymonds, Marita Petzoldt. "Jommelli [Jomelli], Nicolò [Niccolò]." In *The New Grove Dictionary of Music and Musicians.* Edited by Stanley Sadie. Vol. 9, 689-95. London: MacMillan, 1980.

Mckeel, Joyce. "The Harmonic Theories of Kirnberger and Marpurg." *Journal of Music Theory* 4 (1960): 169-93.

Mompellio, Frederico. "Viadana, Lodovico." In *Die Musik in Geschichte und Gegenwart.* Edited by Friedrich Blume. Vol. 13, cols. 1575-81. Kassel: Bärenreiter-Verlag, 1966.

Oberdörffer, Fritz. "Penna, Lorenzo." In *Die Musik in Geschichte und Gegenwart.* Edited by Friedrich Blume. Vol. 10, cols.1016-18. Kassel: Bärenreiter-Verlag, 1962.

Pepusch, John Christoph. "Of the various Genera and Species of Music among the Ancients, with some Observations concerning their Scale." *Philosophical Transactions of the Royal Society of London*, 44 (1746): 266-74.

Perne, François-Louis. "Polémique." *Revue musicale* 6 (1830): 25-31.

Plamenac, Dragan. "An Unknown Composition by Dufay?" *Musical Quarterly* 40 (1954): 190-200.

Planchart, Alejandro. "A Study of the Theories of Giuseppe Tartini." *Journal of Music Theory* 4 (1960): 32-61.

Platt, Peter. "Dering's Life and Training." *Music and Letters* 33 (1952): 41-49.

Prod'homme, J.-G. "Fétis, bibliothècaire du Conservatoire." *La Revue musicale* 116 (1931): 18-34.

Prony, Baron Gaspard Riche de. "Du rapport fait a l'académie des sciences sur cet ouvrage." In Baron Blein. *Principes de mélodie et d'harmonie déduits de la theories des vibrations.* Paris: Bachelier, 1832.

Reaney, Gilbert. "L'Escurel, Jehannot de." In *Die Musik in Geschichte und Gegenwart.* Edited by Friedrich Blume. Vol. 8, cols. 666-67. Kassel: Bärenreiter-Verlag, 1960.

Redlich, Hans Ferdinand. "Monteverdi, Claudio Zuan." In *Die Musik in Geschichte und Gegenwart.* Edited by Friedrich Blume. Vol. 9, cols. 511-31. Kassel: Bärenreiter-Verlag, 1961.

Rivera, Benita V. "The Seventeenth-Century Theory of Triadic Generation and Invertibility and Its Application in Contemporaneous Rules of Composition." *Music Theory Spectrum* 6 (1984): 63-78.

Ruhnke, Martin. "Gasparini, Francesco." In *Die Musik in Geschichte und Gegenwart.* Edited by Friedrich Blume. Vol. 4, col. 1415. Kassel: Bärenreiter-Verlag, 1955.

Schellhous, Rosalie. "Fétis's Tonality as a Metaphysical Principle: Hypothesis for a New Science." *Music Theory Spectrum* 13 (1991): 219-40.

Seay, Albert. "*The Proportionale Musices* of Johannes Tinctoris." *Journal of Music Theory* 1 (1957): 22–75.

Simms, Bryan R. "Choron, Fétis and the Theory of Tonality." *Journal of Music Theory* 19 (1975): 112-38.

Strunk, Oliver. "On the Date of Marchetto da Padova." In *Essays on Music in the Western World*, 39-43. New York: W. W. Norton & Co., 1974.

Szelényi, Istvan. "Der unbekannte Liszt." *Studia musicologica* 5 (1963): 311-31.

Troupenas, Edward. "Correspondance." *Revue musicale* 12 (1832): 125-27.

_____. "Essay sur la Théorie de la Musique." *Revue musicale* 12 (1832): 148-52.

van Hassett. "Sur le manuiscrit des traités de Jean Tinctoris et sur la traduction française de ces ouvrages par M. Fr. Fétis, Membre de l'Academie." *Revue et Gazette musicale de Paris* 28 (1861): 35–6.

Vertrees, Julie Ann. "Mozart's String Quartet K. 465: The History of a Controversy." *Current Musicology* 17 (1974): 96-114.

Volodarsky, A. I. "Nicholaus Fuss." *Dictionary of Scientific Biography*. Editor-in-Chief, Charles Coulston Gillispie. Vol. 5, 209-10. New York: Charles Scribner's Sons, 1972.

Walker, D. P. "The Musical Theories of Giuseppe Tartini." In *Modern Musical Scholarship*, edited by Edward Olleson, 93-111. London: Oriel Press Ltd., 1980.

Wangermée, Robert. "François-Joseph Fétis." *Encyclopédie de la musique*. Edited by François Michel. Vol. 2, 52-53. Paris: Fasquelle, 1959.

Wright, Craig. "Dufay at Cambrai." *Journal of the American Musicological Society* 28 (1975): 175-229.

Index